BUDGET TOOLS

Financial Methods in the Public Sector

Greg G. Chen
Baruch College, City University of New York

Dall W. Forsythe
Wagner School, New York University

Lynne A. Weikart
Baruch College, City University of New York

Daniel W. Williams
Baruch College, City University of New York

CQ PRESS

A Division of SAGE

Washington, D.C.

CQ Press
2300 N Street, NW, Suite 800
Washington, DC 20037

Phone: 202-729-1900; toll-free, 1-866-4CQ-PRESS (1-866-427-7737)

Web: www.cqpress.com

Cover design: Diane Buric Design Illustration, Silver Spring, MD
Cover image: PhotoDisc
Composition: BMWW, Baltimore, MD

⊛ The paper used in this publication exceeds the requirements of the American National Standard for Information Sciences—Permanence of Paper for Printed Library Materials, ANSI Z39.48-1992.

Printed and bound in the United States of America

12 11 10 09 08   1 2 3 4 5

Library of Congress Cataloging-in-Publication Data

Budget tools : financial methods in the public sector / Greg G. Chen . . . [et al.].
    p.   cm.
  Includes bibliographical references and index.
  ISBN 978-0-87289-539-3 (alk. paper)
  1. Budget process.   2. Expenditures, Public.   3. Budget.   I. Chen,
Greg G.   II. Title

  HJ2009.B82 2008
  352.4'8—dc22

                                                                2008017813

Contents

Tables, Figures, and Features

Tables

Figures

Exhibits

Helpful Hints

Preface

As professors of budgeting, we were frustrated by the limited number of explanations and exercises available for our students' use in traditional or theory-based budget texts commonly used in budgeting courses. Theory is essential in any budgeting course, but students need the ability to translate this information into practice and to feel comfortable reading, analyzing, and creating budgets. Thus, we wrote *Budget Tools: Financial Methods in the Public Sector* to fill this need.

Budget Tools teaches students a specific set of skills needed to be successful when creating and tracking budgets, and it focuses on the tools and applications that are commonly used in the budget offices of government agencies and nonprofit organizations. It contains guided examples, data sets, and spreadsheet-based exercises on CD—all class tested and proven to work—and covers a range of topics and skills giving students a hands-on opportunity to master the application of budgeting concepts.

Although we do not dig deeply into the budget process,[*] we use the milestones of the budget process to structure our book, which starts with organizing budget data in the preparation phase and ends with multiyear planning and analysis. Every chapter begins with learning objectives and a brief explanation of the topic. We offer plenty of explanation, teaching tips, and step-by-step examples, and we conclude each chapter with exercises using real budgeting data.

After we introduce the scope of the book in chapter 1, we focus in chapter 2, "Organizing Budget Data," on learning how to use a chart of accounts. We explain why budgeting and accounting are both relevant to budgeting, and we teach students how to organize data and interpret budget data.

We begin to explore the tools used in budget preparation in chapter 3, "Preparing the Operating Budget: The Spending Side." In good times, the executive might ask for new initiatives; in fiscally challenging times, the executive might set targets for reductions and require budget cuts to meet those targets. Thus, we focus on analyzing new initiatives and calculating budget cuts to meet targets. We also discuss approaches to updating our budget base, including a section on projecting payroll.

In chapter 4, "First Steps in Revenue Estimating," we turn to the revenue side, specifically to revenue forecasting methods. From the many techniques,

---

[*]For more on the budget process, see Dall W. Forsythe, *Memos to the Governor: An Introduction to State Budgeting,* 2nd ed. (Washington, D.C.: Georgetown University Press, 2004).

simple and complex, available to forecast revenues, we pick one to review in detail. It is essential that students learn to use spreadsheets in budgeting, and to that end we focus on the use of spreadsheets in forecasting.

In chapter 5, "Preparing the Capital Budget," we concentrate on the capital budget. We examine three areas of capital budgeting: life cycle costs, cost-benefit analysis, and financing capital needs.

We have created a short chapter on the financial plan in chapter 6, "The Financial Plan and Budget Decision Making." Financial plans seem simple, but knowledge of them is essential to the management of an organization, so we take time to understand their importance.

In chapter 7, "Presenting the Budget," we discuss the tools necessary to present the budget. We outline several topics, including performance budgeting and budget justifications.

We explain what kinds of tools are needed to implement a budget in chapter 8, "Implementing the Budget." We demonstrate how to create an operating plan, and we present ways to conduct a variance analysis.

In the final chapter, chapter 9, "Multiyear Plans and Analyses," we discuss multiyear budget plans and analysis. We also spend time on financial statements and present simple tools for analyzing them.

All these tools would be of little account without a thorough understanding of spreadsheets. We have included five appendices, focusing on Microsoft Excel literacy for those needing a tutorial in spreadsheet basics, along with several guided examples of more advanced techniques such as understanding logic functions and developing macros in Excel. These appendices are "Spreadsheeting Basics," "How to Produce Clear, Attractive Reports," and "Advanced Spreadsheeting for Budgeting." Each includes additional exercises to further increase Excel literacy and to perfect skills in creating and analyzing budgets. These special features and appendices make the book an easy reference guide that could be useful to students during their careers.

Using the Companion CD and Instructor Solutions

On the companion CD students and instructors will find data sets, support files, and exercise materials used in the exercises for most chapters in the book and several of the appendices. Users can open the spreadsheets with either Office 2003 or 2007 software. All the spreadsheet files were prepared in Office 2003.

In some instances, when Office 2007 is in use and the file is saved as an Office 2003 document, there may occur noncritical error messages such as these:

- The following features in this workbook are not supported by earlier versions of Excel. These features may be lost or degraded when you save this workbook in an earlier file format.

- Significant loss of functionality. Any effects on this object will be removed. Any text that overflows the boundaries of this graphic will appear clipped.

- Minor loss of fidelity. Some formulas in this workbook are linked to other workbooks that are closed. When these formulas are recalculated in earlier versions of Excel without opening the linked workbooks, characters beyond the 255-character limit cannot be returned.

These errors have no functional effect. The user should select "Continue" (an option that will appear on the screen) and save the file.

Every exercise comes with solutions available to instructors who adopt the book for their courses. To download solutions to *Budget Tools* exercises, instructors must visit http://college.cqpress.com/instructors-resources/budgettools/ and register for a new account. Access is limited to instructors only.

Acknowledgments

During our writing of this book, we have had the support of many people. We are indebted to Kristine Enderle, development editor at CQ Press, for her patience and wisdom. Her guidance has been invaluable. Others on the team—including copy editor Mary Marik, production editor Kerry Kern, and marketing specialist Erin Snow—have been terrific. Many thanks go to John Bartle, University of Nebraska–Omaha; Thad D. Calabrese, New York University; Sang Ok Choi, California State University, Dominguez Hills; Todd Lantin Ely, New York University; Andrew Glassberg, University of Missouri–St. Louis; Glen Krutz, University of Oklahoma; and Daniel L. Smith, Rutgers University–Newark, who reviewed the manuscript and offered valuable suggestions. These reviewers saved us from errors and omissions, yet, as ever, those that might remain are our responsibility alone.

CHAPTER 1

The Craft of Budgeting

We emphasize budget skills and tools in this workbook. As that choice of words suggests, after you work through the material in this book, you are unlikely to think of governmental budgeting as an art form. Neither is budgeting simply an exercise of imagination, although a wide-ranging process of thinking can facilitate the development of options for consideration. Finally, contrary to the impression given by page after page of numbers, budgeting is not a scientific activity. The scientific method, based as it is on careful experimentation and step-by-step changes in single variables, is foreign to budgets, which must be created and managed in the messy world of politics and real-time regional or local economies.

But budgeting is more than educated guesses. Practitioners try to be systematic, and the good ones learn from mistakes and try to correct assumptions found to be in error. With these broad strokes in mind, we might find it helpful to consider budgeting as a craft.

Consider a woodworker.[1] To accomplish the tasks of woodworking well, the woodworker needs to be proficient with a set of tools, and, when faced with a new project, willing to learn to use new ones. Our model woodworker needs to have some tolerance for repetition and must be willing to pay considerable attention to detail. A good woodworker needs to evidence a low tolerance for avoidable error and a sanguine attitude in the face of unavoidable error. Ideally, the woodworker should be appreciative of good design and concerned about reducing waste and misuse of scarce resources, including time and materials. As a project nears its end, the woodworker needs to take extra care with the final finish and remember that thoughtful presentation of the final product is an expression of pride in one's work.

In a small budget office, a budget professional may be called on to employ many different tools in the course of a budget season; this is similar to a woodworker who labors without helpers in a home workshop. In a bigger office, characteristic of a large city or state, a budget examiner may focus tightly on a small set of agencies or programs or even a single large program or tax. In that work, the budget professional may employ a more limited set of tools, similar to a woodworker in a factory that makes only furniture. When a budget professional in a larger office moves on to a different assignment, however, that person is likely to be called upon to learn a new set of tools applicable to the new portfolio of programs or revenue sources. In either case, adaptability—willingness to learn to use a broad range of tools—is characteristic of the successful budget examiner.

In addition to specific skills, a capable budget professional must develop a useful set of work habits and attitudes. For example, during the course of analyzing a budget problem, the budget examiner may employ large data sets, sometimes drawn from different sources and often characterized by embedded errors or missing data. The obvious analogy is to the knots, warps, and other imperfections in the lumber used for building. The skilled budget analyst needs to work through the problems inherent in messy source data, and do so with a passion for eliminating avoidable errors.

Some errors are simply unavoidable. A budget is a set of estimates about the behavior of programs or tax sources in the future, and some of those estimates will be wrong. For that reason, budgeting is, and will always be, an error-prone activity.[2] But the budget professional is passionate about ferreting out avoidable errors. These are the errors produced by inaccurate inputting of data, by incorrect calculations in spreadsheets, or even by poor proofreading. In a strong budget office, considerable time and effort is devoted to catching and correcting such errors before they appear in final products.

Every woodworker needs familiarity with basic tools, and every budget professional needs to master the tools of the trade. For a professional budget examiner, the most important of these tools is the spreadsheet. Although budget examiners use databases regularly, the spreadsheet is the tool of choice for the majority of analytic tasks, and its flexibility and adaptability make it indispensable to the work of professional budgeting. As outlined in Chapter 2 on organizing budget data, spreadsheet literacy includes but is not limited to an understanding of the mathematical functions of the spreadsheet. In much the same way as the woodworker must take care with the final finish of a piece of work, the budget examiner must smooth out the rough edges of a piece of analysis and polish it for presentation. Attention must be paid to the product's eventual consumers, who may include the head of the budget office, the chief executive and legislature of the government, and that small part of the mass media and general public that writes and reads about government finance. Well-designed tables, comprehensible graphics, and, most of all, clear writing are the distinguishing marks of the finished product. In many circumstances, the budget professional will also personally present the analysis to higher-ups, and the ability to organize an oral presentation with findings and recommendations is an increasingly important skill as budget professionals rise higher in their organizations.

Although this discussion has been focused on professionals in an operating budget office, other offices and organizations value and employ people who possess the same habits and skills. In many jurisdictions, budget professionals are employed in offices that monitor and review the budgets presented by the executive branch:

- State legislative analyst's offices, many of which are modeled on the California state office in operation since 1941
- Budget and finance staffs working for finance, ways and means, and budget committees in legislatures and city councils
- Budget analysis shops serving controllers and treasurers in states and large cities
- Nonprofit budget watchdogs at every level of government.

In all of these settings, the skills required to understand and critique budgets and present findings and the budget itself to elected officials are similar to skills of successful budget examiners.

Professionals with these skills and habits are also in demand in a few locations in the private sector, most notably in the credit rating agencies. Working for Moody's, Standard & Poor's, and Fitch, analysts review the finances of state and local governments and their related entities and help investors decide whether to lend them money. Of necessity, the analysts in these agencies spend much more time analyzing debt than most other budget professionals, but the ability of a government to repay its creditors rests in large part on its budget management capability. In this analysis, the skills and habits of work and mind outlined above are central to the work of those professionals.

As suggested earlier, the technical skills outlined in this book can be learned by studying and solving simple and eventually complex problems in the classroom and the workplace. Good judgment and the habits of craftsmanship can be learned only through work and experience, ideally under the tutelage of a seasoned professional. Both technical skill and commitment to the craft of budgeting are essential to the development of a competent budget professional.

When we turn to the financial plans that help us summarize and understand complex governmental budgets, we find that our woodworking analogy has outlived its usefulness. It now may be helpful instead to consider the skills and habits of sailors, especially those skills required before the widespread use of the global positioning system and other precision navigation equipment. In less technologically sophisticated times, ships' captains set a course, used assumptions about wind and currents to estimate the length of time it would take to reach key points, and then set out on their journeys. Several times a day, crew members checked and logged their speed, and crew members used celestial navigation on each clear day to check their position. Wind and currents were never exactly as assumed, so course adjustments were made as the journey progressed. Lengthy delays might mean shortages of resources such as food or fresh water, and changes in course might be necessary to replenish supplies.

Again, the analogies to budgeting seem striking. Long-term plans are based on estimates about revenues, prices, and other key factors, many of which will prove incorrect. So plans are monitored and adjustments made, usually each quarter. Sometimes major changes in resource levels necessitate more serious actions. The clearer the assumptions and the more carefully prepared the plan, the sooner deviations can be identified and analyzed. Clarity, adaptability, and willingness to use available tools and technology—all these are habits of mind and action that are essential in the long-term management of budgets. The task is neither art nor science, and it is certainly not guesswork. The skills required to lay out a plan with care, to monitor it carefully as it is implemented, and to adjust to new data and realities are akin to the skills of the masters and commanders who managed through care, craft, and some good luck to get themselves, their crews, and their ships safely to their destinations. Budgeteers who want to reflect more deeply on this analogy might dip into the novels of Patrick O'Brian.[3]

This introduction aims to evoke both the pleasures and the frustrations of budgeting. The work is difficult enough to be challenging, but it can be mastered by hardworking people who invest time and effort. Skill with tools is rewarded and can be learned, but judgment is critical to success at higher levels of budget organizations. From time to time, the product of a budget analyst's effort has finish and sometimes even elegance. At the same time, budgeting requires considerable effort, and sometimes that effort seems routine or repetitive. At the end of the process, decisions and recommendations by budget offices shape the allocation of resources in their organizations, and their impact can be considerable. For patient and hardworking people who care about the missions of governments and nonprofit organizations, budgeting can be a challenging and satisfying career. We hope this book contributes to their training and work.

Notes

1. This metaphor was first proposed in 1981 in a short, elegant monograph by Edward A. Lehan, and it is still evocative. By suggesting it, Lehan invited us to pick our favorite craft activity and reflect on the analogies to the work done by career budget professionals; see Edward A. Lehan, *Simplified Governmental Budgeting* (Chicago: Municipal Finance Officers Association, 1981).

2. Dall W. Forsythe, *Memos to the Governor: An Introduction to State Budgeting,* 2nd ed. (Washington, D.C.: Georgetown University Press, 2004), 6–7.

3. The full set of those novels was published by W. W. Norton in 2004 as *The Complete Aubrey/Maturin Novels,* by Patrick O'Brian.

CHAPTER 2

Organizing Budget Data

Learning objectives:
- Use a chart of accounts
- Understand accounting codes, particularly object codes
- Understand the role of the chart of accounts in budgeting
- Use spreadsheets to format data
- Use spreadsheets to tabulate (sum) data
- Use spreadsheets to carry sums between tabbed sheets

One of the most important, but also one of the simplest, ideas of budgeting and accounting is that every dollar should be recorded: every dollar an organization receives, keeps, and spends or plans to receive, keep, or spend. How are all of these data organized? If everyone records these transactions using idiosyncratic descriptions, chaos will ensue. Actual transactions will not be coordinated with budget plans. Records of transactions will drift substantially over time as employees change and as people forget how they used to record things and record them with newly invented definitions. Such records would be valueless for budgeting or accountability.

In this chapter, you will learn how to organize budget data by learning to use a chart of accounts and by learning to understand accounting codes, particularly object codes. In the last section, you'll find exercises to practice your skills in organizing budget data by using spreadsheets to format data, to tabulate (sum) data, and to carry sums between "pages."

Understanding the Chart of Accounts

Budget and accounting practice relies on a device known as the **chart of accounts.** The chart of accounts can be simple or complex depending on the nature of the organization. Its most important function is to provide a uniform definition for all normal financial transactions that an organization can experience. For more sophisticated organizations, like a multipurpose state or local government, it should provide a uniform definition for all possible financial transactions. In a more complex organization, the chart will also help identify the subdivision within the organization where the transaction occurs. The full chart of accounts aims to provide for every possible transaction. Budgeting and accounting are coordinated through the chart of accounts because actual transactions are linked to planned transactions through object coding. In this sense, when transactions follow plans, it is appropriate for the accounting staff to defer to the budgeting staff for coding decisions on vague or ambiguous code definitions.

The chart of accounts also provides a guide to budgeting in the form of a checklist of possible expenditures that might occur with respect to planning of future programs. Sorting by these categories can be particularly helpful when such data can be found for other similar programs.

There is an important distinction between budgeting and recording of actual expenditures; it is related to the chart of accounts. Budgeting usually reflects uncertainty; actual expenditure records are records of events, and they are not uncertain. It is, therefore, reasonable to budget at a more aggregate level and to spend at a more specific level. This is where the chart of accounts might force inappropriate links to excessively explicit line-item budgeting if not constrained by judgment and common sense.

Tips and Tools

1. Build your budget from the details at the line item (specific object of expenditure) where possible.
2. Commit your budget at a higher level, such as project, program, or department, distinguishing only between capital and operation and between personnel and other than personnel.
3. Record your expenditures by object of expenditure.

Appendix A provides an example of the 2005 New York State guidelines for a chart of accounts as found at www.osc.state.ny.us/localgov/pubs/arm/arm5.htm.

Understanding Accounting Codes

When an organization consists of a single entity, such as one independent nonprofit organization, the chart of accounts focuses solely on transactions, and that is how this chapter will continue. A chart of accounts includes **classification and coding.** Classification sets out the large categories of financial transactions. Coding sets out labels and definitions for every specific transaction. Coding can be multilayered, which means that a code might have a specific length, say twelve digits, where a particular digit or group of digits has a particular meaning. So, for example, the 1234 in xxxx1234xxxx might always refer to a particular program, no matter what precedes or follows it.

For smaller organizations, the important classifications are **revenues,** capital expenditures, and **operating expenditures,** and the important sources of multiple layers are fund sources and programs. Revenues is a broad general term referring to any money coming to a government or other entity for its own expenditures. Capital expenditures refers to expenditures for expensive and long-lasting goods. Typical organizations set a minimum life expectancy such as five years before they call a good a capital good; these organizations also set a minimum value, such as $50,000, before they classify a good or group of goods bought at once a capital good. So a capital good might be a good that lasts for at least five years and costs at least $50,000. Other organizations might set other values and lengths of time. Operating expenditures are expenditures that are considered consumed when spent; these are expenditures other than capital expenditures.

Fund Sources

A chart of accounts will provide a different code for each **fund source.** This fund code will appear in both revenues and expenditures. There should be one fund code for unrestricted funds. In governments, this is known as the general fund. Restricted funds are those that can be used only for specified purposes. Through a fund code and a program code the chart of accounts provides a method of determining that restricted funds are used for the purposes for which they are received.

Programs

An organization expends its money for purposes. These purposes are aligned with the agency's strategic plan and, for nonprofits, are often associated with grants. Each purpose or grant should receive its own **program code,** which helps show the end to which expenditures are put.

Object Codes

The remaining part of the chart of accounts lists a set of codes, often four digits, that very specifically identifies each financial transaction. Each code might be called an expenditure code, a revenue code, or something else. A general term is **object code.** Object codes may be grouped in sets of 10, 100, or 1000 to help categorize similar transactions. The 1000-level grouping may reflect the classification scheme; thus, revenues, capital expenditures, and operating expenditures may be easily identified because of differences in the first digit in their object codes. (Note that this practice is not used uniformly.)

Tables 2.1 and 2.2 are segments of the recommended Uniform Chart of Accounts as recommended

TABLE 2.1

Uniform Chart of Accounts, Personnel-Related Expenses

7	Expenses—personnel-related
7000	Grants, contracts, & direct assistance
7010–***	Contracts—program related
7020–***	Grants to other organizations
7040–***	Awards & grants—individuals
7050–***	Specific assistance—individuals
7060–***	Benefits paid to or for members
7200	Salaries & related expenses
7210–***	Officers' & directors' salaries
7220–***	Salaries & wages—other
7230–***	Pension plan contributions
7240–***	Employee benefits—not pension
7250–***	Payroll taxes, etc.
7500	Contract service expenses
7510–***	Fundraising fees
7520–***	Accounting fees
7530–***	Legal fees
7540–***	Professional fees—other
7550–***	Temporary help—contract
7580–***	Donated professional services—GAAP
7590–***	Donated other services—non-GAAP

Source: "Unified Chart of Accounts," National Center for Charitable Statistics, http://nccs.urban.org/projects/ucoa.cfm.

TABLE 2.2

Uniform Chart of Accounts, Non–Personnel-Related Expenses

8	Non–personnel-related expenses
8100	Non-personnel expenses
8110–***	Supplies
8120–***	Donated materials & supplies
8130–***	Telephone & telecommunications
8140–***	Postage & shipping
8150–***	Mailing services
8170–***	Printing & copying
8180–***	Books, subscriptions, references
8190–***	In-house publications
8200	Facility & equipment expenses
8210–***	Rent, parking, other occupancy
8220–***	Utilities
8230–***	Real estate taxes
8240–***	Personal property taxes
8250–***	Mortgage interest
8260–***	Equipment rental & maintenance
8270–***	Deprec & amort—allowable
8280–***	Deprec & amort—not allowable
8290–***	Donated facilities

Source: "Unified Chart of Accounts," National Center for Charitable Statistics, http://nccs.urban.org/projects/ucoa.cfm.

by the National Center for Charitable Statistics.

Some organizations use off-the-shelf accounting software that includes implicit account coding systems. There is nothing wrong with this as long as the account coding system is consistent with the organization's planning activities, its funding processes, and its legal obligations. Before using such software, the organization needs to know which coding systems will be used and how flexible they might be.

Consider the example of forming a neighborhood association. This association's objectives include reducing nuisance crime, improving the quality of life in the neighborhood by holding semi-annual cleanup days, engaging city agencies to provide better-quality services, and providing neighborhood input into community development. The immediate objective of the organization is to grow large enough to gain city recognition of its concerns and to begin its neighborhood cleanup activities. Although the organization is not ready to become a 501(c)3 tax-exempt organization, it would like to conduct itself in a manner consistent with that status so that it will have fewer hurdles to jump at the time it applies for that status.

Table 2.3 shows the anticipated first-year expenditures for the neighborhood association assigned to a chart of accounts. The largest expenditure is $4,000 in legal expense for pursuit of 501(c)3 status. The $600 in accounting fees is in anticipation that there will be no voluntary donation of accounting services in the first year that the organization seeks 501(c)3 status. Both of these expenses could be considerably less if member volunteers provide these services. The other expenses include the cost of a mailing to all the households in the neighborhood to invite membership and the cost of T-shirts with a logo for promotion during the neighborhood cleanup. These expenses are related to building membership.

TABLE 2.3
Example with Uniform Chart of Accounts, Neighborhood Association Expenses

7	Expenses—personnel-related	Budget	Actual	8	Non–personnel-related expenses	Budget	Actual
7000	Grants, contracts, & direct assistance			8100	Non-personnel expenses		
7010–***	Contracts—program related			8110–***	Supplies	900	
7020–***	Grants to other organizations			8120–***	Donated materials & supplies		
7040–***	Awards & grants—individuals			8130–***	Telephone & telecommunications		
7050–***	Specific assistance—individuals			8140–***	Postage & shipping	1200	
7060–***	Benefits paid to or for members			8150–***	Mailing services		
				8170–***	Printing & copying	200	
7200	Salaries & related expenses			8180–***	Books, subscriptions, references		
7210–***	Officers' & directors' salaries			8190–***	In-house publications		
7220–***	Salaries & wages—other						
7230–***	Pension plan contributions			8200	Facility & equipment expenses		
7240–***	Employee benefits—not pension			8210–***	Rent, parking, other occupancy		
7250–***	Payroll taxes, etc.			8220–***	Utilities		
				8230–***	Real estate taxes		
7500	Contract service expenses			8240–***	Personal property taxes		
7510–***	Fundraising fees			8250–***	Mortgage interest		
7520–***	Accounting fees	600		8260–***	Equipment rental & maintenance		
7530–***	Legal fees	4000		8270–***	Deprec & amort—allowable		
7540–***	Professional fees—other			8280–***	Deprec & amort—not allowable		
7550–***	Temporary help—contract			8290–***	Donated facilities		
7580–***	Donated professional services—GAAP						
7590–***	Donated other services—non-GAAP						

Source: National Center for Charitable Statistics, http://nccs.urban.org/projects/ucoa.cfm.

The chart of accounts provides a convenient way to show the organization's anticipated expenses. As actual expenses are incurred, they should be recorded against specific object codes so that they can be totaled according to item and compared with anticipated values. This provides for improved accuracy in anticipating costs in the future. Nevertheless, actual implementation of the plans should be flexible. If, for example, all the T-shirts in the first batch are given away during the first semiannual neighborhood cleanup, leaving many volunteers disappointed, then more T-shirts should be acquired for the second cleanup using funds intended for other purposes, if possible.

When the association spends money, it will record those expenditures by recording the date, payee, amount, and object code. By recording the object code, the association is able to make summary reports comparing actual expenditures with those in this plan.

Summary

The chart of accounts is a uniform device for classifying financial data in an orderly manner. It can be used for showing expectations, as in the example, and later for showing actual expenditures. By using a chart of accounts, different people can record financial data for an organization without creating confusion.

Exercises

To complete the exercises, use the spreadsheet file titled "Budget Tools Chapter 02 Exercises." The exercise comes in three parts. The first part is intended to help you prepare for the second and third parts; it is a tutorial in the spreadsheet skills that are used in the second and third parts.

✓ 1. The spreadsheet opens on the "Tutorial" tab. Instructions are provided in the two highlighted green text boxes. The left text box first describes how cells F5 through F9 are summed in cell F10 and how all of these cells are formatted. It then asks you to do the same with data in cells F14 through F16. The right text box describes some advanced formatting skills and asks you to learn a very straightforward use of the "=" sign.

   After completing part 1, click on the "Explanation" tab, which gives step-by-step instructions for parts 2 and 3. Before completing these problems, look at the examples (using a different chart of accounts) on the blue tabs.

✓ 2. Copy the information from the "Source" tab to the "Expenses" tab. When you copy the data you will learn the relationship between codes and labels. The table also contains dollar values associated with the labels. Put these data in blocks reflecting the categories shown on the "Summary" tab (look at the "Example Summary" tab first). Format the copied information in a pleasing manner resembling the example of the first block at the top of the "Expenses" tab. Calculate subtotals for blocks, using the "subtotal" function, which should be shown at the bottom of each block as with the example. The "subtotal" function is explained in Appendix C, in the section on spreadsheeting for budgets. *pp. 230-231.*

   page 186

✓ 3. Carry the totals to the "Summary" tab using the "=" sign as practiced on the "Tutorial" tab. Format the "Summary" tab in a pleasing manner. Calculate sums as indicated by the "Total" labels on the "Summary" tab using the "subtotal" function. Validate success by finding that the "Self-Check" column on the "Summary" tab has turned completely to "TRUE."

Additional Readings

Bland, Robert L. *A Budgeting Guide for Local Government.* 2d ed. Washington, D.C.: ICMA Press, 2007.

Ives, Martin, Joseph R. Razek, and Gordon A. Hosch. *Introduction to Governmental and Not-for-Profit Accounting.* 5th ed. Upper Saddle River, N.J.: Pearson/Prentice Hall, 2004.

Office of Management and Budget. "Section 79—The Budget Data System." OMB Circular no. A-11. Washington, D.C.: U.S. Office of Management and Budget, 2007. www.whitehouse.gov/omb/circulars/a11/current_year/s79.pdf.

CHAPTER 3

Preparing the Operating Budget:

The Spending Side

Learning objectives:

- Develop a budget for a new program
- Examine budget cuts
- Update the budget base
- Create a payroll.

Budget preparation begins in the middle of the fiscal year when the central budget office issues circulars or budget memos. These documents outline for budget office and agency staff the calendar for submission of various products associated with the proposed budget for the next fiscal year. They may also include some specific instructions, such as fringe benefit rates or the inflation adjustments for various categories of goods and services purchased by the government. Finally, they may include general guidance about the expected fiscal climate, along with advice to agency managers about the preparation of budget cuts or new initiatives.

In particularly challenging economic conditions, the circulars may include targets for budget cuts for the next fiscal year, or even requirements for savings and cutbacks in the current fiscal year. In good times, the circulars may invite submission of proposals for new initiatives for review by the budget office and the executive, along with hints or suggestions about program areas where proposals might be especially welcome.

Work then proceeds at the departmental level and in budget examination units. As suggested above, some of this work may involve new budget initiatives, including financial analysis and write-up. Some may focus on budget cuts and other savings proposals. And considerable time is also spent on the more routine work involved in updating existing programs for the year to come. We will discuss each of these topics in turn.

In this chapter, you will learn to analyze new initiatives and budget cuts, understand how to think about budget cuts, learn to update the budget base, and become skilled in creating a payroll. At first, you see how to develop a budget for a new program. Next we'll walk you through a payroll simulation, then on to a forecasting payroll example. From there you will be poised to practice various components of preparing an operating budget in four exercise scenarios.

Analyzing New Initiatives and Budget Cuts

Good program managers are always ready with ideas for spending additional money. The job of the budget analyst in the department and later in the budget office is to review and analyze those ideas and to provide full and accurate financial and programmatic information about initiatives that may be top priorities of the department heads or that may be congruent with the chief executive's agenda.

Examination of new initiatives requires careful analysis, and several important technical tools may be employed in this work. These include analysis of the cost structure of the activities proposed; an understanding of **annualization,** or the relationship between full- and part-year costs. Eventually, the budget analyst must also produce a clear and thoughtful write-up of the proposal for review by the head of the budget office and the chief executive. We will review approaches to good memo writing in the chapter on budget preparation. As outlined in Chapter 5 on the capital budget, additional techniques also come into plan in the analysis of long-lived projects funded in the capital budget.

Cost Analysis

Costs are those resources used when operating a program or organization. In budgeting terms, costs differ from expenditures. Expenditures are actual transactions that have been recorded. Costs are all the expenses that can be associated with a program or organization whether or not an actual transaction takes places.

We need to understand several different types of costs in order to make good budgeting decisions. This is especially important in the case of new budget initiatives because the executive may decide to fund a program initiative at a level of workload or service different from that originally recommended by the departmental sponsor. Thus, when a proposal for a budget initiative is prepared, the analyst must be especially careful to set up an analysis so it can be adjusted for changes in workload.

To analyze a proposal properly, a budget analyst needs to understand the difference among at least three types of costs: fixed costs, step-fixed costs, and variable costs. Note that this typology is different from the categories usually used to write up budgets for final presentation.

Fixed costs remain constant over a given period of time (Figure 3.1). These might include rental or other costs of housing a program, insurance costs, or the costs of executive leadership to run a program.

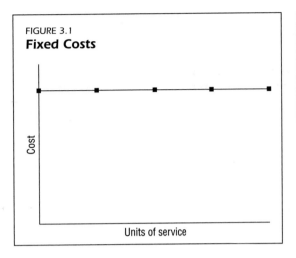

FIGURE 3.1
Fixed Costs

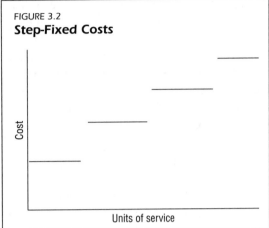

FIGURE 3.2
Step-Fixed Costs

Step-fixed costs remain constant over some relevant range of activity but change when workload or output exceeds that range (Figure 3.2). For example, a kitchen may be able to prepare meals for 1,000 senior citizens each day, but when workload rises above that number a second kitchen might be required.

Variable costs vary directly with service volume or workload (Figure 3.3). When we feed more seniors, the cost of food for their meals increases at a constant rate, assuming no economies of scale in purchasing.

To understand other examples of fixed, step-fixed, and variable costs, consider a projected budget for a child care center. A first step in developing a budget for a new program is to collect information. This task may be simple, as in the example outlined here, or it can take considerable legwork. In general, the more detailed the background work, the better the budget estimate. It would make sense for staff from both the implementing agency and the central budget office to be involved in this search for information. The essential goal is to identify all possible sources of cost for the program initiative, the quantities associated with service provision at different levels of output, and the prices for those inputs. This information is then distilled into the **assumptions** that will be used to construct the budget.

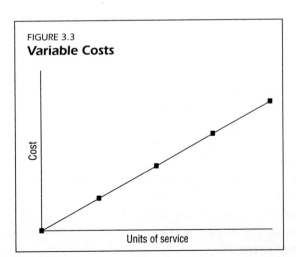

FIGURE 3.3
Variable Costs

Here are the assumptions behind a simplified budget for a child care center: The fixed costs are the director's salary, rent, and utilities. A step-fixed cost is classroom costs for staff. Let's assume that each group of ten children must be supervised by one teacher and one aide. If there are eleven children instead of ten, another teacher and another aide must be added. The variable costs are the food and supplies for each child. Table 3.1 sets out the costs and assumptions associated with this initiative; the table is true only when the additional child causes the group total to be rounded up to the next ten.

Assumptions should always be arrayed separately, often in a separate worksheet. This allows the analysts to update them with new information about prices or other key factors.

The next key question is how many children will be served. A decision about the number of children (or "slots") in the center allows us to calculate levels and costs of staffing as well as variable costs for food and supplies.

We need to be especially careful with the step-fixed costs for teachers and aides. If there were ten children served at the child care center, only one teacher and one aide would be budgeted. Because we cannot hire half a teacher or half an aide, we must round up to the next full unit when we reach the next step in the child-teacher ratio. Thus, if fifteen children needed to be served, two teachers and two aides would be funded.

Variable costs are simpler. We simply multiply the daily cost of food and supplies by the number of children and the number of days that the center will be open.

If we have set up our spreadsheet correctly, we can plug in the number of children and calculate the costs of staff and other resources for that level of service. To convert this into a traditional budget format, we calculate projected expenditures and divide them into two categories: PS (or **personnel services**) for salaries and fringe benefits of staff on payroll, and OTPS (**other than personnel services**) for everything else. You can look back at our discussion of the chart of accounts _page 8_ for a more detailed discussion of classifications in budgeting.

The budget for child care for fifty-five children would look like Table 3.2.

Other cost categories you will sometimes encounter are average costs and marginal costs.

Average costs are the total costs divided by the number of units of production. In the example above, we would calculate average cost by dividing

TABLE 3.1

Costs and Assumptions for Child Care Center

Fixed costs	
Executive director	
Salary	$60,000
Fringe benefits	17,400
Total	$77,400
Rent	$24,000
Utilities	$7,200

Step-fixed costs	
Teacher	
Salary	$45,000
Fringe benefits	13,050
Total	$58,050
Aide	
Salary	$30,000
Fringe benefits	8,700
Total	$38,700

Variable costs (per child per day)	
Food	$4
Supplies	$2

Assumptions	
Child-teacher ratio	10
Child-aide ratio	10
Number of days of operation	260
Fringe benefit rate	29%

TABLE 3.2
Child Care Initiative Budget

	No. of children: 55	
	No. of positions	Expenditures
PS		
Executive director	1	$77,400
Teachers	6	348,300
Aides	6	232,200
Subtotal	13	$657,900
OTPS		
Rent		$24,000
Utilties		7,200
Food		57,200
Supplies		28,600
Subtotal		$117,000
Total budget		$774,900

Note: PS = personnel services; OTPS = other than personnel services.

$774,900 by the number of children served, or fifty-five. Average costs for this level of service are $14,089. Note that the average cost changes as the level of service changes. If we add one more child, variable costs will rise, but by only $1,560—the costs of food and supplies for one child for a year. Fixed costs will be unchanged, and their contribution to average cost will shrink as the denominator—the number of children served—increases. So the average cost for fifty-six children would shrink to $13,865 (Table 3.3).

Marginal costs are the additional costs associated with each extra unit of service. Calculating marginal costs can be a bit tricky. Most of the time, adding one more child will just increase costs by the added variable costs. In the example above, we added costs of $4 a day for food and $2 a day for supplies, multiplied by the number of days of service, or $1,560, when we increased the number of children from fifty-five to fifty-six. However, when a child increases the total number of slots to a new "step"—from sixty to sixty-one, for example—the marginal cost will be the

TABLE 3.3
Child Care Budget with Average Costs

	Number of children			
	55		56	
	No. of positions	Expenditures	No. of positions	Expenditures
PS				
Executive director	1	$77,400	1	$77,400
Teachers	6	348,300	6	348,300
Aides	6	232,200	6	232,200
Subtotal	13	$657,900	13	$657,900
OTPS				
Rent		$24,000		$24,000
Utilties		7,200		7,200
Food		57,200		58,240
Supplies		28,600		29,120
Subtotal		$117,000		$118,560
Total budget		$774,900		$776,460
Average costs		$14,089		$13,865

Note: PS = personnel services; OTPS = other than personnel services.

variable costs (still $1,560) plus the additional staffing costs for one more teacher and one more aide, for a marginal cost of $98,310.

Most government programs are not required to cover all of their costs. But it is possible that elected officials might ask a budget examiner to determine what level of fees would be required to put a program on a **break-even** basis.

To answer this question, we should think back to our discussion of average cost. Presumably fees for each child would have to cover the variable costs for that child, a share of fixed-step costs, and a share of fixed costs. Like the average costs, the break-even level of fees would depend on the number of children served. In our example with fifty-five children served, the average cost was $14,089, and fees set at that level would produce revenue equal to the project expenditures. A program serving sixty children could be staffed by the same number of teachers and aides as one serving fifty-five children. Total expenditures would rise, but only by the additional variable costs. In short, break-even fees, like average costs, change depending on the number of children served.

WHAT GENERATES COSTS?
Organizations experience costs because they do things. Seems simple, but it isn't. Doing something requires using resources—specific resources for specific actions. To determine the cost of a new activity, the first step is to ask: What are we going to do? Then ask: What steps do we take to do that?

Write down the general description, then the steps. For each step, write down the resources required. Sometimes resources are already provided. For example, if you add a small number of new service recipients to a large program, you may already have the resources in the slack time in the work effort of your existing staff.

Be sure to distinguish between new resources and old resources. For most programs, it is advisable to discuss objectives, steps, and resources with experienced program staff who may have greater insight than analysts into the nature of what it takes to accomplish program goals.

Budget Cuts

Budget analysts are also expected to develop and review proposals for budget savings. Just as typical budget initiatives involve increases in services, budget cuts usually call for reductions in services. As you might expect, the analytic issues are often mirror images of the questions that we considered in our discussion of initiatives. Cuts in services will save on the variable costs of the program, for instance, but will not reduce the fixed costs. If we reduce the population of a mental health institution, for example, we will save on food and on staff directly providing care to clients. Unless the cutbacks are large enough to close an entire facility, however, the costs of management and many of the costs of maintenance of the facility will remain. In short, cuts in services do not result in savings based on average costs; cuts in services will save only on variable costs. Similarly, some savings in step-fixed costs may result, but only when service reductions reach the step-down point.

Service reductions yield recurring savings, the most valuable and most difficult to produce. Year after year the reductions in services will reduce spending against the base budget, so a multiyear analysis will show savings in budgets to come. Most of the savings in the annual volume published by the

Costs and Prices

Sometimes analysts become stumped: not because of costs, but because of prices. For example, a cost might be $900 per computer times 100 computers = $90,000; the price is $900 per computer.

How do analysts find prices? There is a hierarchy of options. First, the price, or something very close to the price, may already be known because of an existing contract; or the organization may have rules that set the price, as most organizations do with personnel. Next, existing or recent bids might show closely related prices. Third, for some very standard goods there are published standard price expectations, but this is more likely to arise with industrial goods or commodities. Fourth, there are published catalogues and advertisements. These prices must be treated as somewhat unreliable, and several estimates should be obtained. Last, one may need to seek a proposal (for costly goods) or an informal bid (for less costly goods).

Congressional Budget Office, *Budget Options,* provide recurring annual savings, as do the budget cuts included in the New York City Independent Budget Office's more modest compilation, *Budget Options for New York City.* As those volumes indicate, an analyst also needs to highlight the impacts of budget cuts on affected constituencies if it is to be truly useful to decision makers.

Although recurring savings are more valuable, one-time savings can help to close temporary budget gaps. Nonrecurring savings can be achieved in several ways: Hiring freezes or delays in filling vacant positions produce one-time savings. More broadly, if a new program is being phased in, delaying its implementation will produce nonrecurring savings. Indeed, elected officials often try to reduce the first-year costs of programs by delaying implementation in their first fiscal year. In those circumstances, the budget analyst also needs to calculate and highlight the full costs of the program for a year when it will be fully phased in. In budget jargon, the analyst needs to "annualize" the costs to make clear the full impact of the program when implemented. If a program will be in effect for only four months in its first year, the analyst would multiply the cost of the program in the initial period by three to arrive at full annual spending. In doing this, the analyst needs to be careful to pull out any start-up costs, which are added to the part-year costs in the first year of implementation but should not be included in recurring annualized costs.

Updating the Base Budget

While analysis of new initiatives and budget cuts proceeds, budget examiners must also undertake an important but less visible task: updating the base budget, which details spending estimates for existing services and programs. Most of the spending in the operating budget supports those current services, and it would be an unusual state or local government budget where more than 10 percent of an executive budget proposal represented new spending initiatives or budget cuts. So work on the spending base, while mundane, is important and sometimes technically demanding.

For both the PS category and the OTPS category, the job of the budget examiner is to estimate the cost in the next year of providing services at the current level. With that done, it may also be necessary to estimate nondiscretionary increases or decreases in services levels on the basis of factors like increases in population to be served or changes in federal or state mandates. The school-age population may be growing, for example, requiring more classrooms and teachers. Or new state laws may increase or decrease penalties for felons, leading to changes in prison populations.

We will outline procedures for updating current services budgets, beginning with the simpler problem of estimating OTPS and then moving on to PS. Finally, we will return briefly to the question of estimating the budget impact of changing services levels, a task analogous to budgeting for new initiatives or budget cuts.

Other than Personnel Services (OTPS)

OTPS includes supplies, equipment too small or short-lived to be included in the capital budget, payments to consultants, rent, utilities and heating costs, and spending on the myriad activities of government except support of employees on the payroll. Again, you can look at Appendix A, the chart of accounts, where you will see New York State's rules about how municipalities should categorize spending within OTPS. Higher-level categories include supplies and materials, utilities, insurance, professional and technical services (consultants, in other words), rent or lease payments, operation and maintenance, and miscellaneous.

In general we expect to pay more for goods and services next year than this year. Even in an environment of low inflation, prices will increase by between 2 and 3 percent. For this reason, it is usually necessary to budget more to buy the same amounts of food, fuel, and supplies a year or more from now, and budget examiners "gross up" or increase OTPS estimates accordingly. For spending on items that are important in an agency's budget—food in a corrections department, for example—the budget examiner will look for estimates of expected price levels in the year to come. Sometimes those estimates come from estimates by economic consulting firms. Sometimes industry groups publish estimates of anticipated price levels. Sometimes a budget examiner relies on historical data from the past few years and derives an estimate of price increases if the current trend continues.

With an educated guess about increases in price levels in hand, the calculation required to estimate next year's spending level is simple. The budget analyst multiplies the current year's budget for the category by the estimated increase in price levels, and then adds the product to the current spending level. If anticipated spending on costs for food for a large state's prison system in the current year is $100,000,000, for example, and food costs are expected to increase by 2.5 percent annually in the period in question, the incremental costs are $2,500,000. Add that to the current year's anticipated spending and next year's budget will be $102,500,000.

You may already be familiar with a shortcut for this calculation, which is to multiply the current year's spending by 1.0 plus the anticipated change in prices. If you are using a calculator instead of a spreadsheet, be sure that the change in prices is expressed as a decimal fraction. In this example, we would multiply $100,000,000 by 1.025, yielding the same result. More generally, if S_1 is the current year's spending, and P is the expected change in prices, then next year's estimated spending (S_2) can be calculated as follows:

$$S_2 = S_1 \times (1 + P) \qquad [3.1]$$

You will use this simple shortcut often. The typical budget office, working together with the operating agency, has to do the work to adjust the base budget well before the year has actually ended. If spending in the current year is significantly higher or lower than the budget amount, next year's estimate will have to be adjusted accordingly. Usually, better information is available about spending after the executive submits the budget, so this adjustment is often made during the legislative adoption phase. If the projected spending level is reduced, the savings may then be available to fund other needs, including legislative initiatives.

A budget examiner may also have to change OTPS spending to reflect changes in populations served. Assume for example, that the number of inmates is also expected to grow by 3.5 percent per year. Food is a variable expense that we expected to increase at the same rate as population growth. In this case, we would also have to apply a growth factor for inmate population growth (I), and our new equation would look like this:

$$S_2 = S_1 \times (1 + P) \times (1 + I) \qquad [3.2]$$

To continue our example, we would now expect to spend $106,087,500. After making this calculation, we would document it, noting the assumptions used to arrive at the next estimate. Then we would proceed to adjust prices for every category of spending in the department of corrections.

These calculations illustrate an important point about budgeting. Often the calculations involved are relatively simple, but a very large number of such calculations are required, covering separate budget lines for each agency or program, and complex state and local governments often have many agencies and programs. Budget examiners are expected to make all those calculations accurately and to keep careful track of the assumptions used. The result is considerable complexity, based on the organizational or programmatic structure of the government, even when the calculations used are not themselves complex.

Personnel Services (PS)

Budget examiners also update PS budgets for each program or agency. In broad concept, the task is similar to adjusting the base for OTPS spending.

The analyst is striving to construct a good estimate of next year's costs for the service level currently provided. The key assumption is that those services will be performed by the people currently on the payroll or authorized to hire. While the task may sound similar to updating the OTPS budget base, the calculations can end up considerably more complex, depending on the size and complexity of the agency's payroll. In some governments, this work is done by the central budget office, in others by agency fiscal staff.

In general, government employees get increases in salary on the basis of several factors:

- They may get a cost of living adjustment (COLA) each year, or as otherwise specified by a union contract.

- They usually get paid more when they get promoted to a higher step or grade in the civil service.

- They may get a salary increment for longevity, giving them raises when they pass key milestones in their tenure in government.

Some of these increments will increase their salary base. Some may not. In the payroll example that follows, payment for longevity is a bonus, not an increase in base salary. Employees may get other nonrecurring payments, or bonuses, for superior performance or for success in some special mission.

After the updated salary is estimated, fringe benefits have to be calculated as well. Some are simple, representing either a fixed cost for each employee or a percentage of a worker's salary. Others are more complex. We review the major types of fringe costs below.

Creating a Payroll Simulation

Simulation is a method of forecasting using all the factors and data elements of the existing system. For payroll, where critical elements of information are already in hand, simulation is frequently the optimal method of forecasting. Here we will describe a simulation model to forecast next year's payroll, occasionally referring to the example in the spreadsheet. We will then discuss some special issues of payroll forecasting that do not arise in this example.

The Simulation Model

The simulation model operates on the data contained in a payroll system, which is a specialized database of employee information. In it, all the employees are listed with critical elements of information such as position anniversary dates, payroll grades and steps, length of service in the position (or start date in the position), to name just the most important data elements. Our

TABLE 3.4
Payroll Database

A	B	C	D	E	F	G	H	I	J
Employee no.	Last name	First name	Position title	Grade	Step	Next step	Length of service (years)	Anniversary month	Anniversary day
45123	Stone	Melinda	Supervisor	18	5	5	10	9	15
45124	Delrico	Jose	Team leader	15	3	4	2	7	22
45125	Shaft	George	Office assistant	5	5	5	6	3	1
45126	Vacant		Technician	12					
45127	Mayes	Angie	Technician	12	2	3	1	5	16
45128	Othman	Jerry	Technician	12	4	5	3	6	13

simplified payroll database is shown in Table 3.4 and in the spreadsheet entitled "Budget Tools Chapter 03 Exercises" at the "Payroll Forecast" tab. The model also references data about pay levels in the standard pay scale, as shown in Table 3.5 and in "Budget Tools Chapter 03 Exercises," on the "Pay Scale" tab.

With this information, the "rules" outlined below, a decision, and a bit of empirical information, you can forecast your payroll for the next fiscal year. For many governmental departments, with the notable exception of organizations that make transfer payments, payroll is the chief source of expenditure. Thus, making an accurate payroll forecast goes a long way to making an accurate forecast of the total expenditure needs of the organization. We will return to our example after we review the logical steps needed to create the forecast.

Here are the rules and the decision you need for this simulation:

WHAT IS THE PAY PERIOD? In our example, employees are paid twice a month, with the first period closing on the fifteenth of every month. The pay for the second period does not fluctuate with the length of the month. Twice-monthly or monthly periods are more convenient for simulation than weekly or every other week, but those can

TABLE 3.5
Standard Pay Scale

Grade	Step 1	2	3	4	5
1	$23,500	$24,088	$24,690	$25,307	$25,940
2	25,145	25,774	26,418	27,078	27,755
3	26,905	27,578	28,267	28,974	29,698
4	28,789	29,508	30,246	31,002	31,777
5	30,804	31,574	32,363	33,172	34,002
6	32,960	33,784	34,629	35,494	36,382
7	35,267	36,149	37,053	37,979	38,928
8	37,736	38,679	39,646	40,637	41,653
9	40,377	41,387	42,421	43,482	44,569
10	43,204	44,284	45,391	46,526	47,689
11	46,228	47,384	48,568	49,783	51,027
12	49,464	50,701	51,968	53,267	54,599
13	52,927	54,250	55,606	56,996	58,421
14	56,631	58,047	59,498	60,986	62,510
15	60,596	62,110	63,663	65,255	66,886
16	64,837	66,458	68,120	69,823	71,568
17	69,376	71,110	72,888	74,710	76,578
18	74,232	76,088	77,990	79,940	81,938
19	79,428	81,414	83,449	85,536	87,674
20	84,988	87,113	89,291	91,523	93,811

be handled as well. For weekly or biweekly periods, you will need to list the actual payroll dates, which is not necessary for payment periods of twice a month or every month.

If you pay employees every week, you need to be especially careful. Approximately every five years, a calendar year will start on the closing day of a weekly pay cycle. In this case, it will also end on the closing day of a weekly pay cycle. This means there will be 53 pay cycles in that year, and the cash budget for the payroll will be about 2 percent higher than otherwise.

IS THERE ANY LAGGING WITH RESPECT TO THE PAY? In our current example, there is no pay period lag. But some governments hold over one or two week's pay when employees are hired and pay them at the end of the second or third week. This is a far less common practice with payrolls that use longer pay periods. It is also important to know when step increases, performance increases, and payroll increases due to wage adjustments will be recognized in the pay. In our example, wage adjustments begin with the first payroll in the fiscal year. Step increases begin with the first full pay period after the anniversary date, as do performance increases. Our example assumes a longevity payment that is paid as a nonrecurring bonus at the next paycheck after the tenth anniversary date and every fifth anniversary thereafter.

WHO GETS WHAT KIND OF PAYMENTS, AND DO THEY GO INTO THE EMPLOYEE'S PAY BASE? In our example, the agency pays an annual step increase each year for four years, until the employee reaches the fifth step. The steps go into the employee's pay base. In real systems, there are usually either more steps, or people are likely able to move from one grade to another, having the effect of more steps.

We also posit a 1 percent performance payment that goes to half of the employees. The performance payment occurs every year. It does not go into the employee's pay base, so after one year the employee will see a decline in take-home pay unless the employee receives a step increase. As mentioned earlier, there are also longevity payments at certain anniversaries that do not go into the base.

WHAT DO YOU DO WITH VACANT POSITIONS? Vacant positions (or, more broadly, classes of new hires) should be represented at the correct level of pay. Some organizations hire strictly in entry-level positions. Police officers, teachers, and firefighters are common examples. Other organizations have much more complex rules about hiring at various steps. For example, many governments hire from within at low steps but hire from outside at higher steps. If a person moves from a lower grade within, that employee may be at step 1. If that employee enters from outside and had been paid a competitive salary, the employee's pay might begin at the top step. In our example, we assume that one new employee will be hired near the beginning of the future year and will be paid at the middle step.

WHEN DOES THE FISCAL YEAR BEGIN? In our example, it begins on July 1.

Forecasting Salaries

In this section, we discuss how to use the information outlined above to make a payroll forecast. We will begin by using the spreadsheet, "Budget Tools Chapter 03 Exercises," at the far-left tab, labeled "Payroll Forecast," to simulate the salary base for the next year, and then we will calculate benefits. This spreadsheet tab is shown below as well. In this example, we will use some Excel functions that may not be familiar to you, including some logical expressions, the VLOOKUP function, and the INDIRECT function. For more information about those functions, see the primer in the Appendix or review the Help material in your spreadsheet.

PAY PERIODS. Let us start with Table 3.4 and Table 3.5. These tables have also been stored in our "Budget Tools Chapter 03 Exercises" on tabbed pages labeled "Payroll Forecast" and "Pay Scale."

Tab 3.4

Tab 3.5

	A	B	C	D	E	F	G	H	I	J	K	L
1				Information Basis								
2	Emp. No	Last Name	First Name	Position Title	Pay Grade	Pay Step	Next Step	Length Of Service (yrs)	Anniv. Month	Anniv. Day	Pay Periods after step Increase	Pay Periods Before step Increase
3	45123	Stone	Melinda	Supervisor	18	5	5	10	9	15	19	5
4	45124	Delrico	Jose	Team Leader	15	3	4	2	7	22	22	2
5	45125	Shaft	George	Office Assistant	5	5	5	6	3	1	7	17
6	45126	Vacant		Technician	12	3	4	0	6	30	0	24
7	45127	Mayes	Angie	Technician	12	2	3	1	5	16	2	22
8	45128	Othman	Jerry	Technician	12	4	5	3	6	13	1	23
9												
10												
11												
12											Key	
13											4 OldByPeriod	
14												
15												
16											Key	
17											3 =	NewByPeriod
18											4 =	OldByPeriod
19												
20												
21												
22												
23												
24												
25												
26												
27												
28												
29												
30												

You will see Table 3.5 replicated in columns A through J and rows 1 through 8 of the spreadsheet.

Each employee who has not reached the top of the pay scale will be paid at two different pay rates during the course of the fiscal year. The problem to solve is how many pay periods will be at one pay rate and how many will be at another? If you look back at the rule, it states that a person moves from one step to the next at the beginning of the next pay period after their anniversary, and there is no lag between change in pay status and paycheck.

The formula embedded in the spreadsheet to calculate the number of pay periods after the step increase occurs first on row 3 on the spreadsheet on the tabbed sheet labeled "Payroll Forecast." Notice that column K and column L in Table 3.4 add up to 24 pay periods during the fiscal year. This formula differentiates the pay periods before and after the step increases.

$$(18-I3 - [12*\{I3<7\}])*2 + (J3<16) \qquad [3.3]$$

Note that this and other formulas and expressions are repeated on multiple rows with changing cell references. Only the first entry is cited in this discussion.

M	N	O	P	Q	R	S	T	U	V
Estimating Pay				Fixed Per Person Benefits				Total costs	
Current Periodic Pay	Future Periodic Pay	Expected Pay	Longevity Pay at Yr 10, 15, 20, 25 30	Health Insuranc e	UI	Total	Social Security Wage		Hired
$ 3,999.04	$ 3,999.04	$ 95,977.00	$5,000	$7,500	$364	$7,864	$ 94,200		9/15/1995
$ 3,021.60	$ 3,097.14	$ 74,180.27	$0	$7,500	$364	$7,864	$ 74,180		7/22/2003
$ 1,470.44	$ 1,470.44	$ 35,290.54	$0	$7,500	$364	$7,864	$ 35,291		3/1/1999
$ 2,398.64	$ 2,458.61	$ 57,567.44	$0	$7,500	$364	$7,864	$ 57,567		4/12/1998
$ 2,340.14	$ 2,398.64	$ 56,280.36	$0	$7,500	$364	$7,864	$ 56,280		5/16/2004
$ 2,458.61	$ 2,520.07	$ 59,068.09	$0	$7,500	$364	$7,864	$ 59,068		6/13/2002
		$ 378,364	$ 5,000			$ 45,000	$ 376,587		
	Performance Factor	0.005					6.2%		
		$ 1,892	$ 385,256	Total pay subject to benefits ratio			$ 23,348		
	Proportional Benefits						Total pay	$ 471,711	
	Workers Comp	1.25%				Vacancy Rate Factor	1.07		
	HI	1.45%				Estimated Payroll	$ 441,080		
	Retirement	1%				Turnover	1.12		
	Unspecified Benefits	1%			Estimated Payroll after Turnover		$ 393,869		
	Proportional Benefits Ratio	4.70%							
		$ 18,107							
	Assumption:	$5,000	$7,500	$364			$ 94,200		2005

Explanation of the formula in column K
(18 – M –(12, IF M <7))*2 + (1, IF D<16)
Where, M is month and D is Day
The first part assigns the number 1 to an anniversary month of August,
2 to Sept, etc.... Continuing 7 to January and 12 to June
It multiplies by 2 because there are 2 pay periods a month
The second part adds one more period if employment began before the 16th

	K3			f_x	=(18-I3-(12*(I3<7)))*2+(J3<16)					
	A	B	C	D	E	F	G	H	I	J	K

	A	B	C	D	E	F	G	H	I	J	K
1				**Information Basis**							
2	Emp. No	Last Name	First Name	Position Title	Pay Grade	Pay Step	Next Step	Length Of Service (yrs)	Anniv. Month	Anniv. Day	Pay Periods after step increase
3	45123	Stone	Melinda	Supervisor	18	5	5	10	9	15	19
4	45124	Delrico	Jose	Team Leader	15	3	4	2	7	22	22
5	45125	Shaft	George	Office Assistant	5	5	5	6	3	1	7
6	45126	Vacant		Technician	12	3	4	0	6	30	0
7	45127	Mayes	Angie	Technician	12	2	3	1	5	16	2
8	45128	Othman	Jerry	Technician	12	4	5	3	6	13	1

This formula includes a combination of logical and mathematical expressions. Column I contains the anniversary month value. The expression I3<7 is a logical expression that returns "TRUE" if the anniversary month is before July (entered as "7"). Remember that the fiscal year begins on July 1. If the value is more than 6, the anniversary is July or later, and the expression returns "FALSE." Excel treats "TRUE" as the value "1" and "FALSE" as "0" in mathematical expressions.

The expression (18-I3 – [12*{I3<7}]) leaves the correct number of months remaining in the fiscal year after the anniversary date. Once the expression has adjusted the year end, the multiplication by 2 adjusts for pay periods twice a month. For jurisdictions that use other fiscal years, the 7 should be adjusted to 10 and the 18 to 21 for fiscal years beginning in October, for example. If the fiscal year begins in January, this expression could be simplified to (12-I3)*2.

The expression (J3<16) is a logical expression that returns "TRUE" (or 1) if the entry in column J (anniversary day) is less than the beginning day of the second pay period of the month.

Together, the whole expression provides the number of pay periods in the fiscal year that follow the anniversary date. We will need this information for each employee.

By subtracting this information from the total pay periods in the year, we get the number of pay periods in the fiscal year that precedes the anniversary date, which is why there is the same expression in each cell from K3 through K8 adjusting for row numbers.

For our simulation, this is the most critical information. The procedures for weekly, monthly, and biweekly pay periods are shown on tabs with those labels in the spreadsheet "Budget Tools Chapter 03 Exercises" but are not discussed in detail. The expressions must be changed in columns K and L, and the pay scale must be appropriately adjusted. In addition, for weekly and biweekly pay periods, there is a table in columns J through O and rows 20 through approximately 29 that is used to compute the number of pay periods in the fiscal year.

COMBINING PAY PERIODS WITH PAY AMOUNTS. Table 3.5 is a grid of salary amounts. The rows show salary grades and the columns show salary steps. The spreadsheet shows a new table converting the annual amount to twice-monthly amounts by dividing each value by 24.

Both the original grid and the pay period grid can be found on the tab *— tab 3.5* labeled "Pay Scale." For convenience, this grid is in a range named "OldByPeriod" (Excel does not permit spaces in range names). Excel database functions allow very easy use of this grid to find any value within the *cell B16* table. We will use several Excel functions in this process.

To set up the table, we determined a relationship among all of the cells. The table is structured so that each step is 2.5 percent higher than the step

$979 × 1.025% = $1,004

	J	K	L	M	N	O	P
1							
2							
3							
4			Pay Periods				
5			24				
6			Step 1	Step 2	Step 3	Step 4	Step 5
7		1	$ 979	$1,004	$1,029	$1,054	$1,081
8		2	$ 1,058	$1,084	$1,111	$1,139	$1,167
9		3	$ 1,142	$1,171	$1,200	$1,230	$1,261
10		4	$ 1,233	$1,264	$1,296	$1,328	$1,362
11		5	$ 1,332	$1,365	$1,400	$1,435	$1,470
12		6	$ 1,439	$1,475	$1,512	$1,549	$1,588
13		7	$ 1,554	$1,593	$1,632	$1,673	$1,715
14		8	$ 1,678	$1,720	$1,763	$1,807	$1,852
15		9	$ 1,812	$1,858	$1,904	$1,952	$2,001
16		10	$ 1,957	$2,006	$2,056	$2,108	$2,161
17		11	$ 2,114	$2,167	$2,221	$2,276	$2,333
18		12	$ 2,283	$2,340	$2,399	$2,459	$2,520
19		13	$ 2,466	$2,527	$2,591	$2,655	$2,722
20		14	$ 2,663	$2,730	$2,798	$2,868	$2,939
21		15	$ 2,876	$2,948	$3,022	$3,097	$3,175
22		16	$ 3,106	$3,184	$3,263	$3,345	$3,429
23		17	$ 3,355	$3,438	$3,524	$3,613	$3,703
24		18	$ 3,623	$3,714	$3,806	$3,902	$3,999
25		19	$ 3,913	$4,011	$4,111	$4,214	$4,319
26		20	$ 4,226	$4,331	$4,440	$4,551	$4,664

$979 × 1.08% = $1,058

before it. Moreover, the beginning pay step at each grade is 8 percent higher than the next lower grade. These assumptions allow us to array all the data in the entire table with formulas after entering only the lowest value in the top left cell. In the real world, if such relationships are not so clear in a pay system, you can enter the full array itself instead.

The next thing we did was use an Excel feature to name a range, which included the grade labels and the pay scale, but *not* the step labels. This will allow us to use another Excel feature to change with ease the array referenced, which will come in handy when the pay scale changes.

To find and use a grade and step salary we use this formula:

$$\text{VLOOKUP}(\$E3,\text{INDIRECT}[K\$13],F3+1) \tag{3.4}$$

The VLOOKUP function in Excel takes the general form of VLOOKUP(x,y,z). It looks in an array designated by y, and returns the item designated by z that corresponds to the item identified by x. The referent x will be a label. In this example, x is the cell in column E, which contains the pay grade. The referent z specifies how many columns over in the table to look. Because the label column is counted, we can confidently count the right number as the step (found in column F) plus 1. This annual amount is divided by the number of pay periods, or 24, to find the salary amount for each pay period.

The expression INDIRECT(x) is particularly useful to us. At the cell location specified by x, we can type in the range name of the pay scale, which has been stored in cell K13. (The use of the "$" sign in the middle of the cell address for cell k$13 is explained in the appendix for spreadsheeting, Appendix C.) If we want to compare one pay scale with another, for instance, we can simply replace one range name with another and get the change in the results.

$ = absolute pages 188-189

M3				f_x	=VLOOKUP($E3,INDIRECT{K$13},F3+1)							
	A	B	C	D	E	F	G	H	I	J	K	L	M
1				**Information basis**									
2	Emp. no.	Last name	First name	Position title	Pay grade	Pay step	Next step	Length of service (years)	Anniv. month	Anniv. day	Pay periods after step increase	Pay periods before step increase	Current periodic pay
3	45123	Stone	Melinda	Supervisor	18	5	5	10	9	15	19	5	$ 3,999.0
4	45124	Delrico	Jose	Team Leader	15	3	4	2	7	22	22	2	$ 3,021.4
5	45125	Shaft	George	Office Assistant	5	5	5	6	3	1	7	17	$ 1,470.4
6	45126	Vacant		Technician	12	3	4	0	6	30	0	24	$ 2,398.0
7	45127	Mayes	Angie	Technician	12	2	3	1	5	16	2	22	$ 2,340.1
8	45128	Othman	Jerry	Technician	12	4	5	3	6	13	1	23	$ 2,458.0
9													
10													
11													
12											Key		
13											4	OldByPeriod	

Once we have the pay for the periods of pay at each level, a simple multiplication gives the total pay for each set of periods, and the addition of the two parts gives the regular pay for the employee for the year.

VACANT POSITIONS.   We have included one vacant position during the forecast period, so we need to look back at our hiring expectations to estimate values for columns "Step," "Next step," "Anniversary month," and "Anniversary day." We stated that the hypothetical employee would be hired at the third step and set the anniversary date as the last day of the fiscal year. If we knew an actual anticipated hiring date, we could instead set the step and anniversary date to reflect the actual anticipated information. The inclusion of these assumptions is shown in the yellow highlighted cells on row 6 of the Payroll Forecast tab in the exercise spreadsheet.

OTHER PAY.   In the example, there are two kinds of other pay: longevity pay and performance pay. Neither of these is included in the base for the next year. The longevity pay is paid as if it were a bonus on the longevity date. Performance pay is a 1 percent increment paid over the whole year, and half the work unit is eligible for it. In the Payroll Forecast tab of the spreadsheet, the longevity pay is not included in the base for calculation of the performance pay.

In the spreadsheet the longevity pay is included in the simulation with a logic formula:

$$OR(H3=10,H3=15,H3=20,H3=25,H3=30)*P\$20 \qquad [3.5]$$

P3			f_x	=OR(H3=10,H3=15,H3=20,H3=25,H3=30)*P$20		
A	K	L	M	N	O	P
1			Estimating Pay			
Emp. No	Pay Periods after step Increase	Pay Periods Before step Increase	Current Periodic Pay	Future Periodic Pay	Expected Pay	Longevity Pay at Yr 10, 15, 20, 25 30
45123	19	5	$ 3,999.04	$ 3,999.04	$ 95,977.00	$5,000
45124	22	2	$ 3,021.60	$ 3,097.14	$ 74,180.27	$0
45125	7	17	$ 1,470.44	$ 1,470.44	$ 35,290.54	$0
45126	0	24	$ 2,398.64	$ 2,458.61	$ 57,567.44	$0
45127	2	22	$ 2,340.14	$ 2,398.64	$ 56,280.36	$0
45128	1	23	$ 2,458.61	$ 2,520.07	$ 59,068.09	$0

Remember that the longevity pay is paid after each five-year period of service beginning with the ten-year service anniversary. The expression OR(x, y, . . . ,n) returns the value "TRUE" ("1") if any of the statements within the commas are true. The value in cell P16 is $5,000, the amount of longevity pay. By placing it in a separate cell, we can easily change it if the value changes in future policy.

The performance pay is calculated by summing the expected pay (both before and after the anniversary dates) and multiplying by .005 (.5 percent). See column O, rows 10 through 12 here:

O12				f_x	=O10*O11	
	A	L	M	N	O	P
1				Estimating Pay		
2	Emp. No	Pay Periods Before step Increase	Current Periodic Pay	Future Periodic Pay	Expected Pay	Longevity Pay at Yr 10, 15, 20, 25 30
3	45123	5	$ 3,999.04	$ 3,999.04	$ 95,977.00	$5,000
4	45124	2	$ 3,021.60	$ 3,097.14	$ 74,180.27	$0
5	45125	17	$ 1,470.44	$ 1,470.44	$ 35,290.54	$0
6	45126	24	$ 2,398.64	$ 2,458.61	$ 57,567.44	$0
7	45127	22	$ 2,340.14	$ 2,398.64	$ 56,280.36	$0
8	45128	23	$ 2,458.61	$ 2,520.07	$ 59,068.09	$0
9						
10					$ 378,364	5,000
11				Performance Facto	0.005	
12					$ 1,892	385,256
13					Proportional Benefits	
14					Workers Comp	1.25%
15					HI	1.45%
16					Retirement	1%
17					Unspecified Benefits	1%
18					Proportional Benefits Ratio	4.70%
19						$ 18,107

Together, these calculations allow use to estimate the salary portion of the budget base, and we can move on to calculate fringe benefits.

Forecasting Fringe Benefits

As suggested earlier, we need to think about at least three categories of benefits:

■ Benefits whose cost is unrelated to the employee's salary. For example, health insurance costs do not usually increase with salaries. Some governments may have other such benefits for employees.

■ Benefits whose cost is directly related to the employee's salary. Likely candidates include the employer's contribution to worker's compensation tax, the employer's contribution to retirement plans, the federal Medicare tax, and other similar costs. These are usually expressed as a ratio or a percentage of the employee's salary.

■ Social Security tax, sometimes called OASDI or FICA. At lower salary levels, it is proportional like the items in the second group. But salaries above the Social Security tax ceiling are not subject to this tax during every pay period. In 2007 the maximum taxable amount was $97,500 (it was $90,000 in the example year, 2005).

The Social Security Administration publishes a table at www.ssa.gov/mystatement/maxtax.htm showing the maximum taxable amounts.

In our example, unemployment insurance (UI) at $364 per employee and health insurance, which we have set at $7,500 per employee, are constant costs regardless of the employee's salary.

Our example is, of course, oversimplified. In fact, there are likely to be at least two classes of health insurance costs, one for employees covering only themselves, and a second for employees claiming benefits for families. It may be necessary to develop the spreadsheet to deal with such matters.

Proportional benefits are workers' compensation, estimated at 1.25 percent, HI (Medicare) estimated at 1.45 percent, retirement estimated at an employer's cost of 1 percent, and other unspecified items estimated at 1 percent.

The ratio for the employer's share of Social Security is set at .062 (6.2 percent) as shown by www.ssa.gov/OACT/COLA/cbb.html.

Our calculations follow the same outline. First, we add the constant or fixed benefit per employee amount. These are shown in the spreadsheet with $7,500 in column Q and $364 in column R, totaled to $7,864 in column S. Additional fixed costs can be added simply by adding columns between Q and R. The total of column S is found in cell S10.

To apply Social Security benefits, the wage against which the tax is calculated must be restricted to the maximum taxable amount, which in 2005 was $90,000. The maximum can be found at www.ssa.gov. The spreadsheet applies this maximum taxable rule in column T with the formula:

$$\text{MIN}(O3+P3,T\$20) \hspace{2cm} [3.6]$$

This means that the tax rate is applied to the minimum of either O3 plus P3, which is the annual income (including the longevity pay bonus), or T20,

	A	L	M	N	O	P	Q	R	S	T
1				Estimating pay				Fixed per person benefits		
2	Emp. no.	Pay periods before step increase	Current periodic pay	Future periodic pay	Expected pay	Longevity pay at year 10, 15, 20, 25, 30	Health insurance	UI	Total	Social Security wage
3	45123	5	$ 3,999.04	$ 3,999.04	$ 95,977.00	$5,000	$7,500	$364	$7,864	$ 90,000
4	45124	2	$ 3,021.60	$ 3,097.14	$ 74,180.27	$0	$7,500	$364	$7,864	$ 74,180
5	45125	17	$ 1,470.44	$ 1,470.44	$ 35,290.54	$0	$7,500	$364	$7,864	$ 35,291
6	45126	24	$ 2,398.64	$ 2,458.61	$ 57,567.44	$0	$7,500	$364	$7,864	$ 57,567
7	45127	22	$ 2,340.14	$ 2,398.64	$ 56,280.36	$0	$7,500	$364	$7,864	$ 56,280
8	45128	23	$ 2,458.61	$ 2,520.07	$ 59,068.09	$0	$7,500	$364	$7,864	$ 59,068
9										
10					$ 378,364	$ 5,000			$ 47,184	$ 372,387
11				Performance factor	0.005					6.2%
12					$ 1.892	$ 385.256	Total pay subject to benefits ratio			$ 23,088
13				Proportional benefits					Total pay	
14				Workers' comp.		1.25%			Vacancy rate factor	
15				HI		1.45%			Estimated payroll	
16				Retirement		1%			Turnover	
17				Unspecified benefits		1%			Estimated payroll after turnover	
18				Proportional benefits ratio		4.70%				
19						$ 18,107				
20					Assumption:	$5,000	$7,500	$364		$ 90,000

which contains the maximum taxable amount. It is in a separate cell so you can change it when the Social Security law changes. Because the jurisdiction's fiscal year bridges two years, and the Social Security minimum affects the end of the year earnings, the rule for the first year should be applied.

The totals of the taxable amounts are summed in cell T10 and multiplied by the Social Security rate in cell T11, to find the employer's Social Security contribution in cell T12.

To apply the remaining proportional benefit cost, sum the regular pay and add the performance pay and the longevity pay. In the spreadsheet, these numbers are found in O10, O12, and P10. They are added together in cell P12. This amount is multiplied by the value of the proportional benefits cost in P18 (excluding Social Security), resulting in the amount in cell P19. The value of various components of proportional benefits are summed in the table from P14 through P17.

When we add the benefits (found in P19, S10, and T12) to the expected pay (P12) we get the total expected pay. In the real world, additional adjustments would be required. These would include adjustments for vacancies and an adjustment for new hires at the novice rate. The latter is sometimes called "turnover." A simple calculation for **vacancy rate** is to count the number of

	A	R	S	T	U
1		er person benefits			Total costs
2	Emp. no.	UI	Total	Social Security wage	
12		bject to benefits ratio		$ 23,088	
13			Total pay		$ 473,635
14			Vacancy rate factor		1.07
15			Estimated payroll		$ 442,879
16			Turnover		1.12
17			Estimated payroll after turnover		$ 395,475
18					

periods for which any position is vacant and divide it by the total number of periods times the total number of positions. The result should be a very small fraction. To this fraction add the number 1. In the spreadsheet, cell U14, you will see a "Vacancy rate factor" of 1.07. Total pay, cell U13, is adjusted by this factor to get vacancy adjusted pay in cell U15. The turnover factor is shown in cell U16. Turnover is a complex concept that applies when the mean pay level of resigning employees is higher than the mean pay level of new hires. Calculation is an advanced topic not discussed in this chapter. The "Turnover" factor in cell U16 is used in the same way that the "Vacancy rate factor" is used, resulting in an "Estimated payroll after turnover" in cell U17. This amount becomes the payroll estimate. For both of these factors, multiyear averages or trends are likely to be more reliable than single-year calculations.

Summary

Budget preparation includes analyzing new initiatives and incorporating budget cuts. When conducting these analyses, students must understand the cost structure of the proposed activities. Costs differ from expenditures in that costs are all the expenses associated with a program whether or not those particular costs are included in a budget. There are many different types of costs, including fixed costs, step-fixed costs, and variable costs.

Payroll forecasting through simulation provides an accurate estimate of payroll expense in the future year. It relies on building a model of the payroll system characteristics and applying them to the existing employee base. Because most contributing factors to payroll expense are determined by fixed rules or are within the discretion of the budget authority, prediction can be very accurate. Production of even a very simple simulation requires relatively sophisticated spreadsheet user skills. With practice, these spreadsheets can be modified and developed to make useful estimates under many circumstances.

Exercises

To complete the exercises, use the spreadsheet files entitled "Budget Tools Chapter 03 Exercises."

1. Turning costs into budgets. Each investigator at a human rights agency is required to complete 144 investigations of discriminations a year, while senior investigators are required to complete 180 a year. If the agency wanted to increase the completion of investigations to 5,000 investigations yearly, how many investigators would be needed? Create a budget that would permit the agency this increase. The costs and assumptions are in Table 3.6. $2,898,260   33

2. Thinking about budget cuts. The mayor of Chicago faces a deficit in the coming fiscal year and has decided to consolidate several operations. One part of the solution is to close a firehouse on the north side of town because far fewer fires have been taking place there. Personnel will be laid off; the equipment and firehouse will be sold. How much will the city save in nonrecurring and recurring expenditures? The costs and assumptions for the fire house are in Table 3.7. $1,810,250. and $2,680,000.

3. Creating a payroll simulation. In the spreadsheet "Budget Tools Chapter 03 Exercises" there is a tab labeled "Exercise New Posi-

---

TABLE 3.6
Assumptions in Exercise 1: Turning Costs into Budgets

Fixed costs

Executive director	
Salary	$ 90,000
Fringe benefits (29.0%)	26,100
Total	$116,100
Rent	$ 26,000
Utilities	$ 10,200

Step-fixed Costs

Investigator	
Salary investigator I	$ 60,000
Salary investigator II	75,000
	$135,000
Fringe benefits (29.0%)	39,150
Total	$174,150

Variable costs (per investigator per day)

Supplies	$4

Assumptions

Investigator I/complaint ratio (annual)	144
Investigator II/complaint ratio (annual)	180
Number of days of operation	280
Fringe benefit rate	29%

tions." This tab contains a table with six position numbers 45401 through 45406, as also shown in the image below:

Each position is currently vacant. These are positions for a new function that is to be implemented at the beginning of the 2007 fiscal year, which begins in July 2006. The jurisdiction pays twice each month. In the "Next step" column is the anticipated pay grade at which each employee will be hired. For expenses not described here, assume they are the same as in the example. The twice-monthly pay scale is on the "Exercise New Positions" tab in a named range, "ExerciseScale." For calendar year 2006 the Social Security income cap was $94,200, and for 2007 it was $97,500. However, this is a new function for which new employees will begin in the middle of 2006, so there may be a special consideration. As these are new positions for a new function, vacancy and turnover factors are not relevant in the first year. Use this information to determine the expected first-year cost of these employees. [Hint: it may be much faster to copy this information into the "Information basis" section of the existing "Payroll Forecast" tab of the spreadsheet and then to edit those other elements of the sheet that must be adjusted. Before you do this, be sure you save the spreadsheet with a new file name so you can use the original again.]

TABLE 3.7
Savings in Closing a Chicago Firehouse

Costs	No. of positions	Salary
PS		
Captain	1	$ 75,000
Deputy captain	1	70,000
Lieutenants	2	65,000
Senior firefighters	5	60,000
Firefighters	15	50,000
OTPS		
Maintenance		$ 60,000
Heat, light, power		45,000
Supplies		30,000
Travel		4,000
Training consultant		15,000
Sale of equipment		$180,000
Sale of building		$2,500,000
Assumptions		
Fringe benefits		25%

Note: PS = personnel services; OTPS = other than personnel services.

	A	B	C	D	E	F	G	H	I	J
1				**Information Basis**						
2	Employee No	Last Name	First Name	Position Title	Payroll Grade	Payroll Step	Next Step	Length Of Service (yrs)	Anniversary Month	Anniversary Day
3	45401	Vacant		Supervisor	15		4	0	7	16
4	45402	Vacant		Team Leader	13		3	0	8	16
5	45403	Vacant		Office Assistant	5		1	0	8	16
6	45404	Vacant		Technician	11		1	0	9	1
7	45405	Vacant		Technician	11		1	0	9	1
8	45406	Vacant		Technician	11		1	0	9	16
9										

4. Forecasting payroll. Using the information on the "Payroll Forecast" tab, you need to tell the mayor what the cost would be for three possible general pay increases for the upcoming year. The amounts he would like to consider are 1 percent, 3 percent, and 5 percent. On the "Pay Scale" tab of the "Budget Tools Chapter 03 Exercises" spreadsheet, cell C30 is designed for entering pay increases. For 1 percent, you would enter 1.01 in C30. You then must go back to the "Payroll Forecast" and in cell J3 enter the key for the named range, "NewByPeriod" (the key is 4). The spreadsheet will automatically calculate the new pay amount. After you provide the cost for the three possible increases, the mayor might ask you, "What would we save if we eliminated the performance pay increment?" Write a brief memo to the mayor providing the results of your analysis.

Additional Readings

Behn, Robert D. "Cutback Budgeting." *Journal of Policy Analysis and Management* 4, no. 2 (1985): 155–177.

Levine, Charles H. "More on Cutback Management: Hard Questions for Hard Times." *Public Administration Review* 39, no. 2 (1979): 179–183.

Rabin, Jack, W. Bartley Hildreth, and Gerald J. Miller, eds. *Budgeting Formulation and Execution.* Athens, Ga.: Carl Vinson Institute of Government, University of Georgia, 1996.

Chapter 4

First Steps in Revenue Estimating

Learning objectives:

- Calculate percentages and rate of inflation
- Establish data trends
- Learn difference between current and constant dollars
- Visualize and graph time series data
- Identify and correct outliers
- Forecast nonseasonal data with Holt exponential smoothing
- Use root mean square error and mean error to fit a forecast
- Adjust forecasts for judgmental data

This chapter addresses two topics: developing a budget history through trend analysis and introducing a very simple method for forecasting data. The trend analysis demonstrates the use of both current and constant dollars. The larger the budget office, the more you may have at stake in forecasts. In situations where the stakes are more consequential, it is worthwhile to employ a trained forecaster who can use somewhat more advanced methods or to use this method with more sophistication. If you forecast regularly, you should use appropriate forecasting software such as Forecasting Pro, Autobox, or the forecasting module of SAS. If you forecast infrequently, you may choose to use spreadsheets to forecast and adapt the forecast spreadsheet included with this book to your needs.

Methods for forecasting can be very simple, simple, complex, or very complex. It is not uncommon to find very simple ones in use in budget practice. By way of comparison, the payroll method shown in Chapter 3 is complex. The method offered here is neither very simple, nor is it complex.[1]

In this chapter, after a brief discussion of basic forecasting concepts and terms, we will discuss forecasting with Holt exponential smoothing and learn how to use the root mean square error and mean error to trade off accuracy and bias. The chapter contains a guided example demonstrating how to create an *XY* plot. From there you will be able to do revenue estimating in two spreadsheet exercise scenarios. Forecasting focuses on data in time series; it is not particularly relevant that the data may be revenue or expenditures. Your expenditures are someone else's revenue.

Developing a Budget History in Current and Constant Dollars

It is important to examine past data. What was spent last year? What was spent ten years ago? Twenty years ago? The reason we do this is that the best prediction of what the future brings is the past, particularly the most recent past.

Calculating Percentages

We use percentages to compare data from one year with another year as well as to compare the unit of analysis with a reference group. There are two reasons for using percentages. First, when comparing multiple jurisdictions or components of very different sizes, percentages provide a more realistic basis for comparison than dollar figures; second, large numbers can be confusing, but percentages are something many people understand.

There are three different methods of comparison: **percentage change, percentage of total,** and **reference groups.** Each of these methods can explain data in useful ways. Below are examples of how each of these methods is calculated. The examples are drawn from expenditures of the Health Department of New York City and are portrayed in thousands (see Table 4.1).

TABLE 4.1

Expenditures for Health in New York City, Fiscal Years 1996–2007 (in thousands)

Fiscal years	Health Department	Mental Health Department	Hospitals Department	New York City's total health expenditures	New York City's total expenditures	CPI
1996	$419,308	$319,275	$1,090,173	$1,828,756	$32,066,586	166.9
1997	420,275	345,284	682,924	1,448,483	33,736,152	170.8
1998	472,030	396,095	684,601	1,552,726	34,923,250	173.6
1999	491,603	437,292	722,094	1,650,989	35,858,612	177.0
2000	790,726	251,446	735,127	1,777,299	37,879,886	182.5
2001	906,947	295,114	757,023	1,959,084	40,226,977	187.1
2002	1,049,135	256,064	826,307	2,131,506	40,860,000	191.9
2003	1,414,923	—	826,572	2,241,495	44,340,229	197.8
2004	1,441,247	—	976,875	2,418,122	47,292,395	204.8
2005	1,432,047	—	992,136	2,424,183	52,789,712	212.7
2006	1,467,786	—	1,290,016	2,757,802	53,999,075	220.7
2007	1,513,879	—	758,603	2,272,482	58,705,982	229.5

Note: The Mental Health Department was merged with the Health Department in FY 2003. CPI = consumer price index; CPI Adjusted Index: CUURA101SA0, New York-Northern New Jersey-Long Island, NY-NJ-CT-PA; base period 1982–1984 = 100. CPI figure for FY 2007 is November 2007.

The Department of Health consists of three departments: Health, Mental Health, and Hospitals.

There are two different ways of calculating percentage change, one using current dollars and one using constant dollars. The first example in the next subsection uses current dollars, which are dollars not adjusted for inflation. The second example demonstrates how to control for inflation by converting current dollars to constant dollars. These techniques are useful in examining historical data for both government and nonprofit groups.

PERCENTAGE CHANGE. Percentages can be used in several ways. Percentage change explains changes in data from year to year or for several years. Data in Table 4.1 show the percentage change in the expenditures for the Department of Health from fiscal year 1996 to fiscal year 1997 to be 0.2 percent. When you have several years of data, percentage changes are particularly useful for discovering patterns in expenditure data.

Percentage change is calculated by subtracting the older year from the newer year and then dividing by the older year. This is usually done in a spreadsheet. If this calculation is done on a calculator, the student should multiply times 100. See an example below using the data in Table 4.1:

Newer year – older year / older year * 100 (when using a calculator)

	FY 1997	FY 1996
Department of Health expenditures	$420,275,000	$419,308,000

To find percentage growth of expenditures FY 1997:

$$\$420,275,000 - \$419,308,000 = \$967,000$$

$$\$967,000 / \$419,308,000 \times 100 = 0.2 \text{ percent}$$

Thus, the percentage change for the Department of Health from FY 1996 to FY 1997 is less than 1 percent, or 0.2 percent. Percentage change can be calculated over several years, not just from one year to another. For example, with the data in Table 4.1 we can calculate the total percentage change for an eleven-year period for the Department of Health:

Percentage growth of expenditures for FY 2007 compared with FY 1996:

$$\$1,513,879,000 - \$419,308,000 = \$1,094,571,000$$

$$\$1,094,571,000 / \$419,308,000 \times 100 = 261.0 \text{ percent}$$

Thus, the percentage change for the Department of Health from FY 1996 to FY 2007 is 261.0 percent.

Why bother calculating percentages of change over time? We do it because it is the most useful method for understanding how expenditures have grown or declined over time. In addition, we can gain insight into the cycles of growth and decline over time.

PERCENTAGE OF TOTAL (COMMON SIZING). The percentage of total, or common sizing, explains the proportionality of an item; in other words, how much of the city's total health expenditures are in the Health Department only compared with the expenditures in the hospital system or the mental health system. When several years of data are used, it is possible to examine how proportionality has changed over time. The percentage of the total is calculated by dividing the item by the total. When using a calculator, again multiply the result by 100. See an example below using the data from Table 4.1.

Item / total × 100, when using a calculator

Department of Health Expenditures / Total Expenditures × 100 =

$419,308,000 / $1,828,756,000 × 100 = 22.9 percent

Thus, the proportion of the total health dollars in the city going to the Department of Health compared with the total city investment in health is 22.9 percent.

The advantage of using proportionality is that we see the changes that have taken place for one part of the total health expenditures for the city. And if we compare the proportionality from year to year, we gain in understanding of how types of health resources are being distributed in the city.

COMPARING REFERENCE GROUPS. Another way to analyze the changes in expenditures is to use a reference group, which is a way to compare the trends you have found in your analysis. You choose a reference group that has some relationship to your data. When examining health data, you may want to compare the amount of health expenditures and the changes in those amounts over time in large cities. In the following example (refer to Table 4.1 again), the reference group is New York City's total expenditures.

	FY 1996	FY 1997	Percentage change
New York City's total health expenditures	$1,828,756,000	$1,448,483,000	−20.8
New York City's total expenditures	$32,066,586,000	$33,736,152,000	5.2

The percentage change in total health expenditures over a one-year period is –20.8 percent, while the percentage change in total expenditures for New York City is 5.2 percent. During this period, health expenditures were dramatically cut even as the city's total expenditures grew. Using reference groups can be illuminating. In the exercises at the end of the chapter, you can calculate reference groups over an eleven-year period and gain insight into the extent to which city officials placed health in a prominent place in their policy making.

Calculating the Rate of Inflation (Constant Dollars or Real Dollars)

Constant dollars are the same as current dollars except we control for inflation; that is, we take inflation out of the dollar amount of items. The reason we calculate the effects of inflation is to accurately compare costs of services over time. Using inflation-adjusted numbers (constant dollars) rather than current dollars helps us understand the fluctuations in unit costs over several years. Taking inflation out of the numbers allows us to determine the "real" increase in expenditures or revenues.

An **index** is a benchmark of activity and can be used to examine changes over time. The **Consumer Price Index** (CPI) is one of the most commonly used indices. It is a weighted average of prices of a basket of consumer goods and services that people often purchase. The CPI provides a measure for **inflation,** which is the fall in the purchasing power of the dollar. The CPI is also used as a guide to various cost-of-living adjustments, such as labor negotiations, salary increases, and budgeting increases, from year to year.

An example of how to calculate constant dollars from current dollars is given below.

First, we find the CPI by accessing the Bureau of Labor Statistics Web site at http://stats.bls.gov/. At the Web site, we choose the Consumer Price Index; on the next Web page, we choose the Urban Wage Earners and Clerical Workers CPI because most Americans live in cities and because it best represents the costs in urban areas. We can also choose the region we want. In this case, we chose the New York metropolitan area.

This is an example of the Consumer Price Index for All Urban Consumers used in the following example:

Series Id: CUURA101SA0
Not Seasonally Adjusted
Area: New York-Northern New Jersey-Long Island, NY-NJ-CT-PA
Item: All items
Base Period: 1982–1984 = 100

Year	Annual
1996	166.9
1997	170.8
1998	173.6
1999	177.0
2000	182.5
2001	187.1
2002	191.9
2003	197.8
2004	204.8
2005	212.7
2006	220.7
2007	229.5 (Nov.)

After you determine which CPI you will use, you will choose the base year you are going to use; that is, which year are we going to compare with all the other years? In our example, FY 2007 with a CPI of 229.5 is the base year. The exact formula is:

Current dollar expenditures × [Base year CPI/Current year CPI] = Constant dollars

Here are two examples:

1.3750749

Fiscal year	New York City Department of Health, current dollar expenditures		CPI		Constant dollars
1996	$419,308,000	×	$\frac{229.5^a}{166.9^b}$	=	$576,580,000
1997	$420,275,000	×	$\frac{229.5^a}{170.8^b}$	=	$564,714,000

[a] Base year CPI
[b] Current year CPI

At the end of this chapter are exercises on trend analysis in which students can calculate both current and constant dollars across time.

Basic Forecasting Concepts and Terms

First we need to agree what the term **forecast** means. A forecast is the estimated value for a period based on information from previous periods. With
time series data, we can make serial forecasts of past periods as well as future
periods. Past periods are forecast based on information terminating before that
actual period. Such forecasts give us a way to evaluate the effectiveness of the
forecast model by comparing forecast and actual. Forecast models produce a
mid-point forecast, that is, the forecast of the most likely value. The full forecast also includes an estimate of the confidence interval, which is the range
over which there is a good chance the value will be found. Forecast confidence
intervals are notoriously difficult to determine. A commonsense way to understand the risk in forecast is to keep a record of all forecasts made as each new
observation becomes available and the forecast
is brought up to date.

For discussion purposes, it is assumed that
the data are at the annual **level.** Level refers to
how frequently the data are recorded, and possible levels include weekly, monthly, quarterly,
and annual. However, the methods used here for
annual data are equally effective for data at
other levels, such as monthly or weekly. These
methods outlined here are for **nonseasonal
data.** When the data are nonseasonal and the
methods are of the simple sort explained here,
the level of the data is not relevant to the application of the method. Annual data are naturally
nonseasonal. Other data often have to be made
nonseasonal. Forecast data should also be free of outliers and missing data.[2]
Making data nonseasonal requires considerable effort, which leads to the
chief advantage of working with the naturally nonseasonal annual data. The
chief disadvantage is that annual data provide no means of updating forecasts
or determining how effective the forecast has been before the end of the next
year. In this chapter, we work with annual data or nonseasonal data. In the first
example, we will see an outlier, its effect on the forecast, and a simple solution.

TIPS FOR WORKING WITH DATA
Always graph data. It is important to create graphs of
your data because graphs will provide you with an understanding of your data that would be missing if you
did not see it in graphic form.

Adjust away outliers. Individual data elements that
are extreme must be controlled or else these data elements will skew your results. Outliers can be controlled by omitting them or averaging them.

Keep records of original, unadjusted data. Always
keep an original copy of your data in case you need to
return to your original data. If outliers repeat, you may
decide that earlier events were not outliers after all.

Creating an *XY* Plot for Visualizing Data in Excel

In the following steps we will make an *XY* graph and examine data for outliers. Outliers will be identified but will not be corrected until we have used
the data. That way we will see what happens when there are outliers and what
happens when they are corrected. First, however, we need to make an *XY*
graph. The following guidelines follow the process in Microsoft Office 2007.

1. Highlight the columns that contain the data. (If you would like to practice this yourself, see "Budget Tools Chapter 04 Text Examples and Exercises" on the accompanying disk. Columns can be found in the sheet labeled "Tbl 1" in the support spreadsheet for this chapter.)

	Data	
Period	X_i	
Period 0		
1980	2,210.0	2
1981	2,320.6	2
1982	2,488.3	2
1983	2,767.7	2
1984	3,082.9	3
1985	3,348.8	3
1986	3,430.8	3
1987	3,943.7	3
1988	3,656.3	4
1989	4,083.9	3
1990	4,021.0	4
1991	4,254.9	4
1992	4,772.5	4
1993	4,979.3	4
1994	4,968.9	5
1995	4,894.3	5
1996	5,173.8	5
1997	5,648.2	5
1998	6,547.3	5
1999	6,871.8	6
2000	6,749.2	7
2001	7,209.0	7
2002	5,762.6	7
2003	5,661.4	6
2004	6,653.4	5
2005	7,635.3	6
2006	8,245.0	7
2007	8,647.8	8

The column that will serve as the *X* axis label must be the leftmost of the columns highlighted. Start at the labeled header row. You can skip a column or row by holding the control key down and beginning the highlight again at the next column or row you want to include. If the labels are not immediately above the data, you can either enter labels manually or hold the control key down and then highlight the row that contains the labels. Take note, the labels row must be in the same order as the data.

2. Next, select the insert ribbon (this is a new Microsoft Office 2007 application; see Appendix C for the older approach).

I have the 2004 version of Excel.

Insert
Chart
Scatter

3. On the insert ribbon select *XY* (scatter) see image below.

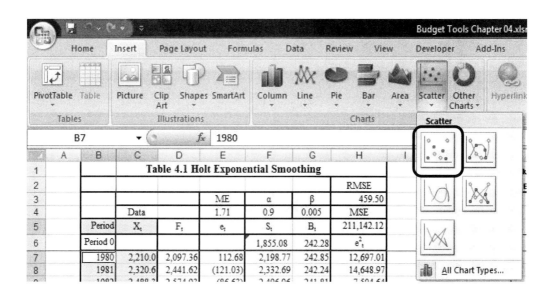

Select the indicated scattergram.

4. The chart will appear in your spreadsheet as seen below, and the ribbon will change to the one seen below.

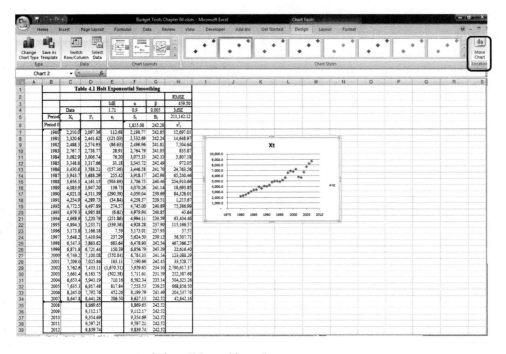

5. Select "Move Chart."

6. In the resultant dialog box,

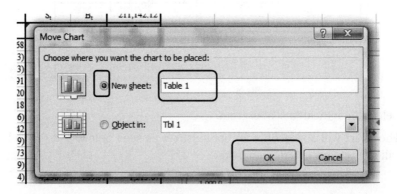

Select the radio button for "New sheet:" and type "Table 1," then click OK.

7. The chart should now look like the following graphic.

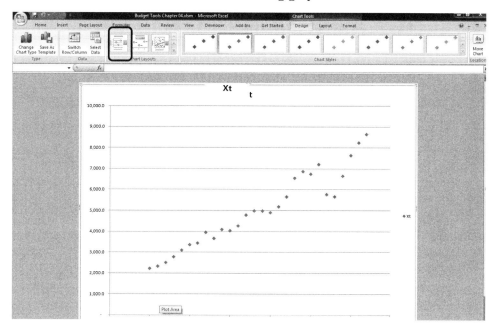

To begin formatting it, select the indicated chart style.

8. Edit the chart title and axes titles directly on the chart as shown in the next two images

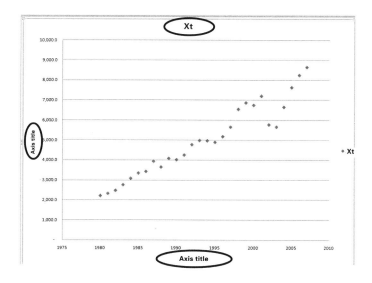

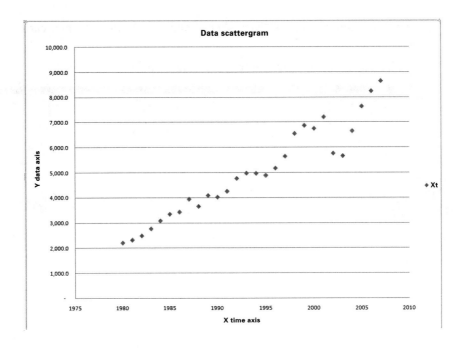

9. Click once on any of the grid lines and press the delete key.

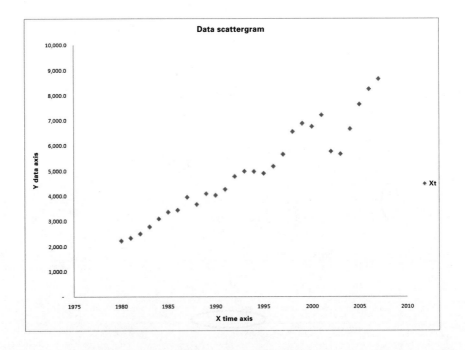

10. Click directly on the 1975, then right click to bring up the following screen:

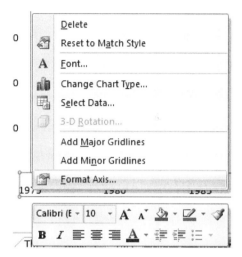

11. Select "Format Axis..." to bring up this screen:

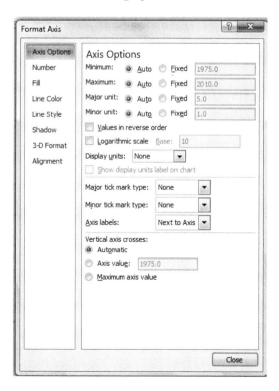

12. Change the indicated radio buttons to "Fixed" and the values to 1980 and 2007 and click the "Close" button.

13. Use the same process to call up the Format Axis menu for the *Y* axis and set the minimum and maximum values to 2000 and 9000.

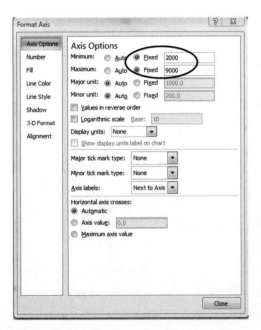

14. Before closing the *Y* Format Axis menu, select the "Number" menu, and set the format to Currency, with zero decimal places.

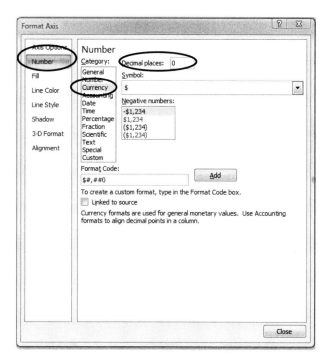

15. The resulting graph should look as follows:

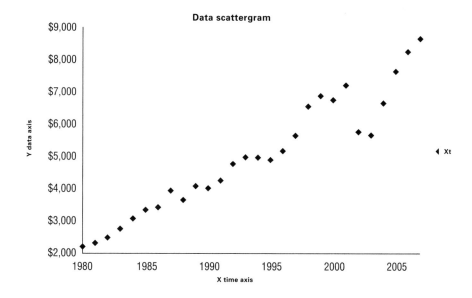

In this graph, the historically oldest data are on the left and the newest data are on the right, so the direction of time is from left to right.

16. In the next copy of this same scattergram, we have marked the outliers. Additional discussion will follow.

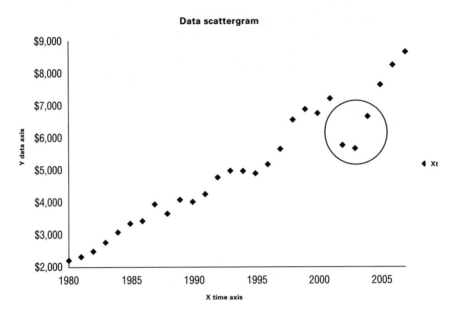

Data scattergram

Two or three observations together usually would not be considered outliers unless there is something very special about them. As subsequent discussion will show, these data are related to personal income tax in New York City, and the three marked observations occur in the three years following the terrorist attack on the city; that fact plus their visually exceptional character provide sufficient reason to treat all three of them as outliers. The first two are quite obviously outliers taken in the context of the whole series. The third is less certain, falling only slightly further out of line than other cyclical low points; however, within the known context, it is not unreasonable to consider it part of the outlier set. In the more typical situation, outliers will be singletons.

In most cases, visual inspection is sufficient to identify outliers. Observations that are uncertain probably are not outliers. The correct treatment of an outlier is to substitute a non-outlier replacement. If there is some reason to believe the outlier is an erroneous entry, identifying the correct entry would be best. Although there are

FORECASTING BASICS
Initialize the forecast. Initializing helps with selecting the best forecast parameters.

Use a grid search. Select parameters that minimize the root mean square error without severely increasing mean error.

Graph the forecast. Compare the forecast with the actual data for a commonsense visual check. Forecasts should not surprise you compared with the end of the historical data.

other plausible solutions, the one used in this chapter is to substitute the average of the two nearest non-outlier values.

Forecasting with Holt Exponential Smoothing

A technique that is widely used for forecasting is Holt exponential smoothing or "Holt's method." The version discussed here is a slight variation developed by T. M. Williams in 1987. **Exponential smoothing,** also called exponentially weighted moving average, is a method of estimating the future of the series using the information contained in the series. The exponential or exponentially weighted part refers to mathematics that put more weight on the most recent observations than on observations from long ago. A variety of techniques go by the name "exponential smoothing." The variety known as Holt exponential smoothing is able to predict both the level and the trend of a data series and has been shown to be relatively accurate compared with many other methods.

The forecast as shown in Table 4.2 is produced through these equations:

$$F_{t+m} = \text{forecast at time } t \text{ of time } t + m = S_t + (B_t * m) \qquad [1]$$

$$S_t = \text{level at time } t = F_t + \alpha e_t \qquad [2]$$

$$B_t = \text{trend at time } t = B_{t-1} + \beta e_t \qquad [3]$$

$$e_t = \text{error at time } t = X_t - F_t \qquad [4]$$

Where:

X_t = the observation at time t m = the number of periods between an observation period and a forecast period
α = alpha, a level smoothing parameter subject to $0 \leq \alpha \leq 1$
β = beta, a trend smoothing parameter subject to $0 \leq \beta \leq 1$
t = a time index.
m = the number of time units into the future

An example use of these formulas is shown in Table 4.2 and Figure 4.1. The source data are inflation-adjusted annual income tax data from a large metropolitan area. There are columns for X_t, F_t, e_t, S_t, B_t, and e^2_t, the last of which is used in calculating root mean square error as discussed below.

As Figure 4.1 shows, these formulas take the recent trends and project them into the future. In examining the plot you will see that historical data are to the left and future data are to the right. Forecasters sometimes put a vertical bar at the point where historical data are exhausted. The larger unconnected round dots are the actual observations. The smaller triangles connected by the line are the results of the forecast model, with the portion to

TABLE 4.2
Holt Exponential Smoothing

Period	Data		ME 1.71	α 0.9	β 0.005	RMSE 459.50
						MSE 211,142.12
	X_t	F_t	e_t	S_t	B_t	$e^2{}_t$
Period 0				1,855.08	242.28	
1980	2,210.0	2,097.36	112.68	2,198.77	242.85	12,697.01
1981	2,320.6	2,441.62	−121.03	2,332.69	242.24	14,648.97
1982	2,488.3	2,574.93	−86.63	2,496.96	241.81	7,504.64
1983	2,767.7	2,738.77	28.91	2,764.79	241.95	835.87
1984	3,082.9	3,006.74	76.20	3,075.33	242.33	5,807.18
1985	3,348.8	3,317.66	31.18	3,345.72	242.49	972.05
1986	3,430.8	3,588.21	−157.36	3,446.58	241.70	24,763.56
1987	3,943.7	3,688.29	255.42	3,918.17	242.98	65,240.46
1988	3,656.3	4,161.15	−504.89	3,706.75	240.46	254,910.66
1989	4,083.9	3,947.20	136.73	4,070.26	241.14	18,693.85
1990	4,021.0	4,311.39	−290.39	4,050.04	239.69	84,328.01
1991	4,254.9	4,289.73	−34.84	4,258.37	239.51	1,213.67
1992	4,772.5	4,497.89	274.57	4,745.00	240.89	75,386.99
1993	4,979.3	4,985.88	−6.61	4,979.94	240.85	43.64
1994	4,968.9	5,220.79	−251.86	4,994.11	239.59	63,434.46
1995	4,894.3	5,233.71	−339.36	4,928.28	237.90	115,166.57
1996	5,173.8	5,166.18	7.59	5,173.01	237.93	57.57
1997	5,648.2	5,410.94	237.29	5,624.50	239.12	56,307.71
1998	6,547.3	5,863.62	683.64	6,478.90	242.54	467,366.27
1999	6,871.8	6,721.44	150.39	6,856.79	243.29	22,616.40
2000	6,749.2	7,100.08	−350.84	6,784.33	241.54	123,088.29
2001	7,209.0	7,025.86	183.11	7,190.66	242.45	33,528.77
2002	5,762.6	7,433.11	−1,670.51	5,929.65	234.10	2,790,617.37
2003	5,661.4	6,163.75	−502.38	5,711.61	231.59	252,387.68
2004	6,653.4	5,943.19	710.16	6,582.34	235.14	504,325.26
2005	7,635.3	6,817.48	817.84	7,553.53	239.23	668,856.50
2006	8,245.0	7,792.76	452.26	8,199.79	241.49	204,537.76
2007	8,647.8	8,441.28	206.50	8,627.13	242.52	42,642.16
2008		8,869.65		8,869.65	242.52	
2009		9,112.17		9,112.17	242.52	
2010		9,354.69		9,354.69	242.52	
2011		9,597.21		9,597.21	242.52	
2012		9,839.74		9,839.74	242.52	

Note: ME = mean error; MSE = mean square error; RMSE = root mean square error.

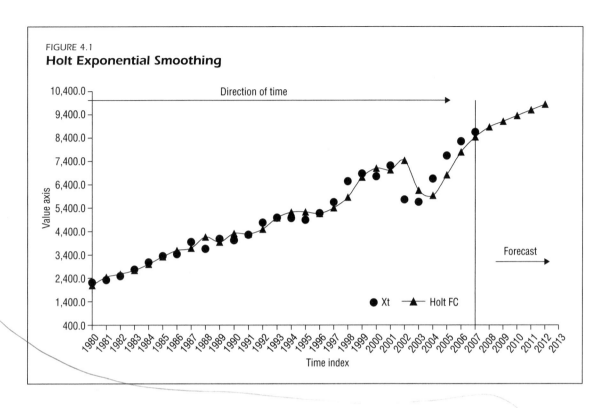

FIGURE 4.1
Holt Exponential Smoothing

the right of the vertical bar reflecting the forecast into the period after the historical data are exhausted.

Initializing Holt

If the data are **annual,** the Holt model is initialized through these steps:

1. Calculate the average of the first three observations. 2,339.633

2. Calculate the average of the fourth through sixth observations.

3. Subtract the first average from the second and divide it by three; we label that number B_0 the initial trend. In Table 4.2, B_0 is found on the row labeled Period 0 in the column B_t and has the value 242.28.

   Multiply B_0 times 2 and subtract the result from the average of the first three observations; we label that number S_0 the initial level. In Table 4.2, S_0 is found in the cell to the left of B_0 and has the value 1,855.08.

   Treat S_0 and B_0 as if they were calculated in the period prior to the period of the first observation, so the forecast value for the first month of actual data is:

$$F_1 = S_0 + B_0 \qquad [5]$$

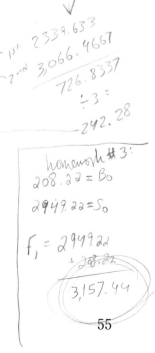

Handwritten annotations:
1st 2339.633
2nd 3,066.4667
726.8337
÷ 3 =
242.28

homework #3:
208.22 = B₀
2949.22 = S₀

F₁ = 2949.22
± 208.22
3,157.44

Use the following process for quarterly and monthly data.

1. Calculate the average of the first year of the data and the second year of the data.

2. Subtract the first-year average from the second-year average and divide by the number of observations in one year; that number is B_0 the initial trend.

   If the data are quarterly, multiply B_0 times 2.5 and subtract from the first-year average; that number is S_0 the initial level.

   If the data are monthly, multiply B_0 times 6.5 and subtract from the first-year average; that number is S_0 the initial level.

3. Continue to use $F_1 = S_0 + B_0$ to find the forecast for the first period.

The data in Figure 4.1 have been initialized according to this process, with S_0 and B_0 shown in Table 4.2 on the row labeled Period 0.

Selecting α and β

At the top of Table 4.2, there are three summary statistics, MSE, RMSE, and ME, which are, respectively, the **mean square error,** the **root mean square error,** and **mean error.** These statistics are called **loss functions,** or summary values that measure the effectiveness of the forecast. The MSE is a standard statistical quantity that is calculated for forecasts the same as it is with other procedures. It is computed as the average of e^2 for the time series. RMSE is the square root of MSE and is identical in concept with the standard deviation. There is no ideal RMSE, but between any two values, the smaller is better.

The ME is the sum of the errors divided by the count of the errors. An unbiased forecast will have an ME of zero. Forecasts are somewhat biased, but it is desirable to minimize the bias. When comparing two forecasts of the same data, one is clearly better if it has a smaller RMSE and a smaller ME, or if one of these is smaller and the other is constant. If one is smaller and the other is larger, there must be a trade-off between accuracy and bias. Often forecasters must make this trade-off and judge where to break even. There is no rule.

These two quantities are used in selecting the optimal values of parameters of Holt. The first Holt parameter is α, a number that is multiplied times the error (also known as deviation, the distance between observation and forecast; see equation 4) to determine the current level of the forecast model. The second parameter is β, which is used to find the current trend of the forecast. In combination the level and trend are used to find the predicted next value of the forecast.

Choosing a particular value of α and β is called "fitting a forecast." Common practice requires that α and β each be set between 0 and 1. Normally, α is more than zero and less than 1. For β the value is less than 1, but

TABLE 4.3
Grid Search for Holt Exponential Smoothing

α, β	(β)	Beta (β) 0.005		0.05		0.2	
A	(α)	ME	RMSE	ME	RMSE	ME	RMSE
L	0.1	−69.86	514.41	10.69	553.84	39.50	795.61
P	0.2	−33.79	517.91	11.79	558.78	55.29	742.38
H	0.4	0.34	515.63	22.72	547.42	58.44	649.57
A	0.6	12.69	495.38	22.72	515.96	46.94	571.56
(α)	0.9	14.65	461.74	20.87	472.65	29.91	500.44

Note: ME = mean error; RMSE = root mean square error.

in one particular circumstance discussed later, it can be zero. A common method for selecting a specific value for α and β is to use a grid of possible α and β values such as in the α and β areas of Table 4.3. The analyst calculates a forecast with each pair of values, determines the value of the loss functions as shown in the ME and RMSE columns of Table 4.3, and selects the best α, β combination. The ME information is shown simply for reference. The best α, β combination is the one with the lowest RMSE value. Using the grid search of Table 4.3, we select α = 0.9 and β = 0.005, which are the values that have been used in Table 4.2.

As an example, consider the data in Table 4.2 and Figure 4.1. These reflect personal income taxes in New York City. The amounts are in millions of dollars. With this method, the average absolute forecast error (a commonly used comparative statistic) is just under 6 percent. If one excludes the immediate aftermath of September 11, 2001, an unpredictable event that is unlikely to recur, it is 5 percent. This error can be reduced, keeping in mind that the period from 2002 through 2004 is exceptional (an outlier as discussed earlier in the chapter). For those three years we substitute the average revenue from only the years 2001 and 2005 (this is a simple method to replace the outliers), which is $7.4 million; the error then falls to 4 percent. Figure 4.2 shows the forecast after this change. An expert forecaster might dispute whether 2005 is an outlier (typically, three years in a row would not be considered outliers); however, with the clear explanation why they should be so considered and the eventual graphic evidence of the return to the previous trend, it seems reasonable to treat that three-year span as an outlier.

New York City will likely spend substantial sums of money to make much more sophisticated forecasts and will, for that expenditure, reduce the forecast error from 4 percent to something closer to 2 or 3 percent. It is likely worth it to spend tens or hundreds of thousands of dollars to reduce the error from 4 percent to 2 or 3 percent because each one percentage point reduction represents almost

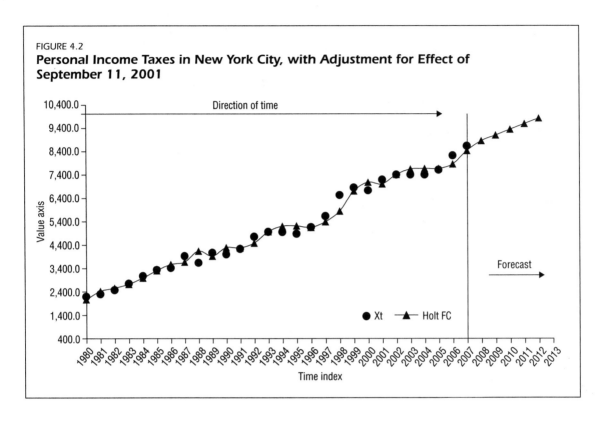

FIGURE 4.2
Personal Income Taxes in New York City, with Adjustment for Effect of September 11, 2001

$100 million, a large absolute sum of money compared with the cost of increasing forecast accuracy although only a small part of the budget. For most municipalities, however, such a reduction reflects a much smaller value, so Holt exponential smoothing is likely to provide an adequate forecast.

The New York City case is only one example, but the approximately 4 percent absolute error is consistent with many results with exponential smoothing. Income tax is relatively volatile, although likely not as volatile as sales tax, so one might expect slightly higher error rates with sales tax forecasts. Property tax valuation does not require forecasting as it should be computable in an accounting sense, with a little uncertainty for the most recent changes. Property tax collections, however, may require forecasting. Because property tax is a relatively stable tax, Holt exponential smoothing should be quite reliable for forecasting these collections. The reliability of forecasts for other revenue sources depends on the consistency of the underlying data series.

In New York, the personal income tax revenue is forecast by the mayor's Office of Management and Budget and separately by the Independent Budget Office, which serves in an advisory role. Other organizations that have an interest in the forecast include the City Council, the Public Advocate, the

Comptroller, and several outside good-government organizations such as the Citizens Budget Commission. All of these organizations may make their own forecasts whether they publish them or not. Many local governments have far fewer participants in forecasting, with the executive budget office being the most likely participant. Most state governments have two to four participants, one from the governor's office, one or two from the legislature, and potentially one from the office of the treasurer. Revenues from nonprincipal sources, such as user fees generated by various agencies, may be forecast by the agency responsible for collecting the revenue.

Doing a Grid Search

There are several ways to conduct a grid search. One is to manually enter each combination of parameters into the forecast spreadsheet (or other software) and compute the results. Another is to write a "macro" and let it cycle through all combinations of the parameters. The approach taken in the supporting part of Table 4.3 (which can be examined in the accompanying spreadsheet, "Budget Tools Chapter 04 Text Examples and Exercises") is a variation of the second approach; it is to make numerous copies of Table 4.2 within the spreadsheet and to simultaneously try all pairs of parameters. Thus, the tab labeled "Tbl 4.3" in "Budget Tools Chapter 04 Text Examples and Exercises" contains fifteen copies of Table 4.2, which differ principally in that they test fifteen different pairs of α and β. As computer power and memory grows larger, this approach may be the most realistic for obtaining quick results. The grid search demonstrated in Table 4.3 produced the parameters used in Table 4.2, which are $\alpha = 0.9$ and $\beta = 0.005$.

Macros can be used to try a much more exhaustive set of combinations, but they can be slow. Software such as SAS or Forecast Pro use other approaches that are more sophisticated and likely to provide parameter fits that are slightly more accurate. Macros are discussed in Appendix E.

Other Cases

Sometimes the forecaster thinks there is no trend. There is a special case of Holt exponential smoothing known as simple exponential smoothing (SES), which is used for data that have no trend. Holt can be used to achieve SES by setting β to zero (0), initializing B_0 to zero (0), and initializing S_0 to the average of the first year or, for annual data, the first three observations.

Some statisticians demonstrate the use of time indexed regression for forecasting. It is not impossible for time indexed regression to be successful. However, time indexed regression is not robust. Robust means that the method will work pretty well even in unfavorable circumstances. The reason Holt exponential smoothing is explained here is that it is known to be robust, and it is not difficult to use.

SPECIAL CASES OF HOLT EXPONENTIAL SMOOTHING

Sometimes forecasters think there is a trend now, but it will later fade away. There is a special case of Holt exponential smoothing known as damped trend.

Damped trend is beyond the scope of this chapter, but it is explained in

Daniel Williams, "Forecasting Methods for Serial Data," in *Handbook of Research Methods in Public Administration,* 2d ed., ed. Kaifeng Yang and Gerald J. Miller (Boca Raton, Fla.: CRC Press, 2008), and

Spyros G. Makridakis, Stephen C. Wheelwright, and Rob J. Hyndman. *Forecasting: Methods and Applications,* 3d ed. (New York: Wiley, 1998).

Many other special cases are also explained in these texts.

Empirical evidence has shown that judgment can improve a forecast if judgmental factors are committed to before the technical forecast is in hand. Otherwise, judgment is merely used to adjust the forecast to the hoped-for number. If, for example, you believe a series is reaching a limit and cannot grow or shrink as fast as it has in the past, then you might commit to adjusting the trend to a less steep trend before seeing the forecast results. Making that decision afterward is inadvisable. One could also make such a decision if, for example, an upward trend in revenue included a recent increase in the assessment rate. The size, or at least the fact, of the adjustment should be agreed to before the results of the technical forecast are in hand.

Judgmental adjustments should usually be quite simple, and they should be made only if the forecaster has information not available to the forecast model. For example, if the forecaster knows that the tax rate will change on a certain date, this fact is information that the forecast model does not know. Suppose the rate increases 5 percent. The adjustment may be simply to increase the forecast by 5 percent beginning with the date of the increase. Or the forecaster might be aware of some lag time in collections; thus, the forecaster may increase the forecast by 3 percent for one month and the other 2 percent for the next month. Simple reasonable decisions are all that is required. For the experienced forecaster, there are methods for minimizing the effect on forecast stability;[3] however, the forecast can be improved by simply making the adjustments to the output to the forecast model. For these sorts of adjustments to be effective, the decision to adjust and the size of the adjustment must be decided before the output of the model is known.

Accuracy and Bias

We learned that RMSE is a loss function that focuses our attention on accuracy, while ME focuses our attention on bias. While reviewing some results, another loss function has been mentioned, **absolute percent error** (or absolute error, presented as a percentage). Forecast literature is, in fact, filled with discussion of various loss functions. These three are not the most perfect, but they have the virtues of being easy to compute, intuitive to understand, and easy to interpret.

RMSE is used to measure how accurate a forecast is. All other things equal, a more accurate forecast is better than a less accurate forecast. Accuracy is the

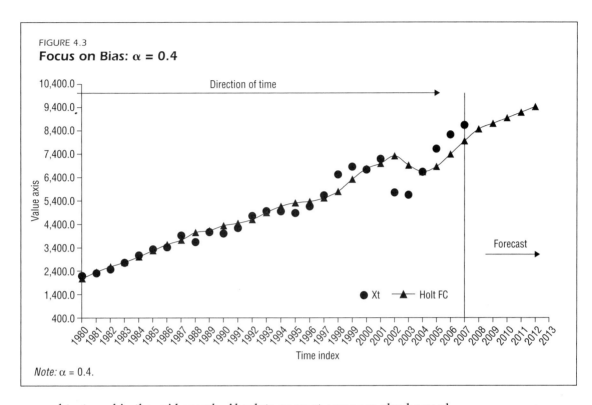

FIGURE 4.3
Focus on Bias: α = 0.4

Note: α = 0.4.

general test used in the grid search. Absolute percent error can also be used to measure forecast accuracy; however, it is not routinely used in fitting a forecast. It is used, instead, for comparative discussion among a variety of forecasts. RMSE is highly dependent on the magnitude of the data that is forecast, absolute percent error is not. So, while a smaller RMSE for one data series is better, between two different data series it is not possible to know whether a smaller RMSE for one is better or worse than the larger RMSE for the other. This limitation does not exist for absolute percent error, which is a relative measure. So the user can compare two entirely different forecasts on the basis of their absolute percent error and determine which is more accurate.

Mean error (ME) is a bias measure, that is, it determines how much the forecast tends to make errors in one direction rather than another (high rather than low, or vice versa). Sometimes when RMSE is reduced substantially, ME will increase. The reasons for this effect are complex. Typically, forecasters pay more attention to accuracy than to bias. Thus, forecast fitting consists largely of minimizing RMSE or some other selected accuracy measure. It is very difficult to simultaneously minimize two statistics. It is, however, unwise to completely ignore ME. In Table 4.3, we see RMSE minimized with α = 0.9 and that ME is minimized with α = 0.4, but the ME would also be improved a little bit with α = 0.6. Figures 4.3 and 4.4 show the forecast with

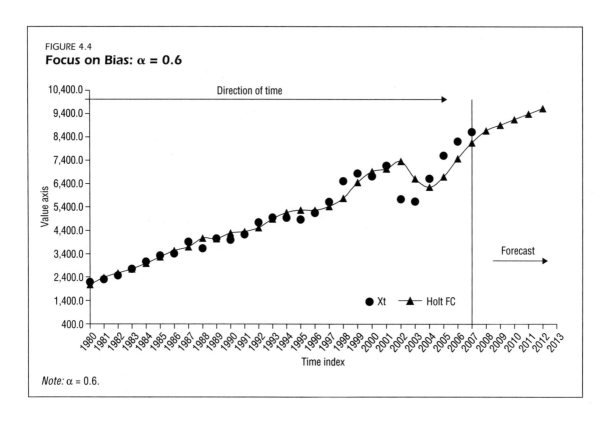

FIGURE 4.4
Focus on Bias: α = 0.6

Value axis

Direction of time

Forecast

● Xt ▬▲▬ Holt FC

Time index

Note: α = 0.6.

these changes. Because of the large incident near the end of the series, these changes have a likely large impact on forecast accuracy, and so it is likely wisest to focus on RMSE. Nevertheless, it is worthwhile examining the effect of reducing ME, particularly, if ME is large.

Summary

In this chapter, we have examined trend analysis using historical data and some basic forecasting concepts, learned how to make an *XY* graph in Excel, examined that graph for outliers, and learned how to make a forecast using Holt exponential smoothing. We learned to use RMSE and ME to select α and β parameters using a grid search. And we learned to decide on any judgmental adjustments to our forecasts before we know the output of the forecast model.

Exercises

To complete the first two exercises in this section, use the tables provided below.

1. Expenditure Analysis in Current Dollars

   a. You are a fiscal analyst in the city's budget office. Complete the current-dollar portion of Table 4.4 analyzing the Health Department's expenditures; use the available data in Table 4.1.

   b. Write a memo from you (as a fiscal analyst) to the budget director explaining the trends.

2. Expenditure Analysis in Constant Dollars

   a. In this exercise, you will complete the rest of the spreadsheet in Table 4.4, conducting the same analysis you did above, only you will convert all the dollars to constant dollars. This exercise allows you to adjust a

Table 4.2 not in spreadsht?

TABLE 4.4

Trend Analysis: New York City's Investment in Health Expenditures, FY 1996 to FY 2007 (in $ thousands)

| Departments | Current dollars | | | | | | | |
	Actual FY 1996	Percent of total	Actual FY 1997	Percent of total	Percent change	Actual FY 1998	Percent of total	Percent change
Health	$419,308	22.9	$420,275	29.0	0.2	$472,030		
Mental Health	319,275	17.5	345,284	23.8	8.1	396,095		
Hospitals (HHC)	1,090,173	59.6	682,924	47.1	−37.4	684,601		
Total health	$1,828,756	100.0	$1,448,483	100.0	−20.8	$1,552,726		
Total health as percentage of New York City's expenditures		5.7		4.3				
Reference group								
New York City's expenditures	$32,066,586		$33,736,152		5.2	$34,923,250		

	Constant or real dollars (controlling for inflation)							
Dept. of Health	$576,580	22.9	$564,714	29.0	−2.1			
Dept. of Mental Health	439,027	17.5	463,950	23.8	5.7			
Hospitals (HHC)	1,499,070	59.6	917,629	47.1	−38.8			
Total health	$2,514,676	100.0	$1,946,293	100.0	−22.6			
Total health as percentage of New York City's expenditures		5.7		4.3				
Reference group								
New York City's expenditures	$44,093,957		$45,330,485		2.8			
Consumer Price Index		166.9		170.8				

Note: HHC = Health and Hospitals Corporation.

TABLE 4.1

Expenditures for Health in New York City, Fiscal Years 1996–2007 (in thousands)

Fiscal years	Health Department	Mental Health Department	Hospitals Department	New York City's total health expenditures	New York City's total expenditures	CPI
1996	$419,308	$319,275	$1,090,173	$1,828,756	$32,066,586	166.9
1997	420,275	345,284	682,924	1,448,483	33,736,152	170.8
1998	472,030	396,095	684,601	1,552,726	34,923,250	173.6
1999	491,603	437,292	722,094	1,650,989	35,858,612	177.0
2000	790,726	251,446	735,127	1,777,299	37,879,886	182.5
2001	906,947	295,114	757,023	1,959,084	40,226,977	187.1
2002	1,049,135	256,064	826,307	2,131,506	40,860,000	191.9
2003	1,414,923	—	826,572	2,241,495	44,340,229	197.8
2004	1,441,247	—	976,875	2,418,122	47,292,395	204.8
2005	1,432,047	—	992,136	2,424,183	52,789,712	212.7
2006	1,467,786	—	1,290,016	2,757,802	53,999,075	220.7
2007	1,513,879	—	758,603	2,272,482	58,705,982	229.5

Note: The Mental Health Department was merged with the Health Department in FY 2003. CPI = consumer price index; CPI Adjusted Index: CUURA101SA0, New York-Northern New Jersey-Long Island, NY-NJ-CT-PA; base period 1982–1984 = 100. CPI figure for FY 2007 is November 2007.

spreadsheet for inflation. The technique is to convert current dollar expenditures using cost of living indexes to constant (real) dollars by removing inflation as a factor.

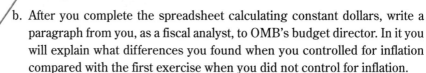

b. After you complete the spreadsheet calculating constant dollars, write a paragraph from you, as a fiscal analyst, to OMB's budget director. In it you will explain what differences you found when you controlled for inflation compared with the first exercise when you did not control for inflation.

To complete the following two exercises, use the spreadsheet file titled "Budget Tools Chapter 04 Text Examples and Exercises."

3. On the "Property Tax" sheet, there are property tax revenues from 1980 through 2006 for a U.S. city. The magnitude (thousand, millions, etc.) is not shown. In 2003 there was an approximately 15 percent tax increase phased in over two years. Assume that you are an analyst working in year 2007; thus, a five-year forecast would continue through year 2012 (five years after 2007).

a. If you were to plan for a judgmental adjustment, what would it be?

b. Using the same grid as used in Table 4.3, make the best forecast through year 2012; do not make your judgmental adjustment.

c. Make an *XY* plot of your forecast beside the original data.

4. On the "Approval" worksheet are the monthly averages of many different polls of presidential approval from September 2001 through July 2007. Past analysis suggests little evidence of seasonality.

a. Make an *XY* plot of these data.

b. Using the same grid as used in Table 4.3, make the best forecast through December 2008.

c. Make a new *XY* plot of the forecast beside the data.

d. Is there any reason why you might think the approval will not reach the forecast December 2008 value?

Additional Readings

Makridakis, Spyros G., Stephen C. Wheelwright, and Rob J. Hyndman. *Forecasting: Methods and Applications.* 3d ed. New York: Wiley, 1998.

Williams, Daniel W. "Forecasting Methods for Serial Data." In *Handbook of Research Methods in Public Administration,* 2d ed., ed. Kaifeng Yang and Gerald J. Miller. Boca Raton, Fla.: CRC Press, 2008.

Williams, Daniel W. "Preparing Data for Forecasting." In *Government Budget Forecasting: Theory and Practice,* ed. Jinping Sun and Thomas D. Lynch. Boca Raton, Fla.: Taylor & Francis, 2008.

Williams, Daniel W. "Seasonality." In *Encyclopedia of Public Administration and Public Policy,* 2d ed., ed. Evan M. Berman and Jack Rabin (founding editor), 1746–1756. Boca Raton, Fla.: CRC Press, 2007.

Williams, T. M. "Adaptive Holt-Winters Forecasting," *Journal of the Operational Research Society* 38 (1987): 553–560.

Notes

1. The two most common very simple techniques are to calculate the average growth or the average percent growth over the last several periods and project whichever into the next several periods. The reason that these are too simple is that they both introduce too much susceptibility to random variation and the percent growth method may introduce a bias toward multiplicative growth.

2. These issues are discussed in Daniel W. Williams, "Preparing Data for Forecasting," in *Government Budget Forecasting: Theory and Practice,* ed. Jinping Sun and Thomas D. Lynch (Boca Raton, Fla.: Taylor & Francis, 2008).

3. See Daniel W. Williams, "Forecasting Methods for Serial Data," in *Handbook of Research Methods in Public Administration,* 2nd ed., ed. Kaifeng Yang and Gerald J. Miller (Boca Raton, Fla.: CRC Press, 2008).

Chapter 5

Preparing the Capital Budget

Learning objectives:

■ Understand fundamental concepts of capital budget and capital budgeting
■ Conduct life cycle costing analysis
■ Conduct cost-benefit analysis
■ Finance capital budget through long-term debt and other mechanisms
■ Learn about new developments in theories and techniques in capital budgeting

A capital budget is a financial plan for the construction, improvement, or acquisition of **capital assets** such as land, buildings, and costly equipment. The planning process for the acquisition of capital assets is called capital budgeting. A capital budget is a key element in the organization's master budget, which also includes an operating budget and a cash budget. Although the building blocks of the operating budget discussed in the earlier chapters are organizational units or programs, it is projects that are the typical units of analysis in the capital budget.

Capital projects are long-lived, costly investments and are usually but not always durable bricks-and-mortar initiatives. Capital projects incur costs beyond the initial purchase price; these might include maintenance, service contracts, or additional personnel required to staff the building or equipment. Conversely, some capital projects can produce expense budget savings. When New York City began to replace its three-man garbage collection trucks with two-man vehicles, the city was able to reduce the workforce of the Department of Sanitation, and it used some of the savings to increase salaries and some to reduce the department's budget.

Given the amount of resources involved and the length of time affected, each capital project needs careful evaluation. Part of the analyst's job is to develop an accurate estimate of the initial outlays required for a capital project. These might include design and construction costs, or the purchase and installation price of equipment. That information is important for the accuracy of plans for cash outlays for capital purposes, and it is also one component of the information required to make decisions among competing capital needs.

The up-front costs are only the starting place for financial analysis of capital proposals. Analysts also need to gather and compare all the costs or savings associated with a capital project over its full life cycle. The future operating and maintenance costs and potential disposal costs and residual values of a project could make a difference in capital budget decisions. New procedures and techniques are required in the analysis and preparation of a capital budget. Because capital assets are long lasting and different capital options may have different periods of probable useful life, analysts will need to use time-value-of-money techniques to create a common framework for evaluating the costs and benefits of long-lived projects. Those data, together with information about the nonmonetary benefits expected from the capital investment, allow decision makers to choose among different ways to meet the same need. This analysis also helps to rank projects from different departments in pursuit of different goals, although a fuller cost-benefit analysis is recommended to support those decisions.

In this chapter, we review two important approaches to analyzing and evaluating capital projects: life cycle costing and cost-benefit analysis. We outline the conceptual framework of the techniques, and we use personal and public organization capital budgeting examples to illustrate their application. We conclude the chapter with a discussion of long-term financing, especially with bonds and the ensuing debt services, linking capital budget to operating budget for potential enabling and limiting effects.

Life Cycle Costing

Governments purchase goods and services primarily through competitive bidding processes. Governments often award contracts on the basis of the lowest purchase price. For capital assets, however, the initial acquisition price does not represent the total cost of ownership. The initial price does not include the recurring cost of operations and maintenance. Nor does it include the potentially large disposal liability if environmentally hazardous materials are involved. Because the downstream cost of asset ownership could be substantial—multiples of the initial purchase price in some cases—governments and other public organizations should factor in all the costs in the capital decision-making process. **Life cycle costing** (LCC) is a simple economic evaluation method in capital budgeting to determine the total cost of ownership. LCC can be, and has been, used to assist management in procurement and other capital budget decision making in addition to a wide range of policy discussions, most conspicuously in issues relating to energy and environment.

This section introduces the LCC concept and its application in public organizations. It first outlines the basic principles and process of LCC. It surveys the development of the technique over time. It then demonstrates the technique by applying it in simple and complex government decision-making processes. The section concludes by pointing to new developments in LCC and providing references for those who would like to continue their studies beyond the scope of this text.

Basic Concept and Application of LCC

LCC is an analytic technique used to determine the total cost of ownership over the lifetime of the asset. The total cost—the life cycle cost—is the sum of all monies attributed to the asset or project from its conception to its disposal. These costs include costs for research and development, purchase or production, installation, personnel to operate and maintain the system, other ongoing support, and eventual disposal. LCC can facilitate the evaluation of alternative projects, assets, and courses of action early on in a project so that the best alternative, the least expensive alternative, can be identified.

The LCC technique finds applications in decision making in our daily lives and in public organizations. For example, the energy efficiency ratings marked on major home appliances sold in the United States are simply a clever way of communicating a component of LCC information to appliance purchasers. The selection of building materials based on initial and operating costs in school construction is an example of LCC in government capital budgeting. Nonprofit organizations may have to consider the recurring operating and maintenance cost in their decisions about whether to accept major contributions of buildings and other facilities. Because of the wide potential and actual applications of LLC and to simplify discussion, we use projects or assets to represent products, systems, goods, and services in the following discussion of life cycle costing.

LCC emerged as a formal analytical method in the United States. Its development can be traced back to the earlier work of the Department of Defense (DOD) in the 1960s. The technique was developed to address the difficulties with total package procurement in DOD. During the past forty years, the basic concept and techniques of LCC have evolved and expanded into public policy decisions and consumer consumption and protection, among other applications. Public policy and consumer information have in turn provided incentives for manufacturers to internalize costs, making cost information more transparent, which improves the technical and allocative efficiency of the economy at large.

Calculating Life Cycle Cost

The total life cycle cost in a typical analysis can be simplified and illustrated in the following formula:

$$\text{Life cycle cost} = A + O + M + D \tag{1}$$

Where:

A = Acquisition cost of a project; this includes the initial capital expenditure for facilities and equipment, the system design, engineering, and installation. These costs usually occur at the beginning of the project.

O = Operating costs; these usually include labor costs, energy costs, material costs, and any additional overhead costs discounted over the life of the project. In some projects, some of those costs may be offset by operating savings, which must also be discounted to their present values.

M = Maintenance cost is the total maintenance and repair costs discounted over the life of the project.

D = Disposal costs include restoration of the local environment and disposal of auxiliary services. Disposal costs turn to negative to represent salvage value when the project has a terminal value. Disposal costs equal the cost or value of the project at the end of the economic life discounted to its present value.

The operating and maintenance costs of a capital project can extend over many time periods. Costs at different times have to be discounted to their present value to allow summation and comparison. To understand discounting, we provide below a review of the concept of time value of money (TVM).

TVM is a fundamental concept in finance. TVM is based on the fact that a dollar today is worth more than a dollar in future times. This concept can be explained by looking at our personal banking activities. For example, we can invest a dollar in a savings account in a bank that offers interest. We will have our one dollar plus interest at the year-end. If we continue the investment, the interest itself will start to earn interest at some future point. This is called compounding. The future amount of an investment with compounding interest is defined as future value and is denoted as FV. It can be calculated by using the future value formula shown in equation 2.

$$FV = PV * (1 + i)^n \qquad [2]$$

Where:

FV = future value
PV = present value
i = discount rate or interest rate

n = number of periods.

Discounting is simply the reversal of compounding. If you know the amount of any future cash flow, you can use discounting to determine its present value of equivalence. The basic equation to discount a future amount to its present value can be expressed in equation 3. The notation of the equation is the same as that in equation 2.

$$PV = \frac{FV}{(1+i)^n} \qquad [3]$$

In the mechanics of LCC, future operating, maintenance, and disposal costs have to be estimated and discounted to their present value. The initial acquisition cost is then added to the present value of these future costs to arrive at the total life cycle cost for each project concerned. The alternatives are then compared on the basis of the total life cycle cost. Other factors being equal, the project with the smallest life cycle cost is most economical and therefore should be recommended for adoption.

As an example, suppose you are an undergraduate student, just enrolled in a four-year university program. You have decided to buy a car, and you are planning to own the car for the next four years while you are in college. After an initial search and investigation, you have narrowed down the choices to two options, car A and car B, that serve your needs equally well; however, they differ substantially in initial purchasing costs, maintenance costs, and fuel efficiency as well as resale prices. Your high credit rating permits you to get a bank loan at an interest rate of 4 percent. The relevant information and assumptions with regard to this car purchase are summarized as follows:

- Car A costs $18,000 and will sell for $5,000 in four years.
- Car B costs $20,000 and will sell for $7,000 in four years.
- You expect to drive 10,000 miles a year.
- Gas mileage is 25 miles per gallon with car A and 30 miles per gallon with car B.
- The price of gas is $2.00 per gallon.
- The yearly average maintenance cost for car A is $200, and for car B it is $150.
- The discount rate is 4 percent. All outlays for operating and maintenance costs occur at the end of each year (this simplifies this case).
- All the above dollar amounts are in current dollars.
- For simplication, inflation is not considered in the analysis.

Which car should you buy from a financial viewpoint?

To address this question, we first organize the relevant data and the assumptions in a spreadsheet program such as Microsoft Excel, as shown in Table 5.1. We then calculate the operating and maintenance costs over the years of the planned ownership, which is shown in Table 5.2. We discount all the future cash flows and summarize their present values to obtain the life cycle cost of the two alternatives. The results of the analysis are presented in Table 5.3. The life cycle cost of car A is $17,356 and the life cycle cost of car B is $16,981. Given that car B is less costly to own than car A, you decide to buy car B, although the purchase price of the car ($20,000) is higher than the alternative ($18,000).

To discount future cash flows to their present value, we need to estimate future costs, and we need to make decisions or assumptions on interest rate. Although the above example gives us exact cost for the next four years, in real life future costs are difficult to forecast precisely. Extrapolation from historical time series data of similar projects or products, or verification of the producer's specification, must be carefully conducted to come up with the estimates of the future costs and possible residual values.

The selection of a **discount rate** is another challenge both theoretically and practically in public organizations, and different organizations may have different rules. The federal government sets guidelines, found in "Circular A-94" from the Office of Management and Budget (OMB), for federal agencies on which discount rates may be used in present value calculations. A state or local government is more likely to use a discount rate that reflects its own cost of borrowing money. There is no universal guideline

TABLE 5.1
Parameters for the Student's Car Purchase

Information and assumptions	Car A	Car B
Gas (price per gallon)	$2.00	$2.00
Distance to drive per year (miles)	10,000	10,000
Discount rate	4%	4%
Purchase price	$18,000	$20,000
Mileage (miles per gallon)	25	30
Maintenance (per year)	$200	$150
Residual value	−$5,000	−$7,000

TABLE 5.2
Calculation of Annual Operating and Maintenance Costs of Car Purchase Alternatives

Annual costs	Car A	Car B
Fuel	$800	$667
Maintenance	200	150
Total	$1,000	$817

TABLE 5.3
Calculation of Discounted Cash Flows of Car Purchase Alternatives

Description	Time	Car A Constant dollars	Car A Present value	Car B Constant dollars	Car B Present value
Purchase price	0	$18,000	$18,000	$20,000	$20,000
Gas and maintenance	1	1,000	962	817	785
Gas and maintenance	2	1,000	925	817	755
Gas and maintenance	3	1,000	889	817	726
Gas and maintenance	4	1,000	855	817	698
Resale	4	−5,000	−4,274	−7,000	−5,984
LCC			$17,356		$16,981

Note: Totals may not add due to rounding. LCC = life cycle costing.

for the selection of a discount rate for nonprofit organizations in practice. To prevent the abuse of the method, a discount rate should be selected consistently across projects of similar risk and should be set in advance of LCC analysis to avoid manipulation. Different interest rates and discount rates can materially affect analysis results and strategically influence capital budgeting decisions in public organizations.

In many cases, the calculation of LCC can be complex and time-consuming. For instance, the life spans of alternative projects can be long and different. Spreadsheet programs such as Microsoft Excel can simplify the calculation, especially when the future cash flows are evenly paced and are in equal amounts—in the form of annuities, for example. Readers who are not familiar with spreadsheet programs or basic financial terms should review the primer chapter for Excel earlier in the book and also the introductory finance books listed at the end of this chapter. The Excel function of PV is handy for the calculation, for example, of discounted cash flow many years into the future. The PMT function is a convenient tool when the alternative projects are of different lifetimes; this function annualizes the present value of the life cycle costs of the alternatives so that meaningful comparison among alternative projects can be made on an annual basis. The project with the lowest annualized costs should be recommended for consideration, other things being equal.

As an example of LCC of public projects with unequal economic lives, let us consider a water-heating system for a newly established laboratory in our college. We have two options: a solar water heater or an electric water heater. The conditions for the two options are outlined below:

- The solar system costs $5,000 to buy and install and $100 to maintain annually.
- The solar system will last for 30 years. The removal and disposal cost at the end of the 30 years will be $300.
- The electric heater costs $500 to buy and install, the electricity bill will be $600 per year, and it does not require regular maintenance.
- The electric water heater will last 15 years. The removal and disposal cost will be $100.
- All the costs are in today's dollars, and all future costs will be paid at the end of the year.
- Money is available to borrow from the local bank at an annual interest rate of 6 percent.

Which system should we choose based on economic considerations?

The relevant data and parameters of the questions are summarized in Table 5.4.

Similar to the car-purchasing example discussed above, we approach this question by determining the life cycle cost for each system and recommend the least costly alternative for decision making. However, because the solar heater has a longer economic life than the electrical heater, simply comparing the life cycle costs of the two systems is invalid; we would be comparing apples and oranges if we did that. One way to resolve this problem is to use the annualized cost method. We will then compare the costs of the projects on an average annual basis, which is independent from the length of the asset's lifetime.

TABLE 5.4
Solar Heater versus Electric Heater

Factors to consider	Solar heater	Electric heater
Purchase and installation costs	$5,000	$500
Energy cost	$0	$600
Maintenance cost	$100	$0
Disposal cost	$300	$100
Number of years in use	30	15
Discount rate	6%	6%

In this approach, we address this question in two main steps: first, to calculate the present value of the life cycle cost of the projects and, second, to amortize the present value of each project to find the annualized cost. The project with the lowest annualized cost is most economical and is therefore recommended for adoption.

Step 1: Calculate the present value (PV) of LCC using formula:

$$LCC = PV(rate, nper, pmt, fv, type)_{recurring} + PV(rate, nper, pmt, fv, type)_{residual} + initial\ outlay$$

After inserting values from the parameters, we get:

$$PV\ of\ LCC\ of\ solar\ heater = PV(0.06, 30, -100,,) + PV(0.06, 30,, -300,) + \$5,000 = \$6,428.72;$$

$$PV\ of\ LCC\ of\ electric\ heater = PV(0.06, 15, -600,,) + PV(0.06, 15,, -100,) + \$500 = \$6,369.08$$

Step 2: Applying the PMT function to annualize the cost using formula:

$$Annualized\ cost = PMT(rate, nper, PV, fv, type)$$

After plugging in values, we get:

$$Annualized\ cost\ of\ solar\ heater = PMT(0.06, 30, -6,428.72,) = \$467$$

$$Annualized\ cost\ of\ electric\ heater = PMT(0.06, 15, -6,369.08,) = \$656$$

As shown in the example, the initial purchasing and installation cost for the solar heater system ($5,000) is much higher than the conventional electrical heater system ($500). The life cycle cost for the solar heater is also higher than the electric heater, $6,428.72 compared with $6,369.08, before taking into consideration the different lengths of the useful life of the two systems. The annualized cost method, however, shows that the solar system is actually more economical to own and operate on an annual basis. Consequently, the solar system should be recommended for installation.

This example illustrates the data dependency of the LCC method. It's necessary to know the different acquisition costs, recurring costs, and disposal costs in order to calculate life cycle cost; these costs are in addition to various assumptions and selections regarding economic lifetime of alternative systems and discount rate. Estimation of future costs and decisions about discount rates, among other parameters, are critical in determining the outcomes. The future is unknown, however, and assumptions can prove to be unfounded. Careful examination of the potential risk caused by potential errors in estimation and assumptions is strongly recommended in the practice of LCC.

In many cases, the uncertainty in the conclusions of LCC can be reduced through sensitivity analysis. Sensitivity analysis consists of calculating LCC under different though plausible assumptions, changing one parameter at a time. A thoughtful sensitivity analysis will provide decision makers with different outcomes for different scenarios. It provides a measure of robustness of the analysis conclusions if the situation shifts away from the assumed. Further discussion of sensitivity analysis is provided in the section on cost-benefit analysis later in the chapter. (See page 85 for more on sensitivity analysis.)

Current Applications

Although LLC has a long history, it has not been widely used in local government and nonprofit organization decision-making practice. Many reasons could have contributed to this phenomenon. Some budget analysts are not technically trained in LLC and the related TVM analysis techniques. Bureaucratic and legal constraints of governments can also prevent wider application of LCC. In many instances, local statutes require that procurement decisions be based on initial acquisition price. If a separate capital budgeting process is not institutionalized, it is also difficult to synchronize life cycle costs with the kind of annual cost analysis carried out for most expense budget analysis. Finally, relevant data are often not available for LCC, or the data are of questionable quality.

A number of steps can be taken to improve the application and utility of LCC in public decision making. Education is often the key, as not all stakeholders are fully aware of the benefits of the technique and not all government agencies are capable of applying it. Second, the regular collection of relevant, reliable, and timely cost data is essential to its wider application. Without access to data, the application of this relatively data-intensive technique cannot be pursued. Finally, government purchasing laws and regulations must change to allow life cycle costs in addition to least bidding price criteria.

The Future of LCC

Like many management tools, LCC is evolving. New and hybrid procedures, such as activity-based life cycle costing, which is a combination of activity-based costing and life cycle costing, have emerged in recent years. Computer programs and real option concepts have been developed and used to model risks, using probability distributions to present uncertain inputs and the resulting LCC output. These new techniques have the potential to provide more comprehensive analysis and richer information to support decision making.

Cost-Benefit Analysis

Cost-benefit analysis (CBA) constitutes a more comprehensive form of economic evaluation than LCC. While LCC focuses on costs, CBA seeks to quantify both the costs and benefits of an intervention and to express both in monetary terms. The monetary measurement allows the evaluation and comparison of projects or programs of different substantive goals. In the CBA framework, we should be able to compare various programs in, for example, health care, education, and correction services in terms of net benefit. Theoretically, CBA gives decision makers the potential to address the major issue of allocative efficiency, that is, how should government allocate the limited public resources most efficiently among the myriad of possible public projects and programs. Practically, the application of CBA is limited, however, because of the bounded rationality of human cognitive capacity, the limited time in decision making, and the potential budgetary constraints. The nature and limitations of CBA will be discussed further in the following sections.

Typologically, there are two main categories of CBA, ex ante analysis and ex post analysis. They are easily distinguished, and they serve different purposes. Ex ante CBA takes place before the project of concern is implemented, and it allows the analyst to investigate and compare potential alternatives of programs or program components to inform program planning. Ex post study is performed after the fact, and its main purpose is to assess the efficiency of an implemented program that can be part of an overall program evaluation.

A Two-Hundred-Year-Old Tool

Cost-benefit analysis found its applications in the public sector in the early nineteenth century. The 1808 "Report on Transportation" by Albert Gallatin, the fourth U.S. secretary of the Treasury, was arguably the first to recommend cost-benefit comparisons for evaluating water-related projects. The concept and the practice of CBA have evolved and expanded over time. One milestone of the application of CBA was the federal Flood Control Act of 1936, which required the U.S. Army Corps of Engineers to assess all benefits and costs accruing to all beneficiaries of water projects. The Bureau of the Budget, the predecessor agency of the OMB, issued the first federally mandated guidelines for CBA of public projects in 1952. Since the 1960s, OMB has been instrumental in integrating the principle of CBA into the decision-making process in U.S. government agencies. The OMB's "Circular A-94" clearly states that the purpose of CBA should be the promotion of efficient resource allocation through well-informed decision making by the federal government. Over time, many terms have been used in CBA for its diverse application in allocative decision making in public organizations. For inclusiveness and consistency, we use the terms *project, program, government intervention,* and *investment* interchangeably in the following exposition of CBA.

Conducting Cost-Benefit Analysis

Although not necessarily carried out in sequence, a number of logically consecutive steps are often found in a thorough and professional CBA:

- Determining standing and perspectives
- Determining alternatives or basis for comparison
- Listing impacts
- Monetizing impacts, including both costs and benefits
- Discounting future impacts
- Calculating program net present value (NPV)
- Performing sensitivity analysis
- Selecting the alternative with the largest net social benefits.

The following subsections intend to provide step-by-step guidance in how to conduct practical CBA in public organizations, especially government agencies.

DETERMINING STANDING AND PERSPECTIVES.   Cost-benefit analysis starts by deciding standing, that is, whose costs and benefits count. In economic evaluation of public programs, the term "social cost-benefit analysis" is often invoked where the interests of all the people in the jurisdiction are taken into consideration. In reality, the decision about who has standing is often determined by the government agency or the project sponsor, and the typical project sponsor is mostly concerned about how a project will affect the sponsor-

WHAT MAKES A THOROUGH COST-BENEFIT ANALYSIS?

During a cost-benefit analysis, special attention should be given to all costs and benefits, including opportunity costs and social benefits that are often imprecise to measure and difficult to quantify in monetary terms. This imprecision could be further exacerbated by the narrow perspective of the sponsoring organization that funds the cost-benefit analysis.

The example in this chapter discusses a cost-benefit analysis of public investment in the construction of a sports facility. To simply the exposition, the example takes only the narrow financial perspective of the city government. It compares the city's tax revenue with its financial costs. The analysis does not include the broader impacts on the lives of the residents in terms of traffic congestion, the environment, the jobs created because of the facility in both the short run and long run, and the convenience for sports fans.

In the real world, professional and comprehensive cost-benefit analysis is often a complicated undertaking. For example, a study of the justice system in Washington State included costs from key government departments, such as the police, criminal courts and prosecutors, jail, juvenile detention, local community supervision, the state department of corrections, and juvenile rehabilitation.[1] A study of traffic law enforcement in British Columbia, Canada, across its northern border accounted for the costs of time lost and the savings on traffic collision injuries and fatalities in addition to government accounting costs and insurance savings. The study looked at the issue from multiple perspectives, including the perspective of the sponsoring insurance company and a broader, societal perspective, where all the people in the province have standing.[2]

Although no study can ever claim to have included all impacts, efforts should be made to account for as many of the impacts as feasible, taking into account the benefits of the information to be generated and the costs involved.

Notes

1. Washington State Institute for Public Policy, "The Criminal Justice System in Washington State: Incarceration Rates, Taxpayer Costs, Crime Rates, and Prison Economics" (Olympia, Wash.: WSIPP, January 2003), www.wsipp.wa.gov/rptfiles/SentReport2002.pdf.
2. G. Chen and R. Warburton, "Do Speed Cameras Produce Net Benefits? Evidence from British Columbia, Canada," *Journal of Policy Analysis and Management* 25, no. 3 (2006): 661–678.

---

ing organization. Project impacts, however, often spill over organizational and jurisdictional boundaries, causing what are often called externalities. Acid rain caused by coal-fired generators, for example, can cause problems beyond the boundary of the power plant and across state and national borders. From government's perspective, comprehensive social cost-benefit analysis is needed to assess the impact of the program on the general public.

Theoretically, a social cost-benefit analysis should include all the people in the jurisdiction—for example, the city, the state, or the nation. In practice and to be comprehensive, a social cost-benefit analysis is often performed from different and sometimes multiple perspectives: a state agency may evaluate a program from its own agency's financial perspective, from the broader state perspective, and from the national perspective as well.

DETERMINING ALTERNATIVES OR BASIS FOR COMPARISON.   A typical project or program is evaluated in comparison with alternative uses of resources in order to generate meaningful information to support allocative decision making. There are at least two explicitly expressed and commonly used bases for comparison: the status quo or an alternative program. Status quo does not necessarily mean no program at all; neither does it imply that the status quo condition is cost-free. A highway has to be maintained under the status quo option even if a decision is made to not implement a newly designed system that will replace the existing one. Consequently, the costs and the benefits of the new programs under consideration should be estimated incrementally, relative to those of the basis of comparison.

Some cost-benefit analyses expressly compare multiple programs in order to select the most efficient one. Theoretically, a thorough CBA should compare the program under study with all the potential alternatives that serve the interest of the groups with standing. In reality, analytic resources, such as funding, time, and technical know-how, are always limited. Cost-benefit analysis, as a rational decision-making process, is necessarily bounded and nonexhaustive. Cost-benefit analysts often compare the study program with one or two alternatives. The validity of the findings in a CBA should, therefore, be interpreted accordingly. An efficient program based on a CBA does not mean the best program in terms of efficiency. Many other programs may be more efficient but are not identified as they are not included in the study in the first place.

LISTING IMPACTS.   An appropriately designed CBA strives to identify and assess all material program impacts. A challenge in identifying impacts is establishing cause-effect relationships and determining what would have happened had the program not been implemented. In some cases, neither the nature of the relationship nor the type of impact is readily known. Whether a given program reduces crime, for example, is difficult to quantify because the causal factors underpinning crimes in some instances are not well understood.

Measurement in social cost-benefit analysis is another challenge. We may not have valid operational measures for concepts that are theoretically important. Sometimes we need proxy indicators for the impacts of interest; for example, we use increases or reductions in the number of convictions as opposed to changes in crime.

Most public programs extend over a lengthy period of time. This requires the quantification of the impacts over the life of the project and beyond if residual effects are expected. Without accurate estimates of program effects, cost-benefit comparison is groundless and possibly misleading. Estimating the physical impact of a program is arguably the most technically demanding task in cost-benefit analysis. The methods and procedures in estimating impacts depend on the timing of the study relative to the stage of program development and implementation. In other words, it depends on whether the CBA is ex ante or ex post.

For ex ante cost-benefit analyses, the impacts over the life of the project have to be predicted, using models, because the planned program has not yet been implemented and the results are by definition not yet observable. The prediction of impacts is often difficult; in most cases, a host of factors beyond the planned program also affects its outcomes. Often simplifying assumptions is necessary to make the analysis possible. In those cases, risk assessment and risk management techniques, such as sensitivity analysis, should be employed to estimate the robustness of the analysis and its conclusions and to explicate the possible scenarios and consequences if the major assumptions are proven factually wrong.

For ex post studies, the program under review should have been partly or wholly delivered, and the physical impacts, given appropriate maturity, should be potentially observable. In these cases, to the extent possible, project impacts should be measured and assessed as opposed to projected or modeled. The estimation of program physical effects requires judicious selection of research methodology and careful collection and analysis of data. Each evaluation to some extent is idiosyncratic in nature, and the analyst should design and conduct CBA correspondingly. Care must be given to the internal validity of the study, that is, the extent to which the observed change, if there is any, could be attributed to the program under investigation.

Monetizing impacts, including both costs and benefits. Almost inevitably, the implementation of public policies requires the use of resources, often referred to as program inputs or costs, depending on the context. These inputs, if not used for the particular program under consideration, could be used for other productive ends. Consequently, the resources used as inputs for government policies should be valued at their opportunity cost. Opportunity cost measures the value of what society must forgo to use the input to implement the concerned program. Opportunity cost is the appropriate way to value input in CBA and to the extent possible should be always considered the first choice in cost estimation.

Accounting costs as reflected in budgets and financial reports should be examined and justified against the principle of opportunity cost if used in CBA. Accounting costs may or may not approximate social opportunity costs and therefore could distort the results of CBA, leading to suboptimal allocation of public resources. One example of inappropriate use of accounting costs to represent program input is the treatment of land that government already owns and that the program under investigation uses or intends to use. The cost of using the piece of land is not usually reflected in government budgets or accounting records, but omitting this cost item as an input to the program will bias the results of the CBA in favor of the program under study and its comparison with alternatives that do not use the piece of government land.

A public project intends to generate positive impacts, the benefit, on the conditions of society. Theoretically, willingness to pay is the appropriate method by which to value the impacts of government policies. For goods and services that are traded in a well-functioning market, the demand curve estimated from market studies can be used to assess the willingness to pay value for marketed goods.

For goods and services not traded in the market, other inferential methods have to be developed. Two main approaches are used in current practices: inferring the value from observed behavior (the revealed preference approach) or inferring values from public surveys (the contingent valuation approach). Each method has its advantages and inherent limits.

As an example of the revealed preference approach, a labor market study observes and examines the additional wage people require as compensation for exposing themselves to greater risk of death or injuries on the job. A statistical value of a typical life can be estimated based on the amount of the extra compensation and the likelihood of job-related deaths. A primary problem associated with this method is the unsustainable assumption that people are fully aware of the risks associated with their jobs. A secondary problem is the assumption that the market is efficient, although, in reality, union bargaining power may affect wages in ways that are unrelated to the level of actual risk associated with a job.

The contingent valuation method relies on subjective information provided by survey respondents. It is relatively easy to administer but is considered less reliable than the revealed preferences of observational studies. Many marketing research studies have demonstrated the discrepancies between survey response and real behavior of consumers. The contingency valuation method supplements the observational studies, however, and more often than not it represents the only way to estimate the values people assign to impacts attributable to social programs.

DISCOUNTING FUTURE IMPACTS. Programs often extend over an extended period of time. The monetized impacts need to be converted into a common metric using the concept of TVM. Future costs and benefits need to be discounted to obtain their present value before summation and comparison. Although discounting future benefits and costs to derive their present values for policy valuation is a relatively straightforward mechanical process, the selection of an appropriate social discount rate is much more theoretically involved. We do not intend to enter into theoretical debate in this book; instead, we focus on the application of CBA in the public setting.

In practice, a number of discount rates are currently being used in CBA. For example, different offices in the U.S. government stipulate different social discount rates for government projects. The OMB, taking a stance that public projects crowd out private investment and therefore the social discount rate should reflect a pretax rate of return on private investment, requires a 10 percent real rate. The Government Accountability Office (GAO) uses a more flexible approach; it bases its discount rate on the real rate of interest on federal borrowing. This approach uses the cost of the source of funds as opposed to the use of the funds. Local governments often use this method in determining a discount rate, in part because their borrowing cost is relatively easy to determine and in part because it provides a link to interest costs in financial statements and other reports. This method is used in the New York City sport facility investment example later in this chapter.

CALCULATING PROGRAM NET PRESENT VALUE. NPV is the difference between the present value of the benefits (the cash inflows) and the present value of the costs (the cash outflows). NPV is the most theoretically sound and practically consistent criterion in evaluating public programs. If the NPV of a project is positive, the program generates more benefits than the resources it costs and therefore is economically efficient relative to the alternative, the basis of comparison. Thus, the program should be recommended for implementation. Computationally, NPV is often obtained by calculating the net benefits by subtracting costs from benefits at different points in the program's lifetime. The net benefits are then discounted and summed to obtain the NPV of the program. Mathematically, NPV can be expressed by the following formula:

$$NPV = \sum_{t=0}^{n} \frac{(b_t - c_t)}{(1+i)^t}$$

[4]

Where:
b = benefit
c = cost
i = discount rate
t = time period
n = number of time periods.

Consider the following case as an example: A prospective student is facing a decision about whether to attend a local university for a course of study leading to a master's degree in public administration. A number of factors enter into the student's decision-making process, but economic issues are her primary concern for the time being. She has learned the basic skills of CBA and intends to use this evaluation tool to solve the problem. Following the step outline above, she narrowed the standing to her interest and identified the alternative for comparison as status quo, that is, not attending the program. She then listed the impact as costs and benefits for attending the university compared with not attending it. She specifically included an opportunity cost of leaving her job, which is substantial and material in the analysis. The parameters and assumptions after her initial investigation are listed below:

- Tuition, fees, books for two years will cost $40,000.
- Opportunity cost of forgone earnings for a period of two years is $100,000.
- Annual extra earnings after graduation will be $10,000 for 20 years.
- All the dollar amounts above are in today's dollars (constant dollars).
- Financial costs are incurred at the beginning of year 1 and year 2, and opportunity costs are incurred at end of year 1 and year 2.
- Benefits are incurred at the end of each year.
- The real discount rate is 2 percent.

Using the data, the student conducted the CBA; see Table 5.5 for the results.

As shown in Table 5.5, the student listed the impacts of attending the program indexed by time. She then calculated the net benefit for each year and discounted the net benefits to their present values to the decision point. She added the present values of the net benefits, the cash inflows as in common financial analysis, to obtain the NPV of the decision to attend college. As shown in the table, the NPV is positive and is more than $20,000. Given the positive NPV and based on economic considerations, she decided to attend the local university's MPA program.

The NPV is recommended as the primary criterion in CBA. Alternative criteria are also available and frequently used in practice. Two theoretically sound criteria other than NPV are benefit-cost ratio (BCR) and internal rate of return (IRR). Although not recommended as the primary criteria for CBA, they are important and warrant further discussion.

The BCR expresses the total benefit and the total cost of a program in a ratio form. It is intuitive to understand and easy to implement. A BCR of greater than 1 indicates efficiency, as more than one dollar is produced in benefit by the program for each dollar of cost. When multiple programs are evaluated, they can be ranked by the BCR. The program with the highest BCR should be considered for adoption first, before programs of lower ranks. The information from the BCR criterion can be insufficient under certain circumstances, however. It may require the supplement of NPV to inform decision making.

Let us assume that two projects are under consideration. Project 1 costs $50 million and generates $100 million in benefits. Project 2 costs $200 million but generates $400 million in benefits. The costs, benefits, BCR, and NPV are illustrated in Table 5.6.

As shown in the table, the BCR for both projects is the same, so we cannot select between these projects on the basis of the BCR criterion alone. The

TABLE 5.5
Cost-Benefit Analysis of Attending Master's of Public Administration Program

Year	Costs Financial	Costs Opportunity	Benefits: extra earnings	Net benefits	Present value
0	−$20,000			−$20,000	−$20,000
1	−20,000	−$50,000		−70,000	−68,627
2		−50,000		−50,000	−48,058
3			10,000	10,000	9,423
4			10,000	10,000	9,238
5			10,000	10,000	9,057
6			10,000	10,000	8,880
7			10,000	10,000	8,706
8			10,000	10,000	8,535
9			10,000	10,000	8,368
10			10,000	10,000	8,203
11			10,000	10,000	8,043
12			10,000	10,000	7,885
13			10,000	10,000	7,730
14			10,000	10,000	7,579
15			10,000	10,000	7,430
16			10,000	10,000	7,284
17			10,000	10,000	7,142
18			10,000	10,000	7,002
19			10,000	10,000	6,864
20			10,000	10,000	6,730
21			10,000	10,000	6,598
22			10,000	10,000	6,468
Net present value					$20,479

TABLE 5.6
Costs, Benefits, Benefit-Cost Ratio, and Net Present Value for Two Hypothetical Projects

Project designator	Costs	Benefits	Benefit-cost ratio	Net present value
Project 1	$50	$100	2	$50
Project 2	200	400	2	200

NPVs of the two projects are substantially different nevertheless; $50 million for project 1 and $200 million for project 2. Assuming that budget and other financing constraints allow both projects to be considered and that no other major projects could be combined with project 1 to generate an equal or greater aggregate return, the decision makers should select project 2 on the basis of the NPV criterion. In any event, the BCR can be used in combination with NPV to better inform decision making.

The IRR approach compares a derived internal rate of return of a project with a predetermined required rate of return. A project's IRR is calculated by solving for the discount rate in the NPV equation (equation 4 presented earlier) so that the NPV equals zero. The IRR of a program measures the return on investment, and it is widely used in business decision making. It is intuitive and can be easily used in comparing different potential investment options. The use of IRR as an evaluation criterion can run into difficulties, too. The NPV equation is nonlinear, so the solution is not always uniquely defined. In that case, the analyst will face difficult choices among multiple and competing solutions. Given this issue, and other conceptually more demanding difficulties, which we do not explore in this text, we do not recommend IRR as the primary criterion for CBA. Similar to BCR, however, IRR can be used to supplement the NPV criterion in CBA.

Theoretically unsound criteria are also used by government and business in CBA and capital budgeting, such as pay back period and accounting rate of returns. The pay back period method concerns the length of time in which a project could recover its costs. The sooner a project can get back initial investment, the more efficient and the safer the project. It is an incomplete measure of efficiency, however, as it omits the cash flows after the payback period. The accounting rate of return rule divides the total earning from the project by its total investment. It is flawed as an evaluation method, as it does not account for TVM. These methods are not recommended as primary rules in evaluating projects in capital budgeting.

PERFORMING SENSITIVITY ANALYSIS.   Sensitivity analysis is an important part of well-conceived and -conducted cost-benefit analyses. New and more advanced techniques have been developed in sensitivity studies in recent years, and the application of sensitivity analysis in CBA is expected to grow in the future. Broadly speaking, there are three different ways to conduct sensitivity analysis: partial sensitivity analysis, the total valuation (extreme case) analysis, and the Monte Carlo analysis. The applicability and limitations of each method are briefly outlined below.

The NPV of a project is influenced by the estimates of impacts, as shown in cash flows and the selection of parameters, such as discount rate. In assessing the impact of the important parameters under different assumptions or due to estimate errors, partial sensitivity analysis is most applicable and convenient. The analysis varies one factor at a time, holding all other factors constant. It is easy to conduct by the analyst and easy to comprehend by decision makers. It is the most frequently used method in current practice. The drawback of the partial sensitivity analysis is its inability to investigate the joint effect of changes in several key parameters concurrently. In reality, more often than not parameters change simultaneously, and interactions of those effects cannot be estimated within the framework of partial sensitivity analysis.

The total valuation method can be used to predict consequences if combinations of influential factors lead into extreme cases. The method can be implemented by changing the key parameter simultaneously to create different scenarios. This will provide the decision maker and program manager extra information of the best, the most likely, and the worst-case scenario so that risk management strategies can be developed in advance. It will also provide an estimate of the robustness of the CBA for the analyst and the decision makers alike. If the program still generates positive net benefits under the worst-case scenario, then the conclusion of the CBA could be deemed robust and the confidence in the efficiency of the program increases. The problem with the total valuation method is the lack of information about the probabilities for the extreme cases. Moreover, the number of scenarios could increase exponentially as more factors are taken into consideration. In theory, brute force analysis could be used to compute the NPV for all possible combinations of parameters with the corresponding potential scenarios, but this approach is impractical and inefficient.

The Monte Carlo method uses modern statistical techniques and powerful computers to simulate a program's net benefit as a function of all plausible variations in the parameters concerned. It is an improvement on the partial and extreme cases sensitivity analysis in two key respects: It makes use of available distributional information about the parameters, and it derives a probability distribution of the net benefit of the project under different scenarios. One of the major limiting factors for the use of the Monte Carlo method is the need to know the probability distributions for uncertain parameters. Moreover, Monte Carlo analysis can be time-consuming and technically demanding. With such heavy requirements for analytical resources, Monte Carlo analysis is often beyond the institutional capacity of state and local governments looking for quick and useful field applications of CBA. Attempts should be made to conduct sensitivity analyses using the Monte Carlo method wherever possible, however, because of its ability to generate much more complete policy-relevant information about risks and rewards.

To study an example of a narrowly defined CBA with different possible discount rates, let us examine the financial impact of government support in the construction of local sports facilities. A proposed redevelopment of Brooklyn's Atlantic Yards area in New York City calls for the construction of an 18,000-seat arena to be the home of the National Basketball Association's Nets.[1] The proposal asks for $100 million in a cash contribution from the city government. You, as the fiscal analyst for the city, are asked to evaluate the proposal's fiscal implications from the city government's perspective. Specifically, you are asked to compute the NPV of the project for city treasury based on two scenarios:

- The city secures approval from federal government to finance the project through general obligation (GO) bonds with a tax exemption; the interest rate or discount rate in this scenario is 6 percent;
- The city could not get federal approval for a tax exemption and it has to issue revenue bonds; the interest rate or discount rate in this case is 9 percent.

Following the steps for conducting a CBA outlined above, you defined the study from the city government's financial perspective, identified the alternative projects under the two bonding scenarios, listed and estimated the revenues and costs for the expected lifetime of the facility, and organized the data in a spreadsheet as shown in Table 5.7. Using equation 4, you computed the NPV of the project under the two scenarios by subtracting costs from benefits in each year to obtain the annual net benefit, discounting the net benefits to their present values, and summarizing the present values to determine the NPV of the project under the two scenarios.

The results of the analysis indicate that if the city can issue a GO bond at an interest rate of 6 percent, the city will make a net financial gain of $35.53 million from the investment. The project under this circumstance should be recommended for implementation. However, if the government cannot get approval to issue a GO bond and has to finance the project with a revenue bond at a 9 percent interest rate, the city will sustain a net loss of $3.83 million. Based on the NPV decision rule and from the city's financial perspective, the project financed by the revenue bond should not be recommended.

This analysis raises an important question of which parameters should be included in sensitivity analysis. The discount rate—the borrowing interest rate in the above case—is apparently important as a change of the rate from 6 percent to 9 percent qualitatively alters the outcome of the analysis. Discount rate is routinely included in professional cost-benefit analyses. Other factors, such as standings and perspectives, potential errors in the estimated program impacts, the methods of monetization are all potentially significant factors. Analysts should work with the project team and other knowledgeable persons, including CBA experts, to select the key uncertain factors to be included in sensitivity analysis. Analysts are recommended to report the CBA under the base case, that is, the most likely case, as well as cases under different and plausible scenarios. The information generated from sensitivity analysis provides decision makers with not only a sense of robustness of the analysis but also time to prepare for outcomes that differ from expectation caused by changes in key assumptions and estimates as time goes by and the situation evolves.

TABLE 5.7
Cost-Benefit Analysis with Sensitivity Analysis of the Atlantic Yards Arena Investment ($ millions)

Period	Year	Costs	Arena construction and operation tax inflow	Net benefit	Present value Discount rate: 6%	Present value Discount rate: 9%
0	2006	$100	3.32	−96.68	−$96.68	−$96.68
1	2007		3.38	3.38	3.19	3.10
2	2008		3.96	3.96	3.52	3.33
3	2009		8.12	8.12	6.82	6.27
4	2010		8.53	8.53	6.76	6.04
5	2011		8.9	8.90	6.65	5.78
6	2012		9.18	9.18	6.47	5.47
7	2013		9.28	9.28	6.17	5.08
8	2014		9.28	9.28	5.82	4.66
9	2015		9.33	9.33	5.52	4.30
10	2016		9.55	9.55	5.33	4.03
11	2017		9.78	9.78	5.15	3.79
12	2018		10.01	10.01	4.97	3.56
13	2019		10.25	10.25	4.81	3.34
14	2020		10.50	10.50	4.64	3.14
15	2021		10.75	10.75	4.49	2.95
16	2022		11.02	11.02	4.34	2.78
17	2023		11.29	11.29	4.19	2.61
18	2024		11.57	11.57	4.05	2.45
19	2025		11.86	11.86	3.92	2.31
20	2026		12.15	12.15	3.79	2.17
21	2027		12.45	12.45	3.66	2.04
22	2028		12.76	12.76	3.54	1.92
23	2029		13.07	13.07	3.42	1.80
24	2030		13.40	13.40	3.31	1.69
25	2031		13.73	13.73	3.20	1.59
26	2032		14.07	14.07	3.09	1.50
27	2033		14.42	14.42	2.99	1.41
28	2034		14.77	14.77	2.89	1.32
29	2035		15.14	15.14	2.79	1.24
30	2036		15.51	15.51	2.70	1.17
Net present value					$35.53	−$3.83

The above example is a simplified version a CBA. It concerned only the narrow financial impacts of the proposed investment from the government's perspective (increased tax flow versus debt service costs). It omitted the many broader factors that should have been involved in a thorough and comprehensive CBA. Factors that can and do enter the larger project-level decision-making process may include relocation of current residents, increased traffic congestion, and new jobs created for the currently unemployed. The quantification of these impacts and the conduct of the more complete analysis are beyond the scope of the present book. For more advanced studies, consult specialized textbooks, such as *Cost-Benefit Analysis,* by Boardman and others, listed at the end of the chapter.

SELECTING THE ALTERNATIVE WITH THE LARGEST NET SOCIAL BENEFITS. If the analyst is satisfied with the technical analysis, the final step of CBA is to recommend to policy makers the most cost-efficient programs for consideration. Following the principle and practice of CBA discussed earlier in this chapter, analysts should recommend the program with positive NPV of social benefits. The recommendation should be supplemented or qualified with a sensitivity analysis, especially when the conclusion is sensitive to errors in forecasts or to assumptions of theoretical contention, such as the determination of the discount rate. Technical competence and professional ethics are important factors in safeguarding the quality and integrity of recommendations regarding capital projects that could have substantial and long-term impacts on the financial health of a government or other public organizations.

Economic and financial analyses, such as CBA, provide information for elected officials to make decisions on behalf of their constituencies. Public decision making is and will remain a normative and political process, however, wherein economic and efficiency measures are but only one piece of data among the myriad of other concerns that feed into the decision-making process. This is especially true for decisions with regard to resource allocation, wherein many interests compete for limited public investment. The results of a well-conceived and rigorously conducted CBA could be, and in reality often are, overruled by political and philosophical considerations. Analysts should be aware of their function in the public decision-making process. A well-designed, -conducted, and -publicized CBA has a better chance of affecting decision making potentially in the best interests of the public, over and above the powerful organized interests in representative democracies.

Despite the limitations, CBA is an important decision support tool that has great potential for rational decision making in capital budgeting. This is especially true at a time of budgetary constraints and government efficiency reforms. CBA has been used increasingly at the federal level during the past two decades, spurred by the Government Performance and Results Act of 1993 and the directives from the OMB and the GAO. State and local governments are also climbing on the bandwagon. Nevertheless, the quality and the breadth of the applications of this rational decision-making method are uneven in public organizations, especially in local governments. To the extent appropriate and possible, better and wider use of CBA in all public organizations in the process of capital budgeting is strongly recommended.

Financing Capital Projects

Some governments or public authorities finance all of their **capital** spending on what is often called a **pay-as-you-go** basis, with taxes or fees for service. Others finance all their capital assets by borrowing in the market for tax-exempt bonds. Most use some combination of debt financing and "pay-go." That ratio is sometimes explicit in a written debt policy, and sometimes it is simply a pattern of practice. In the short run, debt financing expands the ability of a government to fund capital projects. Over the longer term, however, too much debt creates burdensome levels of debt service in the operating budget and can squeeze out other programmatic needs. The credit rating agencies are also sensitive to debt loads, and too much debt can result in rating downgrades and higher interest costs for new bond issuance.

In addition to the comprehensive analysis of costs, savings, and benefits outlined above, an analyst may be asked to include estimates of debt service in the justification of a capital project. The first step is to isolate the initial costs of the project, like design, construction, or purchase price. Unlike maintenance or operating costs, these outlays can appropriately be funded with bond proceeds. Some simple models of bond structures are outlined in the Excel workbook spreadsheets labeled "Bond Structures" in "Budget Tools Chapter 05 Text Examples Bond Structures."

The first spreadsheet, labeled "Cost Components," shows a simplified presentation of upfront costs for a capital construction project. These costs are set out on a separate worksheet because estimates may change. Other worksheets then link to those assumptions, which can be adjusted when necessary. The "Cost Components" spreadsheet (Table 5.8) also contains an estimate of the tax-exempt interest rate at the time when debt is likely to be issued. Because market interest rates fluctuate, most analysts use rates somewhat higher than current borrowing costs, providing a little cushion against changing rates. Finally, the spreadsheet contains an estimate of the underwriting fees and other costs of issuance anticipated in a bond transaction.

Many jurisdictions and authorities issue bonds with level debt service, like payments on a fixed-rate home mortgage. This makes budgeting easy

KEY COMPONENTS OF CAPITAL BUDGETING IN LARGE CITIES

Capital budgeting is a planning tool that can be used to aid policy makers in selecting among many potentially worthwhile and competing capital projects and then financing them. In large jurisdictions the process is often complex and includes the preparation of the capital asset inventory, capital improvement plan (CIP), long-term financial analysis and forecast, and capital budget.

An inventory is the starting point for identifying capital needs and making investment decisions. An inventory compiles information of existing capital assets in terms of age, condition, use, capacity, and the estimated replacement costs. Through analysis of the inventory, decision makers can have a better idea of the state of repair and the new capital assets required to be included in a CIP.

A CIP is a multiyear list of proposed projects and financing resources. It often projects five to six years into the future, although shorter and longer terms are found in some jurisdictions. A CIP is a strategic plan, updated annually. It provides detailed information on the design, cost, and financing of improvements by the requesting agency or for the jurisdiction as a whole. A CIP often includes the estimated impact on the jurisdiction's financing plans.

TABLE 5.8
Project Cost Components and Other Key Assumptions

Acquisition or construction cost	$100,000,000
Design cost	10,000,000
Subtotal	$110,000,000
Costs of issuance @ 1%	$1,100,000
Bond size	$111,100,000
Interest rate	5.875%
Term of bonds (years)	20

TABLE 5.9
Level Debt

Parameters	Excel notation, formula, and values
Principal amount	PV = $111,100,000
Interest rate	rate = 5.875%
Term in years	nper = 20
Annual payment	PMT(rate, nper, −pv) = $9,588,145

and reassures rating agencies, which usually prefer either level debt service or front-loaded debt service and are wary of back-loaded debt service structures. Excel's TVM functions make it simple to calculate annual debt service for a level debt structure. The PMT function gives a quick and accurate estimate of the total principal and interest payment required to retire debt on a given schedule.

The second worksheet (Table 5.9), "Level Debt," restates the relevant assumptions picked up directly from the first worksheet and then uses the PMT function to calculate the annual payment. To make this calculation, the PMT function requires the interest rate (rate), the number of years (nper), and the initial outlays (PV). If you look carefully at the cell containing the calculation of the annual payment, you will see the PMT function introduced with a minus sign. When Excel is asked to calculate a TVM formula using two dollar values (in this case, PV and PMT), the answer always carries a sign different from the dollar variable used as input. The added minus sign restates the answer as a positive number, which makes better sense to most people who will read the analysis.

The total payment is composed of both principal and interest, and, like mortgage or car payments, the interest portion is always higher in earlier years, with the principal portion of the payment growing as the maturity date of the debt approaches. It is also true that typical tax-exempt bond structures pay interest twice a year and principal once a year. To disaggregate these payments into interest and principal and semiannual interest, we need to build a more complex spreadsheet; see Exercise 3 at the end of the chapter.

The tab labeled "Level Principal" shows how to set up a cash flow table with level principal payments, which result in front-loaded payments of total annual debt service (Table 5.10). Statutes in some jurisdictions require this kind of debt structure by mandating equal principal payments each year during the lifetime of the debt. The "Level Principal" spreadsheet again picks up the relevant assumptions but then divides the principal amount borrowed by the maturity of the debt issue to come up with the required principal payment in each year. Interest outlays are calculated by multiplying the principal

TABLE 5.10
Level Principal

Principal amount	$111,100,000
Interest rate	5.875%
Term in years	20
Structure	Level debt service

Year	Principal outstanding	Interest	Principal repaid	Total debt service
1	$111,100,000	$6,527,125	$5,555,000	$12,082,125
2	105,545,000	6,200,769	5,555,000	11,755,769
3	99,990,000	5,874,413	5,555,000	11,429,413
4	94,435,000	5,548,056	5,555,000	11,103,056
5	88,880,000	5,221,700	5,555,000	10,776,700
6	83,325,000	4,895,344	5,555,000	10,450,344
7	77,770,000	4,568,988	5,555,000	10,123,988
8	72,215,000	4,242,631	5,555,000	9,797,631
9	66,660,000	3,916,275	5,555,000	9,471,275
10	61,105,000	3,589,919	5,555,000	9,144,919
11	55,550,000	3,263,563	5,555,000	8,818,563
12	49,995,000	2,937,206	5,555,000	8,492,206
13	44,440,000	2,610,850	5,555,000	8,165,850
14	38,885,000	2,284,494	5,555,000	7,839,494
15	33,330,000	1,958,138	5,555,000	7,513,138
16	27,775,000	1,631,781	5,555,000	7,186,781
17	22,220,000	1,305,425	5,555,000	6,860,425
18	16,665,000	979,069	5,555,000	6,534,069
19	11,110,000	652,713	5,555,000	6,207,713
20	5,555,000	326,356	5,555,000	5,881,356
Total			$111,100,000	$179,634,813

outstanding at the beginning of the period by the interest rate. These interest outlays are added to the level principal payments to calculate the annual debt service in each year. As principal is paid off, interest outlays decline, and so does the total annual debt service payment. Compared with level principal structures, level debt produces lower annual debt service initially but higher debt service later in the maturity schedule. Level debt also produces higher total debt service payments, reflecting the higher interest costs required by slower amortization of principal. We note again that the structure illustrated in this set of cash flows is simplified, and a more complex spreadsheet would be required to calculate debt service with semiannual interest payments.

More complex bond structures can also be modeled, including structures designed to "wrap" existing debt service, maintaining its general profile.

Other structures can be modeled that reshape existing debt service, making total debt service after issuance of the new bonds more or less front-loaded.[2]

Summary

This chapter provides a brief overview of the concepts in a capital budget and key methods in capital budgeting. Two major analytical skills, life cycle costing and cost-benefit analysis, are included for their importance and relevance in capital investment decision making. The chapter first outlines the theoretical underpinning of these methods from a historical perspective. It then presents the methods step-by-step, using examples of student life experience and real case studies of local public organizations, so that the skills can be practiced and applied in real life, real time. The chapter concludes by exposing students to various types of long-term financing for a capital budget, with an emphasis on municipal bonds. Throughout the chapter, students are reminded of the limitations of bounded rationality in technical analysis in public decision making and the political nature and environment of governments. Although very brief by design, the chapter tries to survey a wide range of material and provide a good foundation for preparing and appreciating capital budget and for pursuing more advanced studies in capital budgeting.

Exercises

To complete the exercises, use the data below.

1. The city administration is considering refurbishing the lighting system of its administration building. After an initial investigation, the city procurement office has narrowed down the choices to the following two options:

   - Option 1 is an Urgolight system that costs $500,000 to purchase and install.

   - Option 2 is a conventional system that costs $100,000 to purchase and install.

   - Both systems are expected to last for 20 years.

   - The energy cost for option 1 is $20,000 and maintenance is $2,000 in today's dollars.

   - The energy cost for option 2 is $50,000 and maintenance is $10,000, also in today's dollars.

   - Assume that the discount rate is 4 percent, and all future costs are paid at end of year.

Which lighting system should the city select based on financial (LCC) considerations? *Vrgolight @ $798,987 is $116,433 cheaper.*

2. A city has learned that by buying larger garbage trucks, labor costs for garbage removal would be reduced. You, the analyst, have also collected the following information:

   ■ Cost of the trucks today is $400,000.

   ■ Annual savings in this year's constant dollars is $90,000.

   ■ Trucks will last for four years, then will be sold for $100,000.

   ■ The city can borrow money (discount rate) at 7 percent.

   ■ Inflation (for the next four years) is expected to average 3 percent.

   Note: All the dollar amounts are in this year's dollars (constant dollars).

   Assuming the costs and benefits incur at the end of the year, should the city buy the trucks? *Yes.*

3. A major urban center is planning to issue a $100 million, twenty-year, semi-annual interest municipal bond for the construction of a stadium.

   ■ The interest rate is 5.875 percent, based on the economic and financial conditions of the city and city government.

   ■ The design and issuance costs are estimated to be $10 million and 1 percent, respectively.

   What is the total interest paid if the city decides to adopt a level debt service structure?

   How much does the city still owe on this bond at the end of each year? *$68,534,813*

   See column B.

Additional Readings

Boardman, A. E., et al. *Cost-Benefit Analysis: Concepts and Practice.* 3d ed. Upper Saddle River, N.J.: Pearson/Prentice Hall, 2006.

Cole, Raymond J., and Eva Sterner. "Reconciling Theory and Practice of Life-Cycle Costing." *Building Research and Information* 28, no. 5–6 (September 2000): 368–375.

Emblemsvag, J. "Activity-Based Life-Cycle Costing." *Managerial Auditing Journal* 16, no. 1–2 (2001): 17.

Fabrycky, W. J., and Benjamin J. Blanchard. *Life-Cycle Cost and Economic Analysis.* Englewood Cliffs, N.J.: Prentice Hall, 1991.

Finkler, Steven A. *Financial Management for Public, Health, and Not-for-Profit Organizations.* 2d ed. Upper Saddle River, N.J.: Pearson/Prentice Hall, 2005.

Fuller, Sieglinde K., and Stephen R. Peterson. *Life-Cycle Costing Manual for the Federal Energy Management Program.* NIST Handbook 135. Washington, D.C.: U.S. Department of Commerce, February 1996. http://purl.access.gpo.gov/GPO/LPS16832.

Kreuze, J. G., and G. E. Newell. "ABC and Life-Cycle Costing for Environmental Expenditures." *Management Accounting* 75, no. 8 (1994): 38–47.

Lee, R. C. "Life-Cycle Costing." In *Tools for Decision Making: A Practical Guide for Local Government,* ed. David N. Ammons. Washington D.C.: CQ Press, 2002.

Moussatche, H., and J. Languell. "Flooring Materials: Life-Cycle Costing for Educational Facilities." *Facilities* 19, no. 10 (2001): 333–343.

National Association of State Purchasing Officials, *NASPO State and Local Government Purchasing: Principles and Practices.* 5th ed. Lexington, Ky.: National Association of State Purchasing Officials, 2001.

Rothwell, G. "A Real Options Approach to Evaluating New Nuclear Power Plants." *Energy Journal* 27, no. 1 (2006): 37.

Seldon, M. Robert. *Life Cycle Costing: A Better Method of Government Procurement.* Boulder, Colo.: Westview, 1979.

Notes

1. The data for the Atlantic Yards example are based on "Atlantic Yards: A Net Fiscal Benefit for the City?" New York City Independent Budget Office Fiscal Brief, September 2005, www.ibo.nyc.ny.us/.

2. If more complex calculations are required, the budget office may turn to debt specialists inside the government or to financial advisers or underwriters outside it. They use software specialized for debt service calculations and can produce more detailed and more accurate cash flows quickly and easily. The most widely used such software is created and maintained by DBC. For more information, see the firm's Web site, http://dbcinc.com/.

Chapter 6

The Financial Plan and Budget Decision Making

Learning objectives:

- Understand structurally balanced budgets
- Understand future revenue picture
- Examine projections of future expenditures

The **financial plan** is a high-level summary of revenues and expenditures prepared by the budget office. In the early stages of budget preparation, the first iteration of the preliminary financial plan includes revenue forecasts at existing tax rates and bases, as well as the recommended changes in the spending base. Expenditures in the preliminary plan will also include estimates of capital spending funded out of operating revenues. As review of departmental budgets and proposals proceeds, the plan is updated to include proposed budget initiatives or cuts.

The preliminary financial plan serves three important functions.

- First, it allows the chief executive and other decision makers to see whether revenues from existing sources cover proposed spending, and it thus allows an assessment of whether the budget is balanced. Most state and local governments are required by law to balance their budgets, although the basis for budget balance may change from jurisdiction to jurisdiction.

- Second, the preliminary financial plan provides impetus for the final rounds of executive branch decision making. If the preliminary plan is not balanced, proposals to increase revenues, cut spending, or bond out additional capital projects must be considered. In the happy but infrequent circumstance where the preliminary financial plan shows a surplus, decision makers may consider expanding services, cutting taxes, or funding additional capital needs from pay-as-you-go sources.

- Third, the financial plan also helps to educate legislators and the public about the sources of funding for the budget and distribution of resources among functions or departments in the government or agency.

In a later chapter, we will review methodologies for multiyear financial planning. For the purposes of this chapter, we assume that decision makers are provided with the full annual impact of any budget choices as well as the impact in the year under review. Without such analysis, it is much too easy to make decisions that can create imbalance in years to come, as outlined below.

The Financial Plan

The basic format of the financial plan is simple, although this simplicity can be obscured by detail. At its most schematic, the preliminary financial plan shows projected revenues, projected spending, and an estimated deficit or surplus, which is simply the arithmetic difference between revenues and spending.

The level of detail presented depends on the purpose. The first full-blown preliminary plan is likely to include data on each major tax and other important source of revenue, as well as spending by department or by major program. Although the typical focus is on the jurisdiction's general fund revenues and spending, the plan will also include projected transfers to other major funds, especially pay-as-you-go capital spending. It may also include an itemization of new initiatives proposed by the executive or by departments for inclusion. In the final rush of budget decision making, quick financial plan updates may provide much less detail and may serve simply as a check to see how much progress has been made in achieving budget balance.

As the final budget proposal is pulled together, another complete financial plan will be created to help introduce and explain the full budget proposal. Once again, this plan will include line-by-line information about major revenue sources. It will also usually be based on projections more recent than those in the preliminary plan. It will also include spending only by department or by program, however, with budget cuts or new initiatives included in those spending totals instead of displayed separately. The plan published with the proposed budget will also serve as a benchmark against which to tally changes in the budget during legislative review and adoption.

In some jurisdictions, the financial plan is updated several times throughout the year. For example, New York City revised its financial planning procedures after the fiscal crisis of the mid-1970s, and since then the city has modified its financial plan every quarter on the basis of revised revenue forecasts and updated spending data. The city's fiscal year begins July 1, so the first financial plan of the new year is based on the budget just approved by the city council and is published in late June or early July, shortly after budget adoption is completed. An updated financial plan is issued on or about November 1, and another update is published as part of the city's preliminary budget near the end of January. That budget and its financial plan serve as

TABLE 6.1
New York City Financial Plan, October 2007 ($ millions)

Revenues	FY 2008	FY 2009	FY 2010	FY 2011
Taxes				
General Property Tax	$12,984	$14,100	$15,186	$16,171
Other Taxes	22,215	21,456	22,221	22,696
Discretionary Transfers (1)	546	—	—	—
Tax Audit Revenue	659	559	560	560
Tax Reduction Program	−68	−239	−283	−301
Subtotal: Taxes	$36,336	$35,876	$37,684	$39,126
Miscellaneous Revenue	6,063	5,084	5,101	5,134
Unrestricted Intergovernmental Aid	340	340	340	340
Less: Intra-City Revenue	−1,457	−1,367	−1,368	−1,368
Disallowances against Categorical Grants	−15	−15	−15	−15
Subtotal: City Funds	$41,267	$39,918	$41,742	$43,217
Other Categorical Revenues	1,067	1,007	1,012	1,014
Inter-Fund Revenues	436	411	403	398
Total City Funds and Inter-Fund Revenues	$42,770	$41,336	$43,157	$44,629
Federal Categorical Grants	5,606	5,373	5,358	5,344
State Categorical Grants	10,958	11,424	12,289	12,733
Total Revenues	$59,334	$58,133	$60,804	$62,706
Expenditures				
Personal Service				
Salary and Wages	$21,189	$22,323	$24,082	$25,353
Pensions	5,728	6,265	6,318	6,404
Fringe Benefits	6,406	6,815	7,282	7,795
Subtotal: Personal Service	$33,323	$35,403	$37,682	$39,552
Other Than Personal Service				
Medical Assistance	5,797	5,602	5,756	5,916
Public Assistance	1,187	1,187	1,187	1,187
Pay-as-You-Go Capital	100	200	200	200
All Other (1)	18,044	17,547	17,971	18,376
Subtotal: Other than Personal Service	$25,128	$24,536	$25,114	$25,679
General Obligation, Lease & MAC Debt Service (1,2,3)	3,837	3,896	4,247	5,002
FY 2007 Budget Stabilization & Discretionary Transfers (1)	−4,052	—	—	—
FY 2008 Budget Stabilization (2)	2,255	(2,255)	—	—
FY 2009 Budget Stabilization (3)	—	350	(350)	—
General Reserve	300	300	300	300
Subtotal	$60,791	$62,230	$66,993	$70,533
Less: Intra-City Expenditures	−1,457	−1,367	−1,368	−1,368
Total Expenditures	$59,334	$60,863	$65,625	$69,165
Gap To Be Closed		−$2,730	−$4,821	−$6,459

Source: The complete version of this financial plan can be found at New York City Office of Management and Budget, www.nyc.gov/html/omb/html/finplan10_08.html.

Note: (1) FY 2007 budget stabilization and discretionary transfers total $4.663 billion, including prepayments of subsidies of $639 million, budget stabilization of $3.313 billion, lease debt service of $100 million, debt retirement of $65 million, and a TFA grant that increases FY 2008 revenues by $546 million. (2) FY 2008 budget stabilization totals $2.255 billion. (3) FY 2009 budget stabilization totals $350 million. — = not available.

the baseline for the preparation of the executive budget, which is released in late April or early May, and includes another updated financial plan.[1] When necessary, revised financial plans trigger requests for legislative modification of the budget or, more frequently, changes by the executive. The New York City model of what might be called "continuous budgeting" is unusual among state and local governments, which usually do not provide as much data, nor as often, as New York City.

Financial plans often show changes from prior periods to help readers locate major variances. In the financial plans included in proposed or adopted budgets, the variances will show changes from the prior year. In updates within a fiscal year, the variances may reflect changes from the most recent published plan. The formats may also include simple calculations of percentages representing a tax source or a department as a share of total revenues or spending. As suggested above, this information helps readers understand where resources come from, where they are going, and how these allocations have changed since prior periods.

For example, the projected growth in the general property tax in Table 6.1 is 8.7 percent in the first two years (FY 2008 to FY 2009) while other projected taxes are expected to decline by 3.4 percent during the same period.

Budget Balance and Budget Decision Making

As budget preparation proceeds, executives are often faced with financial plans that show projected deficit in budgets. To close a projected gap, the budget office is as likely as a mayor or government to consider proposals to raise revenues, cut spending, or both. Few elected officials relish either of those sets of choices and will search instead for options that do not involve increases in taxes or fees or cuts in services or jobs. Sometimes the options that avoid those difficult choices provide budget relief in the short run, but they yield no recurring gap-closing benefit. Delays in the initial implementation of a program, for example, might reduce projected spending in its first year, but the full costs of the program will remain in later years when the initiative is fully phased in.

Sometimes options to close projected gaps even increase budget gaps in the future. The sale of a revenue-producing asset—a city-owned building, for example—can produce significant one-time resources for balancing the budget but will reduce receipts every year in the future. Similarly, a decision to reduce pay-go spending for capital and increase borrowing will produce higher spending on debt service as long as bonds are outstanding.

In most jurisdictions, the primary focus of budget preparation is on the year under review, and much less attention is given to budgets further in the future, sometimes called the "out years." As we will see in a later chapter, the process of developing a multiyear plan is slow and cumbersome, and most budget offices cannot produce full updates frequently during budget preparation. However, it is possible to show out-year impacts for individual new initiatives and budget-balancing actions, or at least show the full annual impact of the proposal. Thus, the recommendation to delay program implementation discussed above would be presented in a format similar to what is shown in Table 6.2.

TABLE 6.2
Sample of Table Showing the Effect of Out-Year Spending

Proposal	Gap-closing impact	Full annual impact
Delay implementation of expansion of state child health insurance program for six months	$20,000,000	No savings

This presentation helps the decision maker understand that this portion of the budget gap will recur in the year following and that closing it will require additional difficult choices.

A presentation that shows out-year impacts will also help the analyst who maintains the multiyear plan make adjustments after decisions are made. All budgets for large jurisdictions include some nonrecurring spending, savings, and revenues, but overreliance on one-time actions to solve recurring budget gaps simply pushes the day of reckoning into the future. Permanent savings or recurring revenues will eventually be needed to achieve long-term budget balance.

Summary

A financial plan is a summary of projected revenues and expenditures. Financial plans are useful because they permit policymakers to determine whether future budgets are balanced, they strongly encourage policymakers to choose alternative spending plans if the financial plan is unbalanced, and they educate the public about the sources of revenue in a city's budget.

Exercise

1. Examine Table 6.1 (a spreadsheet version of which is available on the attached CD in the folder labeled "Budget Tools Chapter 06 Exercise") to answer the following questions:

   ■ Are total revenues growing faster or more slowly than expenditures? Show the annual growth rates for revenues and expenditures in a table.

- What is New York City's fastest-growing category of expenditures during the planning period?

- What percentage of New York City revenues comes from the general property tax? How much is this tax growing in each year of the financial plan?

Additional Readings

Ives, Martin, Joseph R. Razek, and Gordon A. Hosch. *Introduction to Governmental and Not-for-Profit Accounting.* 5th ed. Upper Saddle River, N.J.: Pearson/Prentice Hall, 2004.

Kavanagh, Shayne C. *Financing the Future: Long-Term Financial Planning for Local Government.* Chicago: Government Finance Officers Assocation, 2007.

Note

1. Financial plans and other budget documents can be found at the Web site of the New York City Office of Management and Budget at www.nyc.gov/html/omb/html/budpubs.html#finplans.

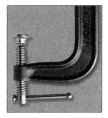

Chapter 7

Presenting the Budget

Learning objectives:
- Understand basic concepts and framework of performance budgeting
- Know which performance measures make sense in budgeting
- Integrate performance measurement with budgeting
- Communicate budgets to the public
- Explain objectives of budget proposals

Preparing the budget is just a first step. The budgets that governors and mayors develop are proposals, requiring amendment and adoption by legislative bodies, typically after considerable public commentary. And recently, questions and comments often focus on performance as well as funding. So budget examiners work to incorporate performance data into their decision making and their presentations and to display their financial data in clear and useful formats. We outline this work here in our discussion of presenting the budget. We want to emphasize the importance of these tasks and warn against the belief that presentation is an afterthought. Citizens are skeptical about government's use of their tax dollars, and legislators have priorities of their own. In that environment, presenting the executive budget as effectively as possible is vital.

Integrating Budgeting with Performance

The purpose of **performance measurement** in budgeting is to exchange **post hoc accountability** for increased **discretion** during budget execution. In the budget proposal, it is usually the operating agency in cooperation with the budget office that proposes target levels of performance achievement that are to be met with the funding provided. As the budget process proceeds, these proposals may be renegotiated. For example, the Department of Transportation and the budget office may suggest target levels, but the mayor's staff or city manager's office may review these suggestions and make changes. In most states, the legislature also engages in adjusting target levels.

During the fiscal year, the operating agency uses these performance targets to measure its success in providing the service it has promised to public officials and budget offices. These measures should be periodically reported to the funding authorities and the public to maintain accountability. Keeping in mind the link between promises made in the budget process and subsequent accountability, budget staff should make sure performance targets are limited in number, meaningful, and linked to the services delivered by the organization.

Beware of simplistic rules. Some will argue that if an agency is overspending or underperforming, the right remedy is to cut the budget until the agency is brought to heel. Others would like a promise that performance reports will never be used "punitively." Neither approach realistically reflects a meaningful implementation of performance budgeting, which requires that variances should be understood before determining a response.

Framework for Performance Budgeting

In the next section, we discuss the selection of elements of performance data. The categories of data will be defined as they are reviewed. First, however, we need a framework, and, because practices vary widely, this framework is prescriptive. Performance budgeting involves four stages: (1) proposal, (2) negotiation and approval, (3) execution, and (4) reporting.

Performance measurement in budgeting should follow all these stages. Thus, the performance data reported at the end of the budget year should reflect the budget targets approved at the end of stage 2. The reporting of performance data that has not been through the first two stages bears little relation to the decision process.

Performance reports should show targets, actuals, and variances. **Targets** can be number of completions, such as, probation officers will complete ten prisoner reviews each week for the year. **Actuals** are what really occurred, such as the fact that probation officers averaged eight reviews a week for the year. **Variances** are the difference between the targets and the actuals. In this example, the unfavorable performance variance was two reviews per week.

Within-year reports should show both the current period and the year-to-date information. Annual reports should also show the same information for one or two previous years as well as targets for the budget year. This form of reporting simply extends a well-established budget reporting framework to performance data. It also encourages stability in performance data. This framework is demonstrated in Table 7.1.

TARGETS. In this chapter, the proposed and budgeted level of performance is called a target. The target should be proposed by the entity that will ultimately be responsible for meeting the

LINK PERFORMANCE MEASURES WITH BUDGET

Some cities have created performance measures, but they are rarely connected to the budget.

Officials in San Jose, California, have created extensive performance reports for each service area, yet the performance indicators are not connected to the budget. The budget itself is extremely detailed, with five years of expenditure data for each service area.

Des Moines, Iowa, however, has extensive performance measures, and they are indeed related to the budget. The Des Moines performance indicators include efficiency ratios for both revenue and expenditures in every service area. City officials have also created effectiveness and productivity ratios.

It can be done.

TABLE 7.1
Framework for Performance Budgeting

Measure	Prior year			Current year			Budget year	Future year
	Target	Actual	Variance	Target	Estimated actual	Variance	Target	Target
Outcome[a]								
Output								
Quality								
Satisfaction								
Other standard								
Process efficiency								
Financial efficiency								
Financial effectiveness								
Equity								

Note: This template is intentionally left blank.
[a]This could also be an interim outcome indicator.

target. As with all budget processes, the central executive and the legislative processes involve a negotiation with the entity that performs the service. Ultimately, these entities have the authority to set the target. However, the target will be meaningless if it does not realistically reflect the empirical basis on which it was originally proposed.

Targets can reflect two sorts of approaches. The first, labeled **benchmarks,** searches for data about achievement in other similarly situated organizations. The target then is to do as well as, or better than, the highest level of success among those organizations. Realistic plans consider the distance to travel to reach this goal and therefore may stage this goal over several periods.

The largest difficulty is with defining "similarly situated." If care is not taken to be sure that other organizations are genuinely similarly situated, benchmarks can be unrealistic, either too difficult or too easy. Organizational design, demographic characteristics, climate, and other factors affecting service success should be considered in identifying similarly situated organizations.

A second approach, labeled **standards,** sets targets based on guidelines established by authoritative bodies. These bodies may be professional organizations, engineering entities, governmental authorities, or many other entities. On some research basis, the entity establishes what a feasible and effective achievement level is. Standards may vary for populations and other characteristics associated with the service delivery, so care should be taken to use the correct standard. One should also be careful to evaluate the source of the standard. Advocacy groups may issue standards that are infeasible, whereas groups of citizens may advocate standards that are ineffective.

ACTUALS. Actuals are the performance data that the agency has committed to use and to report on regularly. The struggle with actual data is the extent to which agency officials report data honestly and in a timely manner. This is not as easy as it sounds. Unfavorable results in performance data can result in agency officials being embarrassed and unwilling to share data with the public. There are no easy answers to this, only the willingness on the part of agency officials to present actual data with a willingness to communicate with the public.

Another difficulty with actuals lies with the reliability of the data collection process. All data elements should be clearly defined before data collection begins. All instruments or devices for data collection should be easy and effective to use. Data collectors should know the data definitions and should have clear protocols for data collection.

VARIANCES. When reporting comparisons of actual performance compared with targets, targets should not be hidden or manipulated to hide variances. Variances should be revealed and analyzed. Clearly, as with all budgets, agencies will not hit their performance targets exactly; there will always be small variances that may not require analysis. Circumstances of the jurisdiction will determine what counts as small; however, in most circumstances, jurisdictions should not be surprised at variances in the neighborhood of 5 to 10 percent until such time that history establishes local expectations. Particular types of programs and particular conditions may change this amount substantially. When variances do call for analysis, a summary of the analysis and findings should be provided either with the budget or in a supplemental report. These findings should be reflected in the next cycle budget proposal.

Reporting Performance Data

There are two types of decisions in reporting performance data. First, one must determine which performance data categories to report. The data categories we will review are outcomes (final, interim, and early stage), outputs, and process measures. Second, one must determine what to count as a reporting element for selected categories.

It is recommended that there be no more than a few lines of performance data for each major budget account. A typical department may have three to six major budget accounts. If your department has twenty budget accounts, you will have to use less space.

OUTCOMES. The focus of performance measurement is outcomes. A major budget account

INTEGRATING EXPENDITURES WITH INDICATORS
Officials in Sunnyvale, California, have created an extensive performance-based budget emphasizing productivity in each of the city's service areas. Each service area is broken down by activity, and each of these activities is further broken into measures of quality, productivity, cost-effectiveness, and finances. The cost-effectiveness measure includes cost per service, cost of repair, and other costs, depending on the activity. Sunnyvale is one of the few cities that integrates expenditures with performance indicators.

should typically have one or at most two outcomes. A measure of an **outcome** reports the degree to which a purpose of a program is met. We have intentionally avoided using the traditional buzzwords such as "mission" or "goal" because we want you to focus on why the agency is running the program, not on some fuzzy academic term. An outcome is an achievement of what you set out to do. An outcome does not focus on short-term production, but on the broader public purpose that public decision makers have in mind when they fund the program under review. Despite difficulties that will become apparent, budgeting for outcomes is the most important step that can be taken in implementing performance budgeting.

An outcome measure might be provided in several forms. One way is to report the absolute number of some accomplishment, such as the number of people who have achieved a goal. One outcome, for example, might be the number of people who have attained self-sufficiency (for example, paying for their own housing for six months) after receiving service from a program.

A second form of measure is a rate. One might report the number of teen pregnancies per thousand female teens after a program has been in action. In general, the rate itself is uninformative, so what should be reported instead is the third form, which is the change in the rate, either alone or as additional information with the rate information.

Examples of reporting rates include an agency that might report the reduction in the number of teen pregnancies per thousand female teens after a program has been in action. Burlington, Vermont, officials have set an outcome of increasing home ownership by 15 percent over the next five years.

Closely related to the form of measure is the population measured. Unless the program in question serves an entire jurisdiction, two distinct populations usually must be measured. One is the population of those people who happen to have been served. The other is the population of the people in the community including similarly situated people who were not served. If a program services one hundred teens in Chicago, it cannot realistically report on a change in teen pregnancy for the whole city; the data will be useful for only the one hundred teens served. If, however, Chicago had a school system–wide program, reporting about the program should show the impact on the city rate, even if some teens were not served.

Outcomes are reported in the context of causality, which addresses the question of whether the program is responsible for the outcome. Causality is usually established through evaluation research, which is more demanding than performance measurement. All that can be accomplished in performance measurement is the collection of data about key characteristics at well-established points of time. Any information from evaluation research should be summarized and appended to the performance report. Otherwise the report should be clear that it reports a measurement of a status at a point in time.

Ideally, a budget should show anticipated outcomes, which, in some circumstances, may be several years in the future. After the budget is approved, the budget should also report the achieved outcomes and demonstrate variances.

Outcomes are not often achieved within the budget horizon. This effect can produce difficulty within the budget model. How does one commit to outcomes, produce results, and report on them within the budget cycle when the outcomes are still pending when the cycle is over? The typical answer is **interim outcome indicators.** An interim outcome indicator is a measure of something that supports the expectation that the outcome will eventually be achieved. This might be an **output,** an **early stage outcome,** or certain **measures of process.**

OUTPUTS.   One sort of interim outcome is an output. A typical output might be the number of graduates of the school system. Graduates can be reported either as the total number graduating (an absolute, but in some ways an uninformative measure) or as the number of graduates compared with the number available to graduate from some starting point such as the ninth grade; this is known as the graduation rate. The graduation rate is also an **efficiency measure,** as discussed below. Burlington, Vermont, has established an output target of fifty-eight buyer-assisted housing units over the next five years to meet its outcome indicator of increasing home ownership by 15 percent over the next five years.

Outputs are distinguished from outcomes in several ways. First, outputs can be counted immediately after the process is over. Second, the link to process is much clearer. And, third, outputs remain part of the causal chain to outcomes. For example, the purpose of an education is not to produce graduates, but to produce social goods for both students and society sometime after the graduation. Graduation is an output in the causal chain to those social goods.

Too often we fail to distinguish between outputs and outcomes. Durham, North Carolina, has stated an outcome of bringing on line eighty-seven more affordable housing units by FY 2007, with the goal of increasing the supply of affordable housing. But eighty-seven more affordable housing units is an output. Durham officials have not stated an outcome. They could have said that their outcome would be increasing the supply of affordable housing by 10 percent.

Early-stage outcomes may be closely linked to the end of the process, but they bear some relationship to the purpose of the program. For K–12 education, college admission rates might be viewed as an early-stage outcome. Early-stage outcomes move beyond the end of the process and begin to attain the actual social goods that are intended in the funding of the program. Often the causal link is a little weaker but still fairly strong. Except for very short-lived programs, early-stage outcomes may still be outside the budget cycle and may be reported in a subsequent year. This weakens the link between the funding and the report.

PROCESS MEASURES. **Process measures,** also called **activity measures,** measure some aspect of how the program goes about achieving its outputs and outcomes. From a management point of view, these measures may be of interest for oversight of the program itself. It is, however, an error to report an excessive number or inappropriate types of process measures in performance budgeting. Of particular interest to budgeting are quality, satisfaction, process efficiency, and a few other well-recognized measures of process. Quality measures are usually standards based, and they report on the delivery. So, in health care, **quality measures** as reported by the Centers for Medicare and Medicaid Services of the Department of Health and Human Services include such hospital quality characteristics as the percentage of heart attack patients who receive aspirin at the time they arrive at the emergency room.[1]

Quality measures serve as interim outcome measures because research suggests and taxpayers perceive that there is a link between the delivery of services reflecting the quality expectation and the achievement of the socially desired outcome.

Quality targets should be set at externally based standards if present performance is near the standards. If present performance is substantially below the standards, targets should show step-by-step progress so that standards will be reached in a realistic but not substantially extended time frame. If performance has exceeded standards, there is no reason to stop increasing the target when the standard is reached.

Measures of satisfaction can determine how various populations perceive the program. These may include service recipients, their proxies, or other populations such as similarly situated people or the populace at large. In reporting the results from satisfaction surveys, it is important to confirm that the survey was conducted using professional research methods, report all significant findings, and report the population surveyed. Satisfaction may measure outcomes or interim outcomes for certain sorts of programs where public satisfaction is a substantial purpose in the first place. For example, streets are not simply clean or dirty; they are clean relative to public expectation. If the public is satisfied, then additional cleaning, although possible, may not be a meaningful goal. Satisfaction is also likely to be of special interest to elected decision makers. Regardless of how absolutely successful a program is, public dissatisfaction suggests need for action.[2]

Targets should be set reflecting progressive increases in satisfaction. It is unrealistic to expect 100 percent satisfaction in every category, but it is also unacceptable to tolerate 80 percent satisfaction when there are reasonable steps that can be taken to improve satisfaction.

Analysts measure efficiency in various ways, but here we focus on **process efficiency,** which is the relationship between critical inputs and their later transformation to outputs. Inputs are resources that are required to perform services. Inputs include personnel (with skills), space, time, equipment, and, in many cases, someone who is to receive a service or something that is to be transformed in some manner through public service. Personnel, space, equipment, and (within certain limits) time can be purchased or hired. Thus, they are financial inputs.

The inputs that should be the primary focus of process efficiency are not financial; instead they are critical inputs such as service recipients or things to be transformed that are essential to the public service delivered. Thus, for education, they would be the students appearing at the beginning of the school cycle or activities. For crime solving, it would be the reports of crimes. Thus, for a school cycle the comparative is:

$$Process\ efficiency = \frac{Completing\ students}{Starting\ students} \qquad [1]$$

This information will be best understood if it is represented as a percentage or, where the number is very small, by the number per thousand or ten thousand. An example would be a high school in which 75 percent of the students complete an academic course of study; that would be 750 students out of a beginning class of 1,000 who would complete an academic course.

Setting targets of this sort provides insight into how well service is delivered and can be delivered. Ideally process efficiency can be raised to 100 percent on a realistic schedule, beginning at current levels. In the real world, it will not be credible to set a short-term goal of 100 percent efficiency unless there is some historical evidence that such success is possible.

Financial efficiency is similar to process efficiency, except that it aggregates the financial inputs, measures them with their cost, and calculates:

$$Financial\ efficiency = \frac{Funds\ spent}{Outputs} \qquad [2]$$

One example—the example of the probation officers who completed eight reviews each per week—is that 416 reviews were completed in that year. Because the average probation officer's salary is $65,000, the financial efficiency of the probation officers is $156 per review. It is then possible to compare the financial efficiency of each individual probation officer to examine each officer's financial efficiency over time.

Financial efficiency communicates how well public resources are used to achieve the outputs of a program. Outputs, however, are not as important as outcome measures, so we also strive to measure financial effectiveness:

$$Financial\ effectiveness = Funds\ spent\ /\ Outcomes \qquad [3]$$

A financial effectiveness measure about probation officers would be, for example, their salaries compared with the outcome of those on probation staying out of prison. The ultimate effectiveness of the probation officers' work is not the number of reviews they complete a week, but their ability to keep ex-prisoners out of jail. Out of the 416 case reviews, 300 ex-prisoners stayed out of jail, for an effectiveness rate of 72.1 percent. The financial effectiveness is $65,000 / 300 = $217 per ex-prisoner who stays out of the criminal justice system.[3]

In reporting financial efficiency, an important consideration is the proper attribution of funds. Jurisdictions are organized differently, so some localities will report direct costs, and others will report similar costs as indirect or allocated costs. Further, cost accounting may not be consistent from jurisdiction to jurisdiction. Consequently, efficiency information may not be comparative with other localities. The International City/County Management Association (ICMA) is building a database to work on this difficulty.[4] The most important comparison is probably with your own jurisdiction's past practice. After that, you can look to similarly situated jurisdictions in your own state, which may have similar organizational factors.

Some programs or services are the focus of widely recognized process measures. For example, emergency services such as fire, police, and ambulance response have well-recognized response time measures. These reflect the time between contact to the emergency phone number and the arrival of the emergency personnel at the site of the emergency. Sometimes standards may be associated with these measures, so they may fall within the general category of quality measures, but they may be difficult to catalogue in the categories listed above. More usefully, one should realize that any such well-recognized process measure is likely to be interesting to the public and decision makers. Rather than trying to categorize or list such measures, the analyst might call this sort of measure to the reader's attention so that an interested reader can seek out more specialized knowledge about such measures.

As with other measures, we should set targets based on past practice with anticipated improvement in the direction of any well-recognized high achievement level. Sometimes, high achievement is controversial or implies policy decisions. In such cases, policy implications should be clearly explained in budgetary documentation. For example, school systems may treat student-teacher ratios as a well-recognized measure, possibly of quality. The general implication is that such ratios should be reduced where there are more than a certain number of students per teacher. However, improving student-teacher ratios is expensive. Thus, setting this as a performance measure without explaining the policy and fiscal implications is merely a backdoor move for a multiyear budget increase and is inappropriate.

Equity

Equity refers to the fair distribution of benefits. Performance measurement cannot speak to the fairness, but it can speak to the distribution. Specifically, it can describe the attributes of the beneficiary population and use those attributes as service targets. Income and geographic distribution, gender and ethnic distribution, age and education distribution, for example, can all be used to measure the fairness of the distribution of program benefits.[5]

Where a program is intended to benefit a narrow population, this information should be revealed as a performance target and subsequently as a performance measure. Where the program is not intended to benefit a narrow population, collect demographic information to demonstrate that the distribution of benefit recipients reflects the makeup of the jurisdiction.

Difficulties in Performance Budgeting

Performance measurement and management take considerable time and effort, but those hurdles can be reduced if bad practices are avoided. We advise against:

- Defining data late in the budget cycle,
- Collecting data inconsistent with data collected in previous budget cycles,
- Collecting data haphazardly,
- Collecting only one or two types of data,
- Reporting too much data,
- Reporting data that are uninteresting to the local public,
- Failing to set targets,
- Failing to track success during the year, and
- Failing to distinguish between outputs and outcomes.

More broadly, performance budgeting is a commitment to using performance data in both the budgeting process and in management. The data should not be collected and reported at the end of the cycle as if the data were somehow informative only at that point. Performance budgeting should begin with planning and budgeting for performance, followed by measurement, reporting, and adjustment in the subsequent budget cycles. The history of public sector performance initiatives reflects rapid growth of interest followed by slow decline and disappearance. To keep this activity alive in a jurisdiction, it is important to establish a framework that draws commitment from both the administrative entity and the funding authority.

Performance budgeting also requires selectivity. This chapter provides insight into what can be reported. The most critical items to report are outcomes or interim outcomes. Beyond that, other measures are negotiable. An effective performance budget does a good job with a few performance items. Once selected, these items should be reported consistently.

Finally, performance budgeting is essentially a blunt weapon aimed at implementing rational methods in the budget process. Wise veterans of the budget wars warn that rational budget methods can increase conflict in the budget process by exposing disagreements and forcing discussion of basic objectives. Implementation requires not only technical competence as discussed in this chapter, but also attention to the political environment.

Writing Budget Justifications

A budget justification is, in effect, a proposal that explains why a particular program is being proposed. This document is usually short—not more than two or three pages—and justifies the proposal to spend funds a certain way. Usually budget justifications are written by budget analysts in government agencies or nonprofit organizations that are advocating a particular initiative that requires increases in their budgets. Managers and professional staff also find themselves in this role from time to time.

Figure 7.1 is a sample of a budget justification format; it provides guidance for the layout of a budget request. Many organizations have their own prescribed format. If no prescribed format is available, this format can be used as a generic guideline or the first page of a budget justification memo. Be sure the table in the budget detail reflects the actual chart of accounts, not the generic one used here. The tables should be modified as needed. Figure 7.2 shows an example of the use of this template.

General Guidelines for Budget Justifications

Analysts should follow certain guidelines as they write a budget justification:

- Be brief. Budget justifications are competing with many other candidates for attention.

- Avoid jargon. The audience for budget justifications may not be familiar with budgetary expressions and vocabulary.

- Avoid hype. Although the audience may not know the subject area, they will most likely be able to tell when the proponent of the initiative is exaggerating.

FIGURE 7.1
Budget Justification Format

AGENCY NAME: _____

PROPOSAL NAME: _____

SUBMITTED BY: _____ **DATE:** _____

COSTS:

Year	Total	General fund	Federal funds	State funds	Other funds
Budget year					
Year 2					
Year 3					

INTRODUCTORY SUMMARY:

STATEMENT OF NEED:

PROGRAM DESCRIPTION:

BENEFITS:

PERFORMANCE MEASUREMENT:

Measurements	Measure	Target
Input:		
Output:		
Outcome:		
Efficiency:		
Effectiveness:		
Quality or process:		
Equity:		

COSTS:

STAFFING IMPACT:

OPTIONS:

FIGURE 7.1 (continued)
Budget Justification Format

Budget allocation	Object codes	Budget year	Year 2	Year 3
Personnel services (PS), Total:				
Full-time personnel services costs				
Other personnel costs				
Nonpersonnel services (OTPS), Total:				
Supplies	100–199			
Equipment	300–399			
Contracts, services, travel benefits	400–499			
Social services	500–599			
Contractual services objects	600–699			
Charges, awards, grants and subsidies	700–801			
Bonds and other	810–870			
Fund, Total:				
General funds				
Federal funds				
State funds				
Other funds:				
Employees, Total:				
Full-time, permanent				
Part-time, temporary, contract				

ACCOMPANYING LEGISLATION:

- Use active sentences. Write directly.

- Avoid personal references (the agent of action is the organization, not the analyst).

- Use standard English.

Section Breakdown

The organization of a budget justification is straightforward. Budget justifications contain an introduction summary, statement of need, a description of the program, issue of benefit, performance measures, costs, staffing impact, suggestions. Figure 7.2 provides an example of how these sections can be filled in.

INTRODUCTION SUMMARY.   There is a short introduction that is really a summary of a few short sentences: "The _____ agency proposes to _____ beginning _____ for \$_____." The introduction is the analyst's chance to get the attention of decision makers. It should not equivocate or use jargon.

FIGURE 7.2
Budget Justification

AGENCY NAME: Department of Sanitation

PROPOSAL NAME: Litter bin placement and service

SUBMITTED BY: Department of Sanitation **DATE:** February 15, 2008

COSTS:

Year	Total	General fund	Federal funds	State funds	Other funds
Budget year	$104,480	$93,980	$10,500		
Year 2	$90,480	$90,480			
Year 3	$90,480	$90,480			

INTRODUCTORY SUMMARY: The Department of Sanitation proposes to place 100 sturdy metal litter receptacles at locations that attract litter, and service these receptacles twice a week using a two-person sanitation crew, beginning on July 1, 2008 (the beginning of fiscal year 2008).

STATEMENT OF NEED: Citizen complaints concerning litter in parks and the business district have increased sharply over the past several years. The annual citizen satisfaction survey shows declining satisfaction over the appearance of public places for the last five years, from a high of 92 percent satisfied or very satisfied in 2001 to 78 percent in 2007.

The Department of Sanitation currently uses part-time minimum-wage workers at each park and high traffic business district location to collect and remove litter. As the volume of activity has increased, this practice has become less effective because the workers are on site for approximately one to two hours at each location, and litter accumulates for approximately eighteen hours, leaving many hours of unsightly conditions. It is anticipated that the presence of easily accessible trash receptacles will substantially reduce the accumulated litter.

PROGRAM DESCRIPTION: The Department of Sanitation has a well-established list of most severely littered locations. These locations are principally in the central business district and in the parks. The program will place litter receptacles in these locations. The purchase of the receptacles is eligible for a federally funded urban environment grant that is funded 75 percent by the federal grant, requiring a 25 percent cash participation by the grantee.

The chief source of cost of this program is not the receptacles, but the service (trash pickup). It is anticipated that every twenty-five receptacles will add five total hours of work to trash pickup (four pickups a week at unusual locations) using a two-person crew. These costs are not eligible for the federal grant. Because of the wide dispersion of locations, the department anticipates adjusting existing routes with the added flexibility provided by one additional full-time position, rather than adding two part-time positions and a special route solely for litter pickup. These services are not anticipated to offset the current part-time litter worker crews because it is anticipated that there will not be 100 percent compliance with voluntary use of litter receptacles.

BENEFITS: The anticipated benefit of this program is the sharp reduction in litter at popular public locations. It is anticipated that this program will reduce complaints received by the city manager and members of the city council. The portion of the public that makes complaints would like no litter at all. The placement of these litter receptacles cannot achieve this level of compliance, but can substantially improve public satisfaction.

PERFORMANCE MEASUREMENT:

Measurements	Measure	Target
Input:	Cost for litter removal through trash receptacles	As budgeted, excluding receptacles
Output:	Pounds of litter removed per week from receptacles	2 million pounds (2,080,000)
Outcome:	Change in citizen satisfaction	5 percent increase in the budget year and 5 percent more in each of the two subsequent years
Efficiency:	Cost per pound of litter removed	23 pounds per dollar ($0.0435 per pound)
Effectiveness:	Cost per 1 percent increment in change in citizen satisfaction	$18,100 per 1 percent change
Quality or process:	Cleanliness evaluation score	95 percent clean by independent raters
Equity:	Change in citizen satisfaction as distributed over demographic categories: income and ethnicity	Equal change in all groups

FIGURE 7.2   (continued)
Budget Justification

COSTS: This project requires the purchase of trash receptacles and a twenty-hour increase in use of a two-person trash pickup crew. The city vendor charges $140 per trash receptacle for a total cost of $14,000, of which three-fourths is paid by the federal share of an urban environment grant. Other nonpersonnel costs are estimated, based on long experience, at 50 percent of personnel costs for trash pickup crews. These costs are principally for the operation and maintenance of equipment. Equipment acquisition is not included, as it will fall under capital budgeting.

STAFFING IMPACT: A total of 40 hours of crew time are added at the standard pay and benefits of $29 per hour for a total of $60,320. This crew member will be added to the total shift time so that numerous shifts can be adjusted to include portions of this service.

OPTIONS: This program is not substantially scalable. The Department of Sanitation has no part-time workers in the trash collection crew and would meet sharp opposition for such positions from the Sanitation Workers Union. A small variation such as addition of five or ten more receptacles (at $140 each) would not substantially affect service, but a larger variation would lead to deteriorating trash collection service. The total identified sites are 106, so it is not necessary to scale up an additional 100 units and add two personnel.

Budget allocation	Object codes	Budget year	Year 2	Year 3
Personnel services (PS), Total:		$60,320	$60,320	$60,320
Full-time personnel services costs		$60,320	$60,320	$60,320
Other personnel costs				
Nonpersonnel services (OTPS), Total:		$44,160	$30,160	$30,160
Supplies	100–199	$14,000		
Equipment	300–399	$30,160	$30,160	$30,160
Contracts, services, travel benefits	400–499			
Social services	500–599			
Contractual services objects	600–699			
Charges, awards, grants and subsidies	700–801			
Bonds and other	810–870			
Fund, Total:		$104,480	$90,480	$90,480
General funds		$93,980	$90,480	$90,480
Federal funds		$10,500		
State funds				
Other funds:				
Employees, Total:				
Full-time, permanent		1	1	1
Part-time, temporary, contract				

ACCOMPANYING LEGISLATION: No legislation is required to implement this action.

STATEMENT OF NEED.   Next comes need. After the short introduction, the analyst explains in narrative form what need is being addressed. Why is this initiative needed? What problems are being addressed? Have there been concrete consequences of these problems? In other words, the analyst is being challenged to tell a brief story that demonstrates how the absence of this initiative has led to socially undesired outcomes.

An example of the statement of need is the statement of the governmental agency, Children's Services, in New York City. Here the need is to reduce the percentage of children who reenter foster care within the year. It is well documented that foster care children who do not obtain a suitable placement are moved constantly from one home to another. The constant changes make it very difficult for children to gain the stability needed for their development.

PROGRAM DESCRIPTION. After discussing the need, it is important to describe the program and to point out differences from or similarities to comparable programs elsewhere.

An example of a program description is the description of the program designed by city officials to reduce the percentage of children who reenter foster care within the year. The program, which seeks to reduce the percentage from 11.3 percent to 5 percent of children who reenter foster care within the year, proposes increasing the number of group homes needed to care for children who cannot adjust to foster homes.

ISSUE OF BENEFITS. Next comes the issue of benefits. If the need is met, who will benefit? What sorts of benefits will accrue? To whom? Next comes the tricky part. Who will be left out? The analyst needs to highlight affected constituencies, political sensitivity, or any risk that should be considered.

One example of benefits is that foster children who were previously shifted from one foster home to another will achieve stability in group homes, which have been proved to be quite successful with many foster children. The risk of such a program is that the city's initial costs will be increased without the city seeing the benefits for at least one or two years. Such a risk is small, indeed, compared with the benefits of added stability for many foster children.

PERFORMANCE MEASURES. How can the operating agency determine whether the program is meeting its objectives and using its resources wisely? Can these measurements actually be accumulated? Will the resultant data be reliable? Are costs associated with collecting and analyzing these data included in the cost estimate? What will the manager or decision maker know from reviewing these data? The section of this chapter on performance measures discusses input, output, outcome, efficiency, effectiveness, quality or process, and equity. These indicators should be considered in any budget justification memo.

An example of performance measures is the extent to which the percentage of foster children who reenter foster care within a year will be reduced from 11.3 percent to 5 percent. It may take two to three years to achieve such a reduction, but the benefits are clear.

COSTS. The next section describes total costs by year and identifies funding sources, identifying each fund source and the amount to be spent from that source. Typical budget requests are for general funds, that is, funds from the general tax revenue in the budget year. Depending on state and local laws, legislative authority may be required to spend funds in other categories as well, even if the funds are not public funds (this statement applies to public agencies). Nonprofit agencies should reveal the whole cost of their program and also the share the public is being asked to contribute, along with the sources of other funding.

This section of the justification should not include money needed at, or saved at, other government departments or other nonprofits. The goal is a brief narrative justifying the cost estimate. More extensive discussion belongs in the work papers. Here, the analyst focuses on major sources of costs and their rationale. It is also helpful to specify savings to be achieved through curtailed activities. However, these savings *must* also be included in the net cost estimate. *Do not estimate savings or costs in other departments without their concurrence.*

An example of cost is the initial cost of establishing more group homes and the savings obtained from no longer sending some foster children frequently from one home to another.

STAFFING IMPACT. This section specifies, in a clear and unequivocal presentation, any personnel increases and reductions. Staffing should be briefly justified here, although complete justification belongs in the work papers. Again, the analyst should not estimate staffing changes at other departments without their concurrence.

An example of the staffing impact is to come up with an estimate of the increased number of staff needed for each of the new group homes. With increased staffing comes increased costs.

OPTIONS. The decision maker will want to see options, so the budget justification should spell out alternatives that require slightly less and slightly more money. The presentation should include at least two elements:

- What benefits will be forgone at the lower funding level? Why? How could the lower level be implemented? What are the out-year implications of the lower funding level? Will this alternative reduce availability of non–general fund money? Why?

- What additional benefits would be obtained by the higher funding level? Are there barriers to implementing at this level? What are the funding-source implications at this level?

For the group home example, the analyst could propose a different group that would cost less. In the case of the foster care agency, a less expensive program would be to establish a media campaign in the city to find new foster care parents. These foster care parents would be trained to work with more difficult children who have had trouble adjusting to foster care.

ACCOMPANYING LEGISLATION. If legislation will be required to implement the initiative, the analyst should identify the relation between the budgetary initiative and the recommended changes in law. Is there parallel proposed legislation under consideration? Are these funds needed to implement legislation that has already passed? Will the implementation of this initiative require legislation that has not yet been proposed?

In this example, no legislation would be required for the foster care agency to implement its proposed program.

Exercises

Below are some exercises for examining performance indicators and budget justification.

1. Categories of Performance Indicators

    Categorize each of these performance indicators:

    ■ Cost of building one unit of housing, $50,000.

    ■ Increasing the housing stock of the city by 15 percent over five years.

    ■ Building forty-five single-family-housing units over five years.

    ■ Locating land to build new affordable housing lands.

2. Using Performance Indicators

    Children's Services has more than 17,006 foster care children in its care. This number has changed over time:

FY 2003	25,622
FY 2004	22,082
FY 2005	18,968
FY 2006	16,807
FY 2007	17,006

    One of the chief goals of the foster care system is to place children in foster care with family members; however, this has been difficult to accomplish. Following are the percentages of children entering foster care who are placed with relatives:

FY 2003	19.2%
FY 2004	19.4%
FY 2005	21.4%
FY 2006	25.5%
FY 2007	28.4%

The number of foster care children in the system is an input and the percentage of children placed in foster care with family members is an output.

Create three performance measures for this exercise. Try to create outcome and equity measures. (There is no right answer to this question.)

3. Budget Justification

Look back to Exercise 1 in Chapter 3. Write a budget justification for this exercise.

Additional Readings

Forsythe, Dall W., ed. *Quicker Better Cheaper? Managing Performance in American Government.* Albany, N.Y.: Rockefeller Institute Press, 2001.

Hatry, Harry P. *Performance Measurement: Getting Results.* 2nd ed. Washington, D.C.: Urban Institute, 2007.

Kelly, Janet M., and William C. Rivenbark. *Performance Budgeting for State and Local Government.* Armonk, N.Y.: M. E. Sharpe, 2003.

Miller, Gerald J., W. Bartley Hildreth, and Jack Rabin. *Performance-Based Budgeting.* Boulder, Colo.: Westview Press, 2001.

Notes

1. See "Glossary of Definitions," Centers for Medicare and Medicaid Services, U.S. Department of Health and Human Services, June 21, 2007, www.hospitalcompare.hhs.gov/Hospital/Static/GlossaryPopUp.asp.

2. A typical discussion of satisfaction surveys is found in Harry P. Hatry, *Performance Measurement: Getting Results,* 2nd ed. (Washington, D.C.: Urban Institute, 2007), ch. 7.

3. When outcomes are measured as a complex number, such as the rate of change, constructing financial effectiveness measures may require considerable effort.

4. At the time of this publication, it is not generally believed that the ICMA database has completely worked out these difficulties.

5. Distribution of benefits should not be confused with tax concepts of horizontal and vertical equity, although programs that serve all portions of the population both across similarly situated people and among differently situated people may receive high public approval. Programs should collect data to show who receives benefits.

CHAPTER 8

Implementing the Budget

Learning objectives:
- Understand and examine the allocative stage of budgeting
- Conduct a variance analysis

Implementing the budget comprises two activities: first, creating an operating plan, and second, performing a variance analysis. Budget implementation should not be confused with "policy implementation." The operating plan is the first step to budget implementation. The operating plan also has two major steps: First, the organization needs to adjust the proposed or requested budget to reflect the budget decisions made by the legislative body. This is the **allocative** stage. Second, the organization needs to plan to spend its money over the fiscal period, generally one year. This is the allotment process.

What we plan to spend and what we actually spend is rarely the same. Variance is the difference between what is budgeted and what is spent. Every month organizations should conduct a variance analysis between budget and expenditures; this consists of comparing the budget with expenditures and examining the difference.

This chapter teaches the skills needed to develop an operating plan and then how to perform a variance analysis. The operating plan and the variance analysis are two of the key elements of budget implementation; that is, spending money as intended and keeping track to make sure that such spending is in fact happening. The chapter contains guided examples. In the first example, we'll look at a budget proposal, legislative action, and the subsequent allocative adjustment. Next we'll look at a variance analysis example. From there you will be poised to practice implementing the budget in three exercises.

Allocation

When an organization requests its budget, it is usually allocated over subdivisions of activity—normally work divisions—and over types of purchases, called objects of expenditure or line items. The line items are specified within each subdivision. We learned about these objects of expenditures in Chapter 2.

Within a typical accounting system, expenditures can be attributed only to **line items,** which must be attributed to broader categories such as work units.

During the legislative or senior executive budget process, decisions are made about total amounts of money, seldom about **objects of expenditure,** and frequently not about work units. These decisions may add sums of money or remove sums of money. In reconciling the executive and legislative budget processes, the differences between proposed and approved budget amounts are normally attributed to "convenience" object codes (or objects of expenditure). These are object codes that are used by legislative analysts and, occasionally, by central budget office budget analysts, but they are not normally available for use by line agencies.

The line agency use of these object codes is to resolve the value of these codes to zero, and the method of this resolution is by attributing the value to some other object code. As the line agency can attribute values only to object codes within its normal work units, the effect is that the agency must allocate the legislative change to a specified subdivision (normally, work unit) and to a specific type of expenditure. Making this attribution is the allocative aspect of an operating plan.

In allocating legislative funding changes, the analyst should pay careful attention to any legislative language associated with the budgetary adjustment. The legislature may designate additional money for particular work, purchases, or hires. It may specify what is too costly when reducing expenditures. The designation may be associated with subdivisions, types of purchases, or activities. If activities are specified, the analyst may need to learn from others within the organization where the activities will occur. Legislative language may be found not only in appropriations law but also in testimony, oral communication, and advice from legislative analysts. The analyst should follow organizational protocol in seeking advice from legislative staff or external individuals concerning unclear adjustments.

An example of a budget proposal, legislative action, and allocative adjustment is shown on the "Allocate & Allot" tab of the spreadsheet, "Budget Tools Chapter 08 Exercises," on the accompanying CD. A portion of the spreadsheet is captured on the next page, so that you can see the overall layout. For the sake of simplicity, only one work unit is shown.

The image on page 124 is the part of the spreadsheet that focuses on allocation. The allocative adjustment is in dollars as shown in column E, but it should be accompanied by text explanation as shown in column G, labeled "Notes." Each adjustment should be associated with a specific legislative or other rationale based on any decision authority. Where decision-maker rationales are not provided, explanations should be associated with any known basis resultant from the budgetary authorization process, including decisions authorized by the organization's chief executive.

		Allocation					Allotment							
2000	Numbers in $Thousands	Proposal	Legislature	Adjust	Operating plan	Notes	Operating plan	Q1	Q2	Q3	Q4	Check	Checked	Notes
2100	**Salaries & Wages**													
2101	Officers & Directors	$ 120.00			$ 120.00		$ 120.00	$ 30.00	$ 30.00	$ 30.00	$ 30.00	$ 120.00	TRUE	Equal amounts per quarter
2102	Salaries	$ 10,000.00		$ (500.00)	$ 9,500.00	Delay new positions	$ 9,500.00	$ 2,250.00	$ 2,250.00	$ 2,500.00	$ 2,500.00	$ 9,500.00	TRUE	$250 K increase for quarters 3 and 4 due to planned staffing increases
2103	Wages	$ 328.00			$ 328.00		$ 328.00	$ 218.67	$ -	$ -	$ 109.33	$ 328.00	TRUE	Equal in "summer" months, June, July, August
	Total Salaries & Wages	$ 10,448.00	$ -	$ (500.00)	$ 9,948.00		$ 9,948.00	$ 2,498.67	$ 2,280.00	$ 2,530.00	$ 2,639.33	$ 9,948.00	TRUE	
2140	**Payroll Taxes & Benefits**													
2141	FICA	$ 783.60		$ (37.50)	$ 746.10	Benefits for delayed positions	$ 746.10	$ 187.40	$ 171.00	$ 189.75	$ 197.95	$ 746.10	TRUE	Follows Salaries and wages
2142	Unemployment Insurance	$ 541.00			$ 541.00		$ 541.00	$ 135.25	$ 135.25	$ 135.25	$ 135.25	$ 541.00	TRUE	Equal amounts per quarter
2143	Workers Comp. Ins.	$ 231.00			$ 231.00		$ 231.00	$ 57.75	$ 57.75	$ 57.75	$ 57.75	$ 231.00	TRUE	Equal amounts per quarter
2144	Disability Insurance	$ 233.00			$ 233.00		$ 233.00	$ 58.25	$ 58.25	$ 58.25	$ 58.25	$ 233.30	TRUE	Equal amounts per quarter
2145	Benefits	$ 111.00			$ 111.00		$ 111.00	$ 27.75	$ 27.75	$ 27.75	$ 27.75	$ 111.00	TRUE	Equal amounts per quarter
	Total Payroll Taxes & Benefits	$ 1,899.60	$ -	$ (37.50)	$ 1,862.10		$ 1,862.10	$ 466.40	$ 450.00	$ 468.75	$ 476.95	$ 1,862.10	TRUE	
	Total Personnel	$ 12,347.60	$ -	$ (537.50)	$ 11,810.10		$ 11,810.10	$ 2,965.07	$ 2,730.00	$ 2,998.75	$ 3,116.28	$ 11,810.10	TRUE	
2160	**Travel & Training**													
2161	Travel	$ 238.00		$ (25.00)	$ 213.00	Reduce travel for conferences	$ 213.00	$ -	$ 71.00	$ 71.00	$ 71.00	$ 213.30	TRUE	No "summer" travel or training
2163	Training & Conferences	$ 543.00		$ (75.00)	$ 468.00	Reduce attendance at conferences	$ 468.00	$ -	$ 156.00	$ 156.00	$ 156.00	$ 468.00	TRUE	No "summer" travel or training
2164	Memberships	$ 145.00		$ (45.00)	$ 100.00	Reduce supported memberships	$ 100.00	$ 25.00	$ 25.00	$ 25.00	$ 25.00	$ 100.00	TRUE	Equal amounts per quarter
	Total Travel & Training	$ 926.00	$ -	$ (145.00)	$ 781.00		$ 781.00	$ 25.00	$ 252.00	$ 252.00	$ 252.00	$ 781.00	TRUE	
2200	**Office Expenses**													
2202	Other Furniture & Equipment	$ 987.00		$ (250.00)	$ 737.00	Make older equipment last longer	$ 737.00	$ 184.25	$ 184.25	$ 184.25	$ 184.25	$ 737.00	TRUE	Equal amounts per quarter
2203	Supplies	$ 400.00			$ 400.00		$ 400.00	$ 100.00	$ 100.00	$ 100.00	$ 100.00	$ 400.00	TRUE	Equal amounts per quarter
2204	Telephone	$ 455.00			$ 455.00		$ 455.00	$ 113.75	$ 113.75	$ 113.75	$ 113.75	$ 455.00	TRUE	Equal amounts per quarter
2205	Duplicating & Printing	$ 333.00			$ 333.00		$ 333.00	$ 83.25	$ 83.25	$ 83.25	$ 83.25	$ 333.00	TRUE	Equal amounts per quarter
2206	Postage & Shipping	$ 345.00			$ 345.00		$ 345.00	$ 86.25	$ 86.25	$ 86.25	$ 86.25	$ 345.00	TRUE	Equal amounts per quarter
2207	Equip. Rental & Maintenance	$ 169.00			$ 169.00		$ 169.00	$ 42.25	$ 42.25	$ 42.25	$ 42.25	$ 169.00	TRUE	Equal amounts per quarter
2208	Subscriptions & Fees	$ 500.00		$ (108.50)	$ 391.50	Eliminate duplicate subscriptions	$ 391.50	$ 97.88	$ 97.88	$ 97.88	$ 97.88	$ 391.50	TRUE	Equal amounts per quarter
	Total Office Expenses	$ 3,189.00	$ -	$ (358.50)	$ 2,830.50		$ 2,830.50	$ 707.63	$ 707.63	$ 707.63	$ 707.63	$ 2,830.50	TRUE	
2220	**Occupancy**													
2221	Rent	$ 432.00			$ 432.00		$ 432.00	$ 108.00	$ 108.00	$ 108.00	$ 108.00	$ 432.00	TRUE	Equal amounts per quarter
2223	Utilities	$ 234.00			$ 234.00		$ 234.00	$ 58.50	$ 58.50	$ 58.50	$ 58.50	$ 234.00	TRUE	Equal amounts per quarter
2225	Janitorial & Similar	$ 123.00		$ (8.00)	$ 115.00	Realize benefits from rebid contract	$ 115.00	$ 28.75	$ 28.75	$ 28.75	$ 28.75	$ 115.00	TRUE	Equal amounts per quarter
	Total Occupancy	$ 789.00	$ -	$ (8.00)	$ 781.00		$ 781.00	$ 195.25	$ 195.25	$ 195.25	$ 195.25	$ 781.00	TRUE	

	A	B	C	D	E	F	G
1					**Allocation**		
2	2000	**Numbers in $Thousands**	Proposal	Legislature	Adjust	Operating plan	Notes
3							
4	**2100**	**Salaries & Wages**					
5	2101	Officers & Directors	$ 120.00			$ 120.00	
6	2102	Salaries	$10,000.00		$ (500.00)	$ 9,500.00	Delay new positions
7	2103	Wages	$ 328.00			$ 328.00	
8	Total	Salaries & Wages	$10,448.00	$ -	$ (500.00)	$ 9,948.00	
9							
10	**2140**	**Payroll Taxes & Benefits**					
11	2141	FICA	$ 783.60		$ (37.50)	$ 746.10	Benefits for delayed positions
12	2142	Unemployment Insurance	$ 541.00			$ 541.00	
13	2143	Workers Comp. Ins.	$ 231.00			$ 231.00	
14	2144	Disability Insurance	$ 233.00			$ 233.00	
15	2145	Benefits	$ 111.00			$ 111.00	
16	Total	Payroll Taxes & Benefits	$ 1,899.60	$ -	$ (37.50)	$ 1,862.10	
17	Total	Personnel	$12,347.60	$ -	$ (537.50)	$ 11,810.10	
18							
19	**2160**	**Travel & Training**					
20	2161	Travel	$ 238.00		$ (25.00)	$ 213.00	Reduce travel for conferences
21	2163	Training & Conferences	$ 543.00		$ (75.00)	$ 468.00	Reduce attendance at conferences
22	2164	Memberships	$ 145.00		$ (45.00)	$ 100.00	Reduce supported memberships
23	Total	Travel & Training	$ 926.00	$ -	$ (145.00)	$ 781.00	
24							
25	**2200**	**Office Expenses**					
26	2202	Other Furniture & Equipment	$ 987.00		$ (250.00)	$ 737.00	Make older equipment last longer
27	2203	Supplies	$ 400.00			$ 400.00	
28	2204	Telephone	$ 455.00			$ 455.00	
29	2205	Duplicating & Printing	$ 333.00			$ 333.00	
30	2206	Postage & Shipping	$ 345.00			$ 345.00	
31	2207	Equip. Rental & Maintenance	$ 169.00			$ 169.00	
32	2208	Subscriptions & Fees	$ 500.00		$ (108.50)	$ 391.50	Eliminate duplicate subscriptions
33	Total	Office Expenses	$ 3,189.00	$ -	$ (358.50)	$ 2,830.50	
34							
35	**2220**	**Occupancy**					
36	2221	Rent	$ 432.00			$ 432.00	
37	2223	Utilities	$ 234.00			$ 234.00	
38	2225	Janitorial & Similar	$ 123.00		$ (8.00)	$ 115.00	Realize benefits from rebid contract
39	Total	Occupancy	$ 789.00	$ -	$ (8.00)	$ 781.00	

(*Note:* This image is a composite of multiple screen captures. Explanation of this table is shown on page 125. Also refer to the spreadsheet on the CD, Budget Tools Chapter 08 Exercises.)

Where legislative and other decision authority guidance is not provided, internal decisions must be made based on managerial decisions. These decisions may be made by the organization head, the work unit head, the management team, or some other entity designated by one of these authorities. It is undesirable for the budget analyst to assume this responsibility unless designated by an appropriate authority. What this means is that, although the budget analyst might calculate numbers and determine balances, the authorization to take money from some areas or give it to others should be based on written decision documents or decisions from the highest levels of decision making within the organization.

The essential characteristic is that the final result must be that there are no funds (negative or positive) remaining in the legislative convenience object code, as determined in this spreadsheet by cell E62 (highlighted in yellow in the spreadsheet for Chapter 8 on the CD). This objective is met when the total adjustment in the "Adjust" column (cell E59) is exactly equal to the amount of the legislative adjustment in the convenience object code in the legislative adjustment column (cell D62), so that the remaining amount (cell E62) in the legislative object code is zero. The "Adjust" column is then combined with the original proposed budget to obtain the final budget allocation. This process is shown in Columns C through G of Image 2. Column C is the budget as submitted to the legislature. Column D, which has an entry only near the bottom (shown only on the CD) is the legislative change. Column E is used to move the legislative change from the legislative line to particular object codes. Column F shows the net result. Column G shows that each row that has an adjustment in column E is given an explanation.

Allotment

The term **allotment** refers to any budgetary process that plans the expenditure of money by dividing it among smaller fiscal periods. This process is also called "calendarization," in accounting technology. The point of allotment is to avoid two budgetary failures, overspending and underspending, by keeping track of actual budget implementation at a micro-periodic level.

It takes no argument to demonstrate that overspending is a budgetary failure. Before the end of the budgetary period, the authorized funds will be exhausted. Either the activity must be curtailed or more funds must be authorized. Unless curtailment is intended, overspending is effectively disobedience of the budgetary authority. Overspending for genuine emergencies should be authorized by top-ranking elected officials and, if law requires, quickly referred for legislative confirmation.

The difficulty with underspending is less apparent. Assume that the budget-making process has produced an effective estimate of budgetary needs. This estimate is produced by a compromise between technical estimates and priorities of decision makers. At the end of the process, allocation of funds should reflect no more than the minimum necessary to achieve the objectives of the decision makers on the basis of the technical needs of the program. Spending less than this amount, therefore, is the equivalent of not attempting to meet the objectives of decision makers. The best alternative interpretation is that poor estimates were made in the budget-making process.

		I	J	K	L	M	N	O	P
									Allotment
1									
2	2000	Numbers in $Thousands	Operating plan	Q1	Q2	Q3	Q4	Check	Checked	Notes
3										
4	2100	Salaries & Wages								
5	2101	Officers & Directors	$ 120.00	$ 30.00	$ 30.00	$ 30.00	$ 30.00	$ 120.00	TRUE	Equal amounts per quarter
6	2102	Salaries	$ 9,500.00	$ 2,250.00	$2,250.00	$2,500.00	$ 2,500.00	$ 9,500.00	TRUE	$250 K increase for quarters 3 and 4 due to planned staffing increases
7	2103	Wages	$ 328.00	$ 218.67	$ -	$ -	$ 109.33	$ 328.00	TRUE	Equal in "summer" months, June, July, August
8	Total	Salaries & Wages	$ 9,948.00	$ 2,498.67	$2,280.00	$2,530.00	$ 2,639.33	$ 9,948.00	TRUE	
9										
10	2140	Payroll Taxes & Benefits								
11	2141	FICA	$ 746.10	$ 187.40	$ 171.00	$ 189.75	$ 197.95	$ 746.10	TRUE	Follows Salaries and wages
12	2142	Unemployment Insurance	$ 541.00	$ 135.25	$ 135.25	$ 135.25	$ 135.25	$ 541.00	TRUE	Equal amounts per quarter
13	2143	Workers Comp. Ins.	$ 231.00	$ 57.75	$ 57.75	$ 57.75	$ 57.75	$ 231.00	TRUE	Equal amounts per quarter
14	2144	Disability Insurance	$ 233.00	$ 58.25	$ 58.25	$ 58.25	$ 58.25	$ 233.00	TRUE	Equal amounts per quarter
15	2145	Benefits	$ 111.00	$ 27.75	$ 27.75	$ 27.75	$ 27.75	$ 111.00	TRUE	Equal amounts per quarter
16	Total	Payroll Taxes & Benefits	$ 1,862.10	$ 466.40	$ 450.00	$ 468.75	$ 476.95	$ 1,862.10	TRUE	
17	Total	Personnel	$ 11,810.10	$ 2,965.07	$2,730.00	$2,998.75	$ 3,116.28	$11,810.10	TRUE	
18										
19	2160	Travel & Training								
20	2161	Travel	$ 213.00	$ -	$ 71.00	$ 71.00	$ 71.00	$ 213.00	TRUE	No "summer" travel or training
21	2163	Training & Conferences	$ 468.00	$ -	$ 156.00	$ 156.00	$ 156.00	$ 468.00	TRUE	No "summer" travel or training
22	2164	Memberships	$ 100.00	$ 25.00	$ 25.00	$ 25.00	$ 25.00	$ 100.00	TRUE	Equal amounts per quarter
23	Total	Travel & Training	$ 781.00	$ 25.00	$ 252.00	$ 252.00	$ 252.00	$ 781.00	TRUE	
24										
25	2200	Office Expenses								
26	2202	Other Furniture & Equipment	$ 737.00	$ 184.25	$ 184.25	$ 184.25	$ 184.25	$ 737.00	TRUE	Equal amounts per quarter
27	2203	Supplies	$ 400.00	$ 100.00	$ 100.00	$ 100.00	$ 100.00	$ 400.00	TRUE	Equal amounts per quarter
28	2204	Telephone	$ 455.00	$ 113.75	$ 113.75	$ 113.75	$ 113.75	$ 455.00	TRUE	Equal amounts per quarter
29	2205	Duplicating & Printing	$ 333.00	$ 83.25	$ 83.25	$ 83.25	$ 83.25	$ 333.00	TRUE	Equal amounts per quarter
30	2206	Postage & Shipping	$ 345.00	$ 86.25	$ 86.25	$ 86.25	$ 86.25	$ 345.00	TRUE	Equal amounts per quarter
31	2207	Equip. Rental & Maintenance	$ 169.00	$ 42.25	$ 42.25	$ 42.25	$ 42.25	$ 169.00	TRUE	Equal amounts per quarter
32	2208	Subscriptions & Fees	$ 391.50	$ 97.88	$ 97.88	$ 97.88	$ 97.88	$ 391.50	TRUE	Equal amounts per quarter
33	Total	Office Expenses	$ 2,830.50	$ 707.63	$ 707.63	$ 707.63	$ 707.63	$ 2,830.50	TRUE	
34										
35	2220	Occupancy								
36	2221	Rent	$ 432.00	$ 108.00	$ 108.00	$ 108.00	$ 108.00	$ 432.00	TRUE	Equal amounts per quarter
37	2223	Utilities	$ 234.00	$ 58.50	$ 58.50	$ 58.50	$ 58.50	$ 234.00	TRUE	Equal amounts per quarter
38	2225	Janitorial & Similar	$ 115.00	$ 28.75	$ 28.75	$ 28.75	$ 28.75	$ 115.00	TRUE	Equal amounts per quarter
39	Total	Occupancy	$ 781.00	$ 195.25	$ 195.25	$ 195.25	$ 195.25	$ 781.00	TRUE	

(*Note:* This image is a composite of multiple screen captures.)

Of course, budgeting is imperfect, so small variances can be expected. Also, sometimes substantial innovations occur after budget decisions occur, but these should be easy to explain.

A typical allotment first divides an annual budget into quarters; then it divides quarters into months. The example given in the "Allocate & Allot" tab of the spreadsheet goes to quarters only. Although money may be divided into quarters, not every object of expenditure will be equally spent in each quarter. New hires may be deliberately delayed until later in the year in order to reduce first-year costs. Certain purchases of goods may occur predominately at one point in the year. Seasonal work may lead to costs during only some parts of the year.

In the spreadsheet, legislative reductions lead to postponing new hires to the midpoint of the year. Thus, more money is allotted to salaries in the second half of the year than in the first half. Wage employees are for seasonal work, which occurs only in the last month of Q4 (Quarter 4) and the first two months of Q1 (Quarter 1). The computer purchases are planned at a specified point in the year. The allotment plan reflects these intentions. As with the allocation, the allotment spreadsheet should include a text explanation in column P. On the CD you will see that the spreadsheet also includes an area for math factors that are used to calculate how funds are divided for the four periods; this math area is provided in columns Q through W, but it could easily be extended as far as necessary into the spreadsheet. Finally, the column labeled "Checked" (column O) verifies that the sum of the four periods totals the amount available to allocate.

At the end of the chapter, Exercise 1 provides a discussion of a more advanced allocation involving monthly periods and the use of unallotted funds.

Budget or Accounting?

Much of what occurs in producing an operating plan involves the attachment of dollars to object codes and fiscal periods. These are the sorts of technical activities that occur at the intersection of budget and accounting. Nevertheless, they are essentially budget activities for several reasons.

- First, as with other budget activities, these activities are planning activities. For the most part, fiscal planning belongs with budgeting.

- Second, allocative decisions are made in the making of the operating plan. Allocation is a budgetary process and should be made in the context of other budgetary decisions.

- Third, allotment is closely related to another budgetary tool, encumbrances. Both of these tools are used in the budget implementation period to prevent intentional and unintentional evasion of budgetary decisions. While encumbrance is used in the expenditure process and is therefore essentially an accounting process, allotment is a planning step and is more closely aligned with budgeting.

Advanced Allocation and Allotment Example

The advanced example in the spreadsheet on the CD, found on the tab "Advanced Allocate & Allot," extends the concepts beyond the initial example. The chart of accounts used here (columns A and B on the spreadsheet) is the same as the chart of accounts used with the example for Chapter 2 on organizing budget data, which may be somewhat more useful for the student who incorporates these materials for actual projects.

This demonstrates the allocation step. The allocation problem is complicated by the fact that the funds are divided over two subprograms, and the funds must be transferred between the two programs to achieve the legislative intent. Sometimes transferring funds between subprograms requires special approval. Subprogram 1 is shown in columns C through H and Subprogram 2 is shown in columns I through N. Only in the whole combined program, columns P through T, is the funding brought into balance with the legislative adjustment. Adjustments for Subprogram 1 are entered in column E and adjustments for Subprogram 2 are entered in column K, with explanations for adjustments in each subprogram entered in the "Notes" column two columns to the right of each adjustment column.

We see that at the subprogram level (see the "Allot" image, a composite of multiple screen captures, on the accompanying CD), the legislative adjustments do not go into balance (cells E87 and K87). Only when the totals of the two subprograms are combined does the whole program go into balance (cell R87). It is very important that once a spreadsheet section such as this one is established and the correct initial "proposed" values are entered, the only entries that should be made are those in the "Adjust" column for the subprograms and those in the "Notes" column. The correct proposed values are those that were submitted with the budget request to any central budget entity. Following this process ensures that there is a specific account for changes from initial budget proposals to the final implemented budget.

In this example, the allotment problem has two complicating factors beyond the basic allotment problem. First, there is a new category called unallotment (see Allotment spreadsheet 5, column W). While this category is not universally used—and when it is used it is often given differing names and accounted for in differing ways—the function of this category is to reserve a small sum of money for unplanned emergencies. Also, unallotment is not a device for transferring money between programs or departments. This sum cannot be much and cannot remain reserved all year. A typical amount is 1 percent in the first two or three quarters, excluding certain expenses. In column W, object code 8260 is exempted (cell W47). In an attempt to attain roughly 1 percent savings without that amount, some back-of-the-envelope calculations are performed at the bottom of columns W and X, producing a new target amount of 1.02 percent. (This number has been converted from a formula value to a fixed number to avoid a spreadsheet circular reference.) Roughly at the end of the third quarter, if no emergency has emerged, this unallotted amount would be allotted to the fourth quarter.

Calling this practice unallotment and revealing it is a transparent government version of this practice, similar to simply budgeting a reserve. The point is to be prepared for emergencies ranging from urgent needs for money to disappointing revenue. This is an executive process and cannot supplant the legislative process, so as the year progresses and no emergency arises, such prudence must be replaced by fulfilling legislative objectives.

The second new complication is the extension of the allotment from quarters to months. This extension is found in columns AF to AQ. With few exceptions, the monthly expenditures can usually be planned as simply one-third of quarterly expenditures. The main exception is when there is a targeted expenditure with a known date. Quarterly allotments must become monthly allotments in order to implement budget tracking through a practice known as **variance analysis.**

Variance Analysis

What we budget and what we actually spend is rarely the same. Variance is the difference between what is budgeted and what is spent. Every month organizations should conduct a variance analysis between budget and expenditures that consists of budget, expenditures, and the difference.

Although it is easy enough to examine the difference between what is budgeted and what is spent every month, it is not so easy to determine why there are differences. It takes careful analysis. Table 8.1 shows a typical variance analysis.

This variance analysis shows that the revenues are coming in lower than expected. At the end of the first month, only 5 percent of city taxes have been recorded instead of 8.33 percent or $\frac{1}{12}$ of the revenues. This variance analysis also demonstrates that expenditures (actuals) for the first month totaled $181,258, which is 7.3 percent of the budget. However, the percentage of the budget that should have been spent is 8.33 percent (one-twelfth of the year). The result is that the fire department has a surplus of $27,075 for the first month while the total surplus for the year is only to be $13,200. There is underspending going on. That underspending is in the PS side of the budget, in which only 7.2 percent of the budget has been spent instead of 8.33 percent.

On closer examination, it is discovered that the problem is in the number of firefighters. Two lines show the underspending: the firefighter lines. Six positions are vacant, three in each of the firefighter lines, and it is these vacancies that are creating the large surplus. If these vacancies continue, the surplus by the end of the year could be quite large. Thus, it is important to examine carefully the number of positions that are filled.

Table 8.2 shows a different picture of the ABC Fire Department after three months.

Clearly, the revenue is now flowing as scheduled. After three months, 25 percent of the budget can be expended and 25 percent of the revenue should have been collected, and indeed 25 percent of the revenue budget has been collected. But on the expenditure side, only 21.5 percent of the PS has been spent, which indi-

WHAT CAUSES VARIANCES?

Variances can be caused by many factors. The most common factor lies in personnel changes. Unexpectedly, someone leaves, and we are left with extra funds for the remainder of the year unless we decide to replace that person. Other factors may be changes in the costs of nonpersonnel services, supplies, or energy. And we find that increased energy costs mean that we have spent more on heat, light, and power than we intended. We have a negative variance.

These types of changes require the budget analyst to carefully examine variances every month to ensure that negative variances are immediately noticed and surpluses can be put to good use.

TABLE 8.1
ABC Fire Department, First Month Variance Analysis, 2007

			Actuals		Difference
		Annual budget	First month	Percentage spent	Budget—first month
Monthly (percentage)				8.3	
Revenues					
City taxes		$2,100,000	$100,000	4.8	$2,000,000
State revenue		400,000	33,333	8.3	366,667
Total		$2,500,000	$133,333	5.3	$2,366,667
Expenditures					
PS	Positions				
Chief	1	$98,000	$8,167	8.3	$89,833
Shift commander	3	220,500	18,375	8.3	202,125
Firefighter 2	12	705,600	44,100	6.3	661,500
Firefighter 1	26	1,146,600	84,525	7.4	1,062,075
Clerical (.5 PT)	1.5	44,100	3,675	8.3	40,425
Subtotal	43.5	$2,214,800	$158,842	7.2	$2,055,958
NPS					
Supplies		$145,000	$11,833	8.2	$133,167
Equipment		90,000	7,500	8.3	82,500
Travel		12,000	1,000	8.3	11,000
Consultants		25,000	2,083	8.3	22,917
Subtotal		$272,000	$22,416	8.2	$249,584
Total PS and NPS		$2,486,800	$181,258	7.3	$2,305,542
Difference between revenue and expenditures		$13,200	−$47,925		$61,125

Note: PS = personnel services, PT = part time, NPS = nonpersonnel services.

cates a sizable surplus. Those lines remained unfilled. At the same time, the equipment line in NPS has been overspent. Instead of spending 25 percent of the budget, the fire department has spent 72.2 percent, according to the equipment line in Table 8.2. What happened? That problem needs to be investigated. It turns out that ten new breathing apparatuses at $6,500 per piece were budgeted for and bought that month. Although the line indicates that the equipment line is overspent, it is not. It is simply that the volume of equipment was consumed during one month and not spread throughout the fiscal year.

Many jurisdictions use **calenderization** to distribute the yearly budget into monthly or even more detailed expenditure reports for control purposes.

TABLE 8.2
ABC Fire Department, First Quarter Variance Analysis, 2007

| | | Annual Budget | Actuals | | Difference |
			Third month	Percentage spent	Budget— actuals
Monthly (percentage)				25.0	
Revenues					
City taxes		$2,100,000	$525,000	25.0	$1,575,000
State revenue		400,000	100,000	25.0	300,000
Total		$2,500,000	$625,000	25.0	$1,875,000
Expenditures					
PS	Positions				
Chief	1	$98,000	$24,500	25.0	$73,500
Shift commander	3	220,500	55,125	25.0	165,375
Firefighter 2	12	705,600	132,300	18.8	573,300
Firefighter 1	26	1,146,600	253,575	22.1	893,025
Clerical (.5 PT)	1.5	44,100	11,025	25.0	33,075
Subtotal	43.5	$2,214,800	$476,525	21.5	$1,738,275
NPS					
Supplies		$145,000	$35,500	24.5	$109,500
Equipment		90,000	65,000	72.2	25,000
Travel		12,000	3,000	25.0	9,000
Consultants		25,000	6,250	25.0	18,750
Subtotal		$272,000	$109,750	40.3	$162,250
Total PS and NPS		$2,486,800	$586,275	23.6	$1,900,525
Difference between revenue and expenditures		$13,200	$38,725		−$25,525

Note: NPS = nonpersonnel services, PS = personnel services, PT = part time.

This is useful because some jurisdictions have seasonal programs. Schools, for example, expend fewer dollars in the summer when most students are not in school.

Volume can make a difference that is hard to notice. For example, supplies in Table 8.2 have been budgeted for $145,000; within this lies an assumption that each of the thirty-eight firefighters has been budgeted for $500 a year in personal supplies that are provided by the department. But there are not thirty-eight firefighters; this year there are thirty-two, with six vacancies. So $500 multiplied by 6 is $3,000 that should not be spent for the year. This works out to $250 a month for those six vacancies. It is such a small amount that it is hardly noticeable; after three months, 24.5 percent has been spent rather than 25 percent. But if these vacancies remain throughout the year, the surplus will become $3,000, which is not a small amount of money. It is important to track the smallest differences between what is expected for the month and what is actually spent.

Notice that because extra dollars are being spent on the NPS side, the surplus on the PS side, which is growing, has been hidden. After three months, the surplus on the PS side is three times what it was in the first month.

Both quantity and volume of expenditures must be closely examined when a variance analysis is conducted.

Price is also a consideration. Prices change; therefore, the budgeted price is not necessarily what is used when the supplies are purchased. It is rare, however, that staff will overspend a line; rather, the staff will reduce the number of items to stay within its budget.

The secret to a smooth fiscal year is the careful monthly examination of the variance between revenue and expenditures. Budget staff must pay special attention to issues of quantity, volume, and price.

Summary

We create an operating plan with the adopted budget. Given what we have actually received, we will need to plan how we are going to spend that money. We need to carefully examine any changes in the legislative funding to ensure that we create an accurate operating plan. After we create an operating plan, we need to turn to tracking our spending. What we plan to spend and what we actually spend will be different. This difference is the variance, and we need to carefully track this variance throughout the year.

Exercises

1. Develop an allocation and an allotment plan. To complete this exercise, use the spreadsheet file on the CD entitled "Budget Tools Chapter 08 Exercises." On the tab labeled "Exercise" in the spreadsheet is the proposed budget for a health care finance program. From this, develop an allocation and an allotment plan.

It is worth noting that the $400 million in object code 2241 is for health care claims, and the $10 million in 2501 is for claims-processing costs. The legislature has provided $50 million for new benefits but no money for the estimated $50,000 in processing costs for new claims; these costs are to be achieved through administrative savings. The legislature has also demanded other administrative efficiencies. Little guidance has been given for achieving administrative efficiencies. Based on past payroll patterns, you may want to anticipate that 48 percent of the pay will occur in the first half of the year and 52 percent will be in the second half. There are no special purchases. The

TABLE 8.3
Variance Analysis for San Jose Operating Budget, 2007–2008

	Annual budget	Actuals		Actuals	
		First month	Percentage spent	Third month	Percentage spent
Expenditures			8.33		25.0
Fire	$134,685,340	$11,000,000		$32,500,000	
Police	279,740,088	23,500,000		71,000,000	

building lease for the departmental office is $125,000 per month. Net legislative adjustments are $48.75 million.

2. Examine and Discuss San Jose's Variance Report

In Table 8.3 we have used San Jose's operating budgets to create a hypothetical variance report. Find the variances for the expenditure side and discuss what you think might prove to be problematic for the agency in the coming months.

3. Examine and discuss the Department of Transportation's Variance Report

Table 8.4 is a hypothetical variance report from the department of transportation in a large city in the Northeast. Find the variances for both the

TABLE 8.4
Variance Report from the Department of Transportation, 2007–2008

	Annual budget	Actuals		Actuals	
		First month	Percentage spent	Third month	Percentage spent
Revenues			8.33		25.00
Federal aid	$30,000,000	$2,000,000		$6,000,000	
State aid	80,000,000	8,000,000		30,000,000	
Local aid	20,000,000	1,700,000		5,400,000	
Total	$130,000,000	$11,700,000		$41,400,000	
Expenditures					
Central fleet maintenance	$2,267,724	$180,000		$530,000	
Public works and transportation	1,606,402	130,000		390,000	
Public works department	86,176,802	7,300,000		22,000,000	
Snow removal	12,292,072	—		—	
Transportation department	27,618,759	2,300,000		2,100,000	
Total	$129,961,759	$9,910,000		$25,020,000	

Note: — = not available.

revenue and expenditure sides and discuss what you think will be problematic for the agency in the coming months.

Additional Reading

Finkler, Steven A. *Financial Management for Public, Health, and Not-for-Profit Organizations*. 2nd ed. Upper Saddle River, N.J.: Pearson/Prentice Hall, 2005.

Chapter 9

Multiyear Plans and Analyses

Learning objectives:
- Examine assumptions in multiyear financial plans
- Understand fund accounting
- Read simplified financial statements
- Analyze financial statements

City and state budget officials focus on more than the projected year. They focus on several years into the future. Such an emphasis becomes more important as dollars become scarce. The purpose of this chapter is to understand how to establish a multiyear financial plan for your agency and to learn some simple tools for analyzing multiyear financial statements. From there you will be poised to practice planning and analyzing multiyear financial plans, which is an exercise scenario at the end of the chapter. In this chapter the focus is on operating budgets, not capital budgets.

Financial Plans

Financial plans are projections of future year (outlying year) budgets, revenues, expenditures, and net. Why bother? The projection of future budgets makes current decision making more thoughtful. What is the impact of raising salaries next year? What is the impact of agreeing to increased health benefits for the workforce in a contract negotiation?

Financial plans contain assumptions for the future about the agency's goals, examine levels of service, define the financial condition of the agency, examine trends in revenues, and provide descriptions of both the capital and operating budget objectives. Financial plans encourage long-range thinking and discourage irresponsible decision making in the near term. It becomes much more difficult for an elected official to advocate raising salaries or undertake major projects when a five-year financial plan illustrates the deficit that may be incurred with the implementation of these goals.

The first requirement is to agree on the number of years involved in the financial plan. Many financial plans are four or five years in length. Once the time frame is decided, attention must be turned to building a consensus about the agency's goals during this agreed period of time. The goals are dependent on the levels of service that the municipality or nonprofit group wants to provide during these years.

Environment

After the participants agree on goals, the financial condition of the municipality or agency must be determined. The financial condition is heavily dependent on numerous assumptions about the external environment:

NATIONAL LEVEL. To what extent will the health of the national economy affect the agency's operating funds? How reliable are the projections that the agency has made in the past? Many municipalities have an extensive number of factors to be considered in their analysis. For example, San José, California, considers the following projected factors about the federal level for the next five years:

- Real gross domestic product (percentage of change)
- Prime rate
- Mortgage rate
- U.S. unemployment rate
- Total U.S. employment rate (percentage of change)
- U.S. automobile sales (percentage of change)
- OPEC oil prices (percentage of change)
- U.S. Consumer Price Index (CPI).

After all these factors are considered, San José will project what possible effect each of these factors will have on future municipal revenues and expenditures.

STATE LEVEL. The state financial environment is vitally important to municipalities and nonprofit organizations. Sometimes a municipality has a built-in insulation from the state's economic condition because of a municipality's unique financial structure. The municipality, for example, might be a university town and not dependent on the state's economic health. In most instances, however, municipalities are extremely dependent upon the fiscal condition of the state. Nonprofits usually depend on state revenues for some of their programs. Any decline in the state's economy usually directly affects the fiscal health of its municipalities.

REVENUE MIX. Many municipalities depend heavily on the property tax, which has been considered fairly inelastic; that is, property tax revenue fails to keep pace with increases in population and inflation. The consequences of this are that the property tax is a relatively stable tax and is not as dependent on the local economy as other taxes. In recent years, there has been more volatility in property tax collections. Other taxes—the sales tax, for example—are quite elastic as they are quite dependent on increases in population and the health of the economy. Hence, an analysis must be conducted examining the types of revenues and the extent to which these revenues are stable or easily respond to the peaks and valleys of a financial cycle.

Internal factors within a municipality or agency can also be important:

DEBT. Almost all municipalities have incurred debt through selling bonds for major projects. Such debt results in the municipalities paying interest and principal on that debt annually out of the operating budget. Questions about future debt obligations need to be answered in order to predict annual payments. In addition, refinancing current debt can result in extra cash for the coffers because bonds can sometimes be refinanced at a lower interest rate.

RESERVE FUND. Most organizations, whether small nonprofit groups or large municipalities, wish to build reserve funds. The questions become: How big will the reserve fund be? When will the reserve fund be used? How disciplined is the organization going to be when it needs to add to the fund in tight times? These kinds of decisions will have an impact on any projected budget.

Trends in Revenue Growth, Revenue Diversification, and Operating Costs

Some trends in revenue and expenditures are common throughout the United States.

REVENUE GROWTH. Municipalities can have quite complex revenue packages, with several different streams arriving at different times of the fiscal year, and with different levels of volatility. The same is true for nonprofit organizations. A typical municipality may have property taxes, sales taxes, utility taxes, income taxes, and a variety of user fees. A typical nonprofit organization can have what seems like countless revenue streams: city contracts, state grants, federal contracts, endowment income, business income, user fees, and donations of all kinds, including real estate. Regardless of the revenue, each revenue stream must be examined over time. Ten-year and twenty-year histories are common; with those histories, projections can be made to determine as close as possible what will happen to a particular revenue during the next four or five years. The section on forecasting in Chapter 4 is useful here.

DIVERSITY OF REVENUES. Municipalities must understand not only the amounts of revenue entering the coffers but also the extent to which the diversity of revenues is changing. This analysis must be closely examined in terms of what the optimum diversity of revenues is for that particular organization. Certainly, a rule of thumb is that diversity of revenues is important because no municipality or nonprofit organization wishes to depend largely on one revenue stream. Diversity ensures some stability in collection. But what types of diversity? Which type of tax? What kinds of user fees? And how has that diversity changed over time? These are the types of questions that must be answered to ensure the stability of a revenue structure.

OPERATING EXPENDITURES. The growth rate among the various categories of expenditures must be examined to ensure that there are no surprises among the changes in expenditures. The best way to conduct this analysis is over time: not over five years, but over ten or twenty years. Some expenditures—pensions and employee benefits, for example—are particularly important, for these are often the fastest-growing categories. Because most operating budgets are largely made up of personnel costs, it is important to examine these categories. An updated analysis is important for understanding how expenditures are growing.

It is necessary to consider many different categories of expenditures:

- Number of personnel
- Wages and union contracts
- Health care expenditures
- Pension expenditures
- Workers' compensation
- Economic development expenditures.

Some cities use a limited number of assumptions for a five-year financial plan. The city of Champaign, Illinois, for example, uses these factors in its assumptions about its five-year plan: percentage of change over the preceding year, federal inflation rate, construction cost index, federal funds rate, per capita income growth, population growth in the county, growth of salaries, step and longevity growth in salaries, police and fire pension increases, increases in the costs of the Illinois Municipal Retirement Fund, and increases in the cost of health insurance. These indicators are carefully calculated and are used to create a five-year financial plan for the city.

Capital Budget Planning

Chapter 5 of this book reviews the capital budget, debt structure, and debt analysis. In addition, the impact of the capital plan on the operating plan must be carefully measured. For example, a renovation of a public library with state-of-the-art lighting can result in an increase in the operating budget because of the need to purchase expensive light bulbs and because the renovation may call for additional cleaning. At the same time, maintenance in other areas may be less than it was before the renovation. It is important to develop the capital plan in close collaboration with the operating plan.

Closing the Gap

Multiyear planning can result in gaps between projected revenues and expenditures in future years. Indeed, this is a principal reason for creating a four- or five-year financial plan. The municipality may have a balanced budget for the upcoming year, but when projected revenues and expenditures are laid out, the municipality may not be able to project a balanced budget for the fourth year out. An example of this type of problem is the financial picture for the Metropolitan Transit Authority (MTA) in New York State. Six years are listed below, of which the first two—2005 and 2006—are actuals. The remaining years are projections. Beginning in fiscal year 2008, the MTA projects a deficit of more than $1 billion. The 2007–2010 financial plan clearly demonstrates the gaps, and also the gap-closing actions that can be taken to close them.

July Financial Plan
With Policy and Gap Closing Actions
($ in millions)

	2005	2006	2007	2008	2009	2010
July Plan Baseline	**$1,182**	**$1,121**	**$290**	**($1008)**	**($1,781)**	**($2,146)**
Policy Actions:						
Pension Liability Reduction / Pension Earnings	($450)	$21	$42	$42	$42	$42
2004 Real Estate Tax Stabilization Account	0	200	0	0	0	0
2005 Capital Security Addition / Security Initiatives	(100)	(100)	0	0	0	0
2005 Holiday Fare Program	(50)	50	0	0	0	0
Anti-Graffiti Campaign	0	0	(6)	(3)	(5)	(6)
Service Marketing Campaign	0	0	(5)	0	0	0
Gap Closing Action:						
2007 Agency Program to Eliminate the Gap	$0	$19	$47	$60	$61	$61
Post-2007 Agency Program to Eliminate the Gap	0	0	0	13	22	22
Shared Services	0	0	0	5	10	15
2007 Increased Fare and Toll Yields	0	0	78	237	242	243
2009 Increased Fare and Toll Yields	0	0	0	0	247	255
Reorganization Legislation	0	0	0	5	25	25
Change in Cash Balance from Previous Year	0	(600)	(410)	(254)	0	0
July Plan Closing Cash Balance	**$582**	**$711**	**$36**	**($905)**	**($1,137)**	**($1,488)**

The following contributions are accounted for in the above Baseline Labor Expenses:

Contribution to GASB Fund	$0	$173	$97	$80	$88	$97

Metropolitan Transportation Authority   July Financial Plan 2007   2010

Below the first line that shows the deficit are actions that demonstrate how the deficit may be reduced. Clearly, at this point, the MTA does not have a plan to balance the FY 2008–2010 budgets, but the gap-closing actions demonstrate a deficit reduction.

San Diego, California, issued its first five-year financial plan in November 2006, and in this plan the city does not have a resolution for its deficits in any future years (Table 9.1). Its gap-closing actions (corrective actions) reduce the annual deficits but do not eliminate the deficits, although the deficit for FY 2008 is fairly small ($24.6 million).

San Diego has taken an important step by creating and distributing a five-year financial plan. It allows the decision makers to examine the long term. It also puts decision makers on notice that short-term decision making is now out of fashion. We need to consider current steps to eliminate the gaps be-

TABLE 9.1

San Diego's Financial Plan FY 2008–2012, General Fund Corrective Action Steps (in millions)

	Fiscal Year				
	2008	2009	2010	2011	2012
Surplus/deficit	−$87.4	−$173.8	−$175.9	−$178.8	−$178.3
Corrective actions					
Positions					
Elimination of 446.34 FTEs	$11.1	$11.1	$11.1	$11.1	$11.1
Elimination of 100 FTEs	6.8	6.8	6.8	6.8	6.8
BPR streaming					
Salary and wages	5.3	10.6	15.9	15.9	15.9
Nonpersonnel expenses	1.9	3.8	5.7	5.7	5.7
Employee benefit adjustments/furlough	4.3	4.3	4.3	4.3	4.3
Debt refinancing: Petco Ball Park	3.8	3.8	3.8	3.8	3.8
Reallocation of transient occupancy tax	6.0	10.0	10.0	10.0	10.0
Budget cleanup					
Corrected general government services bill	3.2	5.3	5.3	5.3	5.3
Inactive fund balances	2.1	—	—	—	—
Release of encumbered funds	3.0	—	—	—	—
Leveraging city assets	15.3	21.8	21.8	21.8	21.8
Managed competition	tbd	tbd	tbd	tbd	tbd
Subtotal for corrective actions	$62.8	$77.5	$84.7	$84.7	$84.8
Net surplus/deficit	−$24.6	−$96.3	−$91.2	−$94.1	−$93.6

Source: "City of San Diego Five-Year Financial Outlook, Fiscal Years 2008–2012," www.sandiego.gov/mayor/pdf/five_year_plan_11_15.pdf.
Note: BPR = Business Process Reengineering; FTE = full-time employee; tbd = to be determined; — = not available.

tween revenues and expenditures not just in any current year but in future years. Decisions made today can affect the gap in future years.

Tools for Analyzing Multiyear Financial Statements

When students are confronted with **financial statements,** they often feel overwhelmed with numbers and are unsure how to analyze the maze of numbers before them. There are methods that can be used to make sense out of all these dollar figures.

Fund Accounting

Fund accounting is a system of accounting where records are kept for separate revenue and expenditure streams. For example, local and state governments create an operating fund (sometimes called the general fund) with which they track revenues and expenditures of everyday transactions. Local and state governments have three basic categories of funds:

- **Governmental funds.** Governmental funds comprise general funds, debt service funds, and special revenue funds.
    - **General fund.** General funds, sometimes called operating funds, are the funds that track the day-to-day operations of the organization.
    - **Debt service fund.** These are funds that track payments of principal and interest in debt that has been acquired by a government entity.
    - **Special revenue fund.** These funds are used for a designated purpose of government.
    - **Capital fund.** These funds track transactions about capital projects when major projects are undertaken or acquired. See Chapter 5 on capital budgeting for more information.
- **Proprietary funds.** These funds track transactions of activities that are run like businesses.
- **Fiduciary funds.** These are funds that track transactions in which government acts as a trustee, such as collecting and tracking workers' compensation or Social Security payroll taxes and then depositing those funds with the state.

Nonprofit groups also operate using fund accounting. Nonprofits are required to have three funds and three funds only:

- **Unrestricted funds.** Unrestricted funds, also called operating funds, pay for the day-to-day operations of the organization.

- **Temporarily restricted funds.** These funds are restricted in their use and cannot yet be spent but may be spent in the future.

- **Permanently restricted funds.** These funds cannot be spent, although the interest earned on the funds may be used.

Oversight

The United States has developed a high degree of consistency in its accounting standards for governments and nonprofits. This is due to two organizations. The Governmental Accounting Standards Board (GASB) organized in 1984 is the body within the accounting profession that established standards of financial accounting and reporting for local and state governments. Its standards follow generally accepted accounting principles (GAAP), which are agreed upon by the accounting community. Nonprofits are subject to a different board, the Financial Accounting Standards Board (FASB). Both of these boards are administered by the Financial Accounting Foundation, which selects the members of the GASB and FASB.

Financial Statements

Financial statements are the audited accounting of the revenues and expenditures in each fund. Local and state governments as well as nonprofit organizations usually create financial statements for each fund once a year.

Financial statements are made up of the balance sheet (statement of net assets or statement of financial position), the income and expense statement (also known as the statement of activities), and the cash flow statement. In addition, nonprofits are required to issue a statement of functional expenses. Although a thorough review of financial statements must be undertaken for in-depth study, a balance sheet and income statement are presented here so that students with some practice using financial statements can create a simple analysis of the financial position of a government entity or of a nonprofit.

BALANCE SHEET. The **balance sheet** shows the total amounts of assets, liabilities, and net assets (often called the fund balance) at the end of the fiscal year. Local and state governments create a governmentwide financial statement that includes all of the agencies for which a particular government entity is responsible. In addition to a governmentwide financial statement,

---

PUBLIC STATEMENTS OF SPENDING

Analysis of local and state government typically focuses on the governmental funds statements, and the most important of those use modified accrual accounting.

The Financial Accounting Standards Board requires some nonprofits, namely voluntary health and welfare organizations, to produce a statement of functional expenses. This statement divides expenses into two primary classifications: program expenses and supporting expenses. Within supporting services, the FASB defines three sections: administrative, fund-raising, and membership development. The FASB requires a statement of functional expenses so that donors and others who wish to assess the organization's service efforts will have a statement that addresses their concerns. The National Charities Information Bureau and the United Way have established that at least 60 percent of an organization's expenses should be devoted to program services.

local and state governments also issue fund financial statements for each grouping of related accounts such as the operating fund and the capital fund.

Assets equal liabilities plus the net assets. **Assets** are the uses of capital and are the resources of an organization, which can range from cash to fixed assets. **Liabilities** are the sources of capital and are the amounts owed. **Net assets** is the amount by which assets exceed liabilities. Net assets become the financial worth of the organization.

An example of a fund financial statement for the statement of net assets (balance sheet) for the city of Charlottesville, Virginia, can be seen in Table 9.2. There are four funds within the government funds: the general fund, which is the day-to-day operating fund; the capital projects fund; the social services fund; and other funds.

INCOME AND EXPENSE STATEMENT. The **income statement** shows all the revenues and expenditures for the fiscal year of the organization. For local and state governments, revenues are usually taxes, fees, intergovernmental revenue, fines, and investment earnings. Expenditures can be categorized in different ways. Programmatically, expenditures can be all dollars spent in that fiscal year for police, parks, education, and other departments. Categorically, expenditures can be all dollars spent on salaries or on nonsalary items such as supplies and equipment. The income statement will tie into the balance sheet in that these are all the revenues and expenditures for the year in which the balance sheet ends. The income statement for Charlottesville, Virginia, is shown in Table 9.3.

CASH FLOW STATEMENT. The cash flow statement becomes important because it reports the sources and uses of cash for the agency. It is usually divided among three sections: operating activities, investing activities, and financing activities. Operating activities reflect the revenues used in everyday operations of the organization and the uses of the cash. Investing activities report on the purchase or sale of capital or financial assets. Financing activities relate to the organization's receipts and disbursements from borrowing and the repayment of debt.

RATIOS

A variety of ratios can be used in government or nonprofit financial analysis. Many of these ratios can be found in Web sites and accounting textbooks. The importance of the ratios lies in the student's accurate assessment of the ratios.

To conduct a successful analysis, students should examine at least three to five years of financial statements. If students create a current ratio for just one year, they could be misled if there is excessive liquidity because the agency had just financed bonds and had an influx of cash. What is important is the trend line over a period of time for the current ratio.

Ratio Analysis

It is often difficult to understand what is important in these financial statements. Tools have been created to aid analysts in their analysis; one of the most powerful tools is **ratio analysis.** Ratios must be viewed within context. If only one ratio is highlighted, it will be difficult to develop a comprehensive, in-depth understanding of a city's financial statements.

TABLE 9.2

Balance Sheet for the City of Charlottesville, Virginia, Government Funds Only, June 30, 2006

	General fund	Capital projects fund	Social services fund	Other government fund	Total
Assets					
Cash	$25,540,244	—	$156,943	$5,462,149	$31,159,336
Investments	—	—	—	600	600
Accounts receivable	1,046,166	$2,295	3,893	35,610	1,087,964
Taxes receivable	24,319,651	—	—	—	24,319,651
Special assessments received	—	16,813	—	—	16,813
Due from other governments	5,055,427	5,195,502	705,290	3,178,186	14,134,405
Due from other funds	3,269,698	506	—	—	3,270,204
Loans receivable	—	3,192,556	—	143,723	3,336,279
Accrued interest receivable	9,972	—	—	10	9,982
Total assets	$59,241,158	$8,407,672	$866,126	$8,820,278	$77,335,234
Liabilities and fund balances					
Liabilities					
Accounts payable	$1,727,186	$2,625,763	$111,167	$1,291,934	$5,756,050
Accrued liabilities	3,644,356	8,612	210,905	190,381	4,054,254
Due to other governments	—	—	—	134,281	134,281
Due to other funds	—	1,756,310	—	1,211,616	2,967,926
Deferred revenue	27,581,876	3,215,701	544,054	127,374	31,469,005
Total liabilities	$32,953,418	$7,606,386	$866,126	$2,955,586	$44,381,516
Fund balances					
Reserved	$715,230	$20,257,807	—	$901,885	$21,874,922
Unreserved, designated:	—	—	—	—	—
General fund	3,921,815	—	—	—	3,921,815
Capital projects fund	—	−19,456,521	—	—	−19,456,521
Debt service fund	—	—	—	4,962,807	4,962,807
Unreserved, undesignated:	—	—	—	—	—
General fund	21,650,695	—	—	—	21,650,695
Total fund balances	$26,287,740	$801,286	—	$5,864,692	$2,953,718
Total liabilities and fund balances	$59,241,158	$8,407,672	$866,126	$8,820,278	$77,335,234

Source: Comprehensive Annual Financial Statement for the Year Ended June 30, 2006, City of Charlottesville, Virginia, www.charlottesville.org/Index.aspx?page=1869.

Note: — = not available.

An important question to answer is on which fund should ratio analysis be conducted. For both governmental and nonprofit organizations, it is best to examine the general fund (operating fund), which is the fund for the day-to-day expenditures.

TABLE 9.3

City of Charlottesville Statement of Revenues, Expenditures, and Changes in Fund Balances, Governmental Funds, for the Year Ended June 30, 2006

	General fund	Capital projects fund	Social services fund	Other government fund	Total
Revenues					
Taxes	$80,203,931	—	—	—	$80,203,931
Fees and permits	1,594,542	—	—	—	1,594,542
Intergovernmental	21,984,160	$4,681,286	$9,526,662	$11,399,552	47,591,660
Charges for services	4,204,335	12,198	—	2,484,904	6,701,437
Fines	508,322	—	—	—	508,322
Investment earnings	—	78,312	—	6,956	85,268
Miscellaneous	1,657,780	137,421	22,162	215,119	2,032,482
Total revenue	$110,153,070	$4,909,217	$9,548,824	$14,106,531	$138,717,642
Expenditures					
General government	$11,198,590	$2,379,781	—	—	$13,578,371
Public safety	24,314,230	—	—	$1,875,079	26,189,309
Community services	6,119,250	2,429,279	—	4,569,087	13,117,616
Health and welfare	3,466,120	—	$11,810,684	9,602,318	24,879,122
Parks, recreation, and culture	6,941,920	724,953	—	79,957	7,746,830
Education	32,503,082	904,589	—	—	33,407,671
Conservation and development	3,528,002	1,027,612	—	922,190	5,477,804
Other activities	173,034	148,199	—	—	321,233
Debt services	—	—	—	7,074,419	7,074,419
Capital outlay	—	8,719,385	—	—	8,719,385
Total expenditures	$88,244,228	$16,333,798	$11,810,684	$24,123,050	$140,511,760
Net	$21,908,842	−$11,424,581	−$2,261,860	−$10,016,519	−$1,794,118
Other financing sources					
Transfers from other funds	$3,964,587	$5,991,263	$2,261,860	$11,193,957	$23,411,667
Transfers to other funds	−18,778,273	−965,614	—	−16,502	−19,760,389
Proceeds from debt issuance	—	—	—	—	—
Refunding bond issued	—	—	—	—	—
Payment to refund	—	—	—	—	—
Total other	−$14,813,686	$5,025,649	$2,261,860	$11,177,455	$3,651,278
Net change in fund balance	$7,095,156	−$6,398,032	0	$1,160,936	$1,857,160
Fund balance, July 1, 2005	$19,192,584	$7,200,218	—	$4,703,756	$31,096,558
Fund balance, June 30, 2006	$26,287,740	$802,186	—	$5,864,692	$32,953,718

Source: Comprehensive Annual Financial Statement for the Year Ended June 30, 2006, City of Charlottesville, Virginia, www.charlottesville.org/Index.aspx?page=1869.

Note: — = not available.

1. The first three ratios described here are all about liquidity; that is, the cash and other cash-like assets relative to short-term liability due in the next twelve months. These can be used to solve any short-term problems. The most common ratio is the current ratio.

$$\text{Current ratio} = \text{Current assets} / \text{Current liabilities}$$

Often in financial statements of state and local governments, the current assets will be the total assets because investments and fixed assets may be recorded in another fund. This is not the case for nonprofit organizations. At the minimum, the current ratio should be greater than 1. Each government and organization should be able to pay off its current liabilities with its current assets and remain liquid.

2. Another way to think about the liquidity of an organization is to ask how much working capital exists in this organization. Certainly this should always be positive.

$$\text{Working capital} = \text{Current assets} - \text{Current liabilities}$$

3. There is another ratio, the quick ratio, which focuses on the amount of cash-like assets such as cash, accounts receivable, and short-term securities (which are sometimes called quick assets). Other types of receivables, such as taxes, are not as quick to be recovered and would not be counted.

$$\text{Quick ratio} = \text{Quick assets} / \text{Current liabilities}$$

4. The fourth measure is about long-term solvency; that is, can the government entity or nonprofit group pay off its long-term debts? Such calculations are often called leverage ratios because we are measuring the amount of debt that has been used to leverage the governmental or organizational assets. The most useful ratio examines the total capital of the organization where the debt-to-asset ratio for a financially sound organization is expected to be around 0.6 or less.

$$\text{Debt-to-asset ratio} = \text{Total liabilities} / \text{Total assets}$$

5. Another useful ratio is the days payable ratio, which is an average of the number of days it takes for the organization to pay its bills. The expectation is that accounts are payable in 30 days.

$$\text{Days payable ratio} = \text{Accounts payable} \times 365 \text{ days} / \text{NPS expenses}$$

6. Some ratios use both the balance sheet and the income statement. There is always an issue of profit. Did the government end the year in the black, or did the government end with a deficit? This is all about building for the future. Going into debt is not building for the future. Measuring the surplus is accomplished by using the profit margin ratio with the expectation that there will always be a small profit.

Profit margin ratio = Surplus / Revenue

7. Sustainability can be measured through the degree to which the assets, liabilities, revenues, and expenses are dispersed. The most important category is revenue. How dispersed are the revenues? This ratio is expressed as a percentage of the total.

Common size ratio = Line item amount / Total amount

Each source of revenue can be a percentage of the total revenue. Local governments are often heavily dependent on taxes, and they cannot expect much diversity in their revenues. Sometimes it is difficult to draw any conclusions from examining revenue dispersion in local governments. This is not the case for nonprofit organizations. In nonprofits, if revenues are widely dispersed among several categories, such as government contracts, grants, fees, contributions, and endowment income, the conclusion can be drawn that the resources are sustainable.

For nonprofits that prepare cash flow statements, simple time series can be useful. The trend of cash flow from operations should be positive. Less intuitively, negative cash flows for investing and financing are also positive signs because they mean an organization is increasing its capital assets or reducing its debt.

One example of using these ratios in a financial analysis is shown in the financial statement for a small nonprofit organization shown in Table 9.4. Table 9.5 and Table 9.6 show the statement of financial position (balance sheet) and the statement of activities (income statement) for that same nonprofit organization.

With this information students can calculate a series of ratios that would help explain the financial condition of the nonprofit organization. Clearly, the measures of liquidity are quite solid. The current ratio is over 5 and the quick ratio is 4.5. The working capital is more than sufficient. The long-term solvency ratios are equally solid, with the debt-to-asset ratio being less than 2. The asset management ratios demonstrate that the nonprofit does not pay its payables in a timely manner, which is cause for concern.

TABLE 9.4

Financial Statement for a Small Nonprofit Organization

			FY 2006		
1. Current ratio	Current assets / Current liabilities		$1,289,762 / $248,695	=	5.19
2. Working capital	Current assets—current liabilities $1,289,762	minus	$248,695	=	$1,041,067
3. Quick ratio	Quick assets / Current liabilities		$1,121,492 / $248,695	=	4.51
4. Debt-to-asset ratio	Total liabilities / Total assets		$630,153 / $3,676,115	=	0.17
5. Days payable ratio	All accounts payable × 365 days / NPS expenses		$73,000,000 / $1,161,884	=	62.83 days
6. Profit margin ratio	Surplus / Revenue		−$2,037 / −$3,822,766	=	−0.053%
7. Common size ratio	Line item amount / Total amount	Contributions	$565,032		14.78%
		Grants	1,182,215		30.93
		Government contracts	1,459,639		38.18
		Fees	529,243		13.84
		Interest	86,637		2.27
			$3,822,766		100.00%

The profit margin ratio is problematic because the nonprofit had a slight deficit this year. Questions that need to be answered include: Is this loss a one-time event or has this nonprofit been in this situation before? Is this nonprofit building intergenerational equity over time? What is the trend over five or ten years?

Looking at the degree of diversity in revenues, the analyst can see that this nonprofit organization depends heavily on government contracts; in contrast, contributions are quite a small proportion of the revenues. Certainly, the nonprofit would benefit from a greater emphasis on contributions.

It is possible to conclude that, although the nonprofit does not have immediate concerns about liquidity and solvency, this nonprofit organization needs to stabilize its profit margin and improve its sustainability of resources through revenue diversification. More could be learned through an in-depth examination of the sources and uses of revenue.

TABLE 9.5
Statement of Financial Position (Balance Sheet) for a Small Nonprofit Organization

Current assets

Cash	$271,671
Temporary cash investments	619,941
Accounts receivable	45,918
Pledges receivable	183,962
Prepaid expenses	168,270
Total current assets	**$1,289,762**

Long-term assets

Investments	$2,033,200
Land, buildings	1,612,164
Other assets	30,751
Total long-term assets	**$3,676,115**
Total assets	**$4,965,877**

Current liabilities

Accounts payable	$200,000
Accrued expenses	48,695
Total current liabilities	**$248,695**
Long-term liabilities	
Mortgage	$381,458
Total liabilities	**$630,153**

Net assets

Unrestricted	$2,509,727
Temporarily restricted	825,997
Permanently restricted	1,000,000
Total net assets	**$4,335,724**
Total liabilities and net assets	**$4,965,877**

TABLE 9.6
Statement of Activities (Income Statement) for a Small Nonprofit Organization

Revenue

Contributions	$565,032
Grants	1,182,215
Government contracts	1,459,639
Fees and membership dues	529,243
Interest and gains	86,637
Total revenue	**$3,822,766**

Expenses

Salaries	$2,187,465
Benefits	475,454
Total PS	$2,662,919
NPS	
Accounting fees	$14,500
Legal fees	1,000
Supplies	78,872
Telephone	22,145
Postage and shipping	13,957
Rentals	101,289
Printing and publications	48,062
Travel	170,060
Depreciation	100,242
Food	119,111
Admission fees	77,966
Utilities	124,620
Insurance	115,107
Program equipment	52,572
Maintenance	35,932
Other program expenses	59,250
Payroll processing	14,916
Staff development and training	12,283
Total NPS	$1,161,884
Total expenses	**$3,824,803**
Change in net assets	**−$2,037**

Note: January 1, 2006, to December 31, 2006. PS = personnel services; NPS = nonpersonnel services.

TABLE 9.7

City of Charlottesville Balance Sheet, Government Funds Only, June 30, 2005

	General fund	Capital projects fund	Social services fund	Other government fund	Total
Assets					
Cash	$17,455,863	$3,889,312	$108,907	$4,334,506	$25,788,588
Investments				599	599
Accounts receivable	1,358,985	16,164	6,263	700,456	2,081,868
Taxes receivable	21,203,551				21,203,551
Special assessments receivable		16,813			16,813
Due from other governments	3,363,801	4,819,047	782,115	5,277,677	14,242,640
Due from other funds	3,113,737				3,113,737
Loans receivable		1,826,518		148,543	1,975,061
Accrued interest receivable	216,489	—	—	10	216,499
Total assets	$46,712,426	$10,567,854	$897,285	$10,461,791	$68,639,356
Liabilities and fund balances					
Liabilities					
Accounts payable	$1,467,986	$3,322,474	$92,249	$3,284,540	$8,167,249
Accrued liabilties	2,815,039	24,000	230,255	171,488	3,240,782
Due to other governments				108,543	108,543
Due to other funds				1,848,853	1,848,853
Deferred revenue	23,236,817	21,162	574,781	344,611	24,177,371
Total Liabilities	$27,519,842	$3,367,636	$897,285	$5,758,035	$37,542,798
Fund balances					
Reserved	$979,023	$5,684,987		$788,797	$7,452,807
Unreserved, designated:					—
General fund	1,118,013				1,118,013
Capital projects fund		1,515,231			1,515,231
Debt service fund				3,914,959	3,914,959
Unreserved, undesignated:					—
General fund	17,095,548	—	—	—	17,095,548
Total fund balances	$19,192,584	$7,200,218		$4,703,756	$31,096,558
Liabilities and fund balances	$46,712,426	$10,567,854	$897,285	$10,461,791	$68,639,356

Source: Comprehensive Annual Financial Statement for the Year Ended June 30, 2005, City of Charlottesville, Virginia, www.charlottesville.org/Index.aspx?page=1584.
Note: "—" = not available.

TABLE 9.8

City of Charlottesville Statement of Revenues, Expenditures, and Changes in Fund Balances, Governmental Funds, for the Year Ended June 30, 2005

	General fund	Capital projects fund	Social services fund	Other government fund	Total
Revenues					
Taxes	$73,521,654	—	—	—	$73,521,654
Fees and permits	1,553,833	—	—	—	1,553,833
Intergovernmental	9,629,915	$8,937,858	$9,819,003	$12,830,816	51,217,592
Charges for services	4,420,205	—	—	3,285,459	7,705,664
Fines	541,733	—	—	—	541,733
Investment earnings	—	90,121	—	3,247	93,368
Miscellaneous	1,400,939	237,422	26,751	220,515	1,885,627
Total revenue	$101,068,279	$9,265,401	$9,845,754	$16,340,037	$136,519,471
Expenditures					
General government	$10,293,731	$540,328	—	—	$10,834,059
Public safety	22,388,096	—	—	$3,962,105	26,350,201
Community services	6,299,314	2,066,346	—	4,440,075	12,805,735
Health and welfare	3,385,595	213,015	$11,986,071	9,437,130	25,021,811
Parks, recreation, and culture	6,624,111	753,057	—	136,810	7,513,978
Education	31,133,916	661,986	—	—	31,795,902
Conservation and development	3,259,330	1,898,156	—	1,339,792	6,497,278
Other activities	167,858	—	—	—	167,858
Debt services	—	—	—	5,529,690	5,529,690
Capital outlay	—	23,908,132	—	—	23,908,132
Total expenditures	$83,551,951	$30,041,020	$11,986,071	$24,845,602	$150,424,644
Net	$17,516,328	–$20,775,619	–$2,140,317	–$8,505,565	–$13,905,173
Other financing sources					
Transfers from other funds	$4,403,507	$5,726,162	$2,140,317	$10,652,361	$22,922,347
Transfers to other funds	16,578,460	–1,561,643	—	–20,602	–18,160,705
Proceeds from debt issuance	—	19,962,475	—	—	19,962,475
Refunding bond issued	—	—	—	2,913,333	2,913,333
Payment to refund	—	—	—	–3,043,650	–3,043,650
Total other	–$12,174,953	$24,126,994	$2,140,317	$10,501,442	$24,593,800
Net change in fund balance	$5,341,375	$3,351,375	—	$1,995,877	$10,688,627
Fund balance, July 1, 2004	$13,851,209	$3,848,843	—	$2,707,879	$20,407,931
Fund balance, June 30, 2005	$19,192,584	$7,200,218	—	$4,703,756	$31,096,558

Source: Comprehensive Annual Financial Statement for the Year Ended June 30, 2005, City of Charlottesville, Virginia, www.charlottesville.org/Index.aspx?page=1584.

Note: — = not available.

What would be most helpful in the analysis of this nonprofit's fiscal health would be to examine several years of financial statements instead of only one. Establishing a trend line with several years of data can lead to a more comprehensive picture of this organization's fiscal health.

Summary

In this chapter we learned how to establish a multiyear financial plan for your agency, and we learned simple tools for analyzing multiyear financial statements. The balance sheet, income statement, and cash flow statement were discussed. Several examples from government and nonprofits are included.

Exercises

To complete the exercises, use the data in Table 9.7 and Table 9.8 and the spreadsheet titled "Budget Tools 09 Exercises."

1. Use the financial statements from Charlottesville, Virginia, to conduct your own analysis. Two years are provided so that a comparison between years can be made. Students are advised to use the format in the spreadsheet in Table 9.4 and add an additional column for FY 2005 so that the ratios can be compared side by side. (Please note that NPS used in the days payable ratio is 20 percent of the total expenditures.)

   When students compare the ratios, they should focus on measures of liquidity, long-term solvency, and asset management ratios.

Additional Readings

Bryce, Herrington J. *Financial and Strategic Management for Nonprofit Organizations: A Comprehensive Reference to Legal, Financial, Management, and Operations Rules and Guidelines for Nonprofits.* San Francisco: Jossey-Bass, 2000.

Department of Finance. *Comprehensive Annual Financial Report, Charlottesville, Virginia.* Charlottesville, Va.: City of Charlottesville, June 30, 2007. www.charlottesville.org/Index.aspx? page=596.

Ives, Martin, Joseph R. Razek, and Gordon A. Hosch. *Introduction to Governmental and Not-for-Profit Accounting,* 5th ed. Upper Saddle River, N.J.: Pearson/Prentice Hall, 2004.

Zietlow, John, Jo Ann Hankin, and Alan Seidner. *Financial Management for Nonprofit Organizations: Policies and Practices.* Hoboken, N.J.: Wiley, 2007.

Appendix A

Chart of Accounts

All municipalities in New York State are required to use a standard system for classifying and coding accounting transactions.

Classification

A classification of accounts is a systematic arrangement of accounts based upon a definite scheme. The purpose of classifying accounts is to provide a standard format for recording and reporting financial transactions, which allows comparisons to be made with other municipalities or other financial periods. The classification system serves as a basis for budgeting, accounting, and reporting as well as for administrative control purposes, accountability to the Office of the State Comptroller and the general public, cost accounting, and the compilation of financial statistical data on the state level.

Coding

Coding of accounts facilitates the classification of data on source documents and the posting of entries in the accounting records. It enables identification of transactions quickly and provides consistency in reporting. The coding system used in New York State is an alphanumeric system—a letter or combination of letters followed by a series of digits.

The alpha portion of each code, consisting of one or two letters, identifies the fund. The following funds are provided for municipalities in New York State.

Appendix A is reprinted from *Accounting and Reporting Manual* (Albany: New York State Office of the State Comptroller, n.d.), Chapter 5, Classification and Coding Structure, www.osc.state.ny.us/localgov/pubs/arm/arm5.htm.

Fund	Alpha Code	County	City	Town	Village
Governmental Funds:					
General	A	X	X	X	X
Special Revenue:					
Town Outside Village	B			X	
Special Grant	CD	X	X	X	X
Miscellaneous (1)	C	X	X	X	X
County Road	D	X			
Highway-Town Wide	DA			X	
Highway-Part Town	DB			X	
Road Machinery	DM	X			
Water	FX	X	X	X	X
Sewer	G	X	X	X	X
Public Library	L	X	X	X	X
Special Districts (2)	S			X	
Permanent	PN	X	X	X	X
Capital Projects	H	X	X	X	X
Debt Service	V	X	X	X	X
Proprietary Funds:					
Enterprise (3)	E	X	X	X	X
Internal Service	M	X	X	X	X
Self Insurance	MS	X	X	X	X
Fiduciary Funds:					
Agency	TA	X	X	X	X
Pension Trust	TP	X	X	X	X
Private Purpose Trust	TE	X	X	X	X

1. Miscellaneous Special Revenue Funds include: Refuse (CL), Parking (CP), Recreation (CR), Transportation (CT), Urban Renewal (CU), and Miscellaneous (CM).
2. Special District Funds include: Drainage (SD), Fire Protection (SF), Lighting (SL), Miscellaneous (SM), Park (SP), Refuse and Garbage (SR), Sewer (SS), Parking (ST), and Water (SW).
3. Enterprise Funds include: Airports (EA), Electric Utilities (EE), Health Related Facilities (EF), Hospitals (EH), Infirmaries (EI), Refuse and Garbage (EL), Miscellaneous (EM), Parking (EP), Recreation (ER), Sewer (ES), and Water (EW).

The numeric portion of each code, which immediately follows the alpha portion, identifies general ledger, revenue and expenditure/expense accounts. The same account code number, where applicable, is used in all funds.

General ledger codes have three digits and are arranged in balance sheet order; assets, followed by liabilities and fund equity.

100–499	Assets
600–699	Liabilities
800–999	Fund Equity

For example, 200 identifies the asset CASH in each fund. A200 identifies the asset CASH in the General Fund.

Revenue codes have four digits and are arranged by source (where did the revenue come from):

1000–2999	Local Sources
3000–3999	State Sources
4000–4999	Federal Sources
5000–5999	Interfund Transfers and Proceeds of Obligations

Each category is further subdivided to better identify the revenue source. For example 2401 identifies INTEREST AND EARNINGS in each fund.

GAAP requires revenues to be classified by fund and by source. Thus General Fund INTEREST AND EARNINGS would be classified A2401.

Expenditure/expense codes have 5 digits and are arranged by functional unit and object of expenditure/expense. The term function refers to the primary classification and description as to purpose (what was the purpose of the expenditure/expense). The first four digits identify the function:

1000–1999	General Government Support
2000–2999	Education
3000–3999	Public Safety
4000–4999	Health
5000–5999	Transportation
6000–6999	Economic Assistance and Opportunity
7000–7999	Culture and Recreation
8000–8999	Home and Community Service
9000–9099	Employee Benefits
9700–9799	Debt Service
9900–9999	Interfund Transfer

Each function is further subdivided to better classify the expenditure/expense. For example expenditure code 1325 in the General Governmental Support function identifies the Treasurer's Office within the financial office of the municipality.

Expenditures should be further classified by character, that is, on the basis of the fiscal period they are presumed to benefit. The major character classifications are: current, capital outlay and debt service. Character classifications may be accomplished by grouping the object classifications, discussed below, which are subdivisions of the character classification.

The object of the expenditure/expense (the fifth digit in the code) is a secondary classification and identifies the item purchased or service obtained in order to carry out a function. The object is identified by the fifth and final digit:

.1	Personal Services
.2	Equipment and Capital Outlay
.4	Contractual
.6	Debt Principal
.7	Debt Interest
.8	Employee Benefits
.9	Interfund Transfer

Code 1325 from above can then be further classified as 1325.4 to indicate Contractual Services within the Treasurer's Office.

GAAP requires expenditures to be classified by fund, function, character, and object. Thus a General Fund expenditure for Contractual Services within the Treasurer's Office is coded A1325.4.

The coding of expenditures/expenses may be expanded to include more detail such as department, location, and/or activity accounting. This can be accomplished at the local government level by further expanding the object of expenditure/expense code by adding additional digits. As an example, contractual expenditures (.4) listed above could be further refined:

.41	Supplies and Materials
.42	Utilities
.43	Insurance
.44	Professional and Technical Services
.45	Rent or Lease
.46	Operation and Maintenance
.47	Miscellaneous

Employee benefits, including such items as the localities share of social security, retirement, and various types of insurance, may be recorded in two ways. The first method would be to use the Employee Benefits Codes (9000–9099) with the .8 object of expenditure. The alternative method would be to charge the employee benefits to the various functional units using the .8 object of expenditure.

Appendix B

Further Discussion of Data Organization

In a typical textbook the worst problem you encounter is a word problem that has been intentionally obfuscated to test whether you can untangle it. In the real world, untangling the nature of the problem is merely the first step to analysis. The larger problem has to do with data. It is not necessarily the case that data are not available. Indeed, the data may be too numerous. The problem is in figuring out which data are relevant and making the data ready to analyze.

Budget circumstances usually do not afford the luxury of collecting new **primary data** for the purpose of analysis. The only time you will have data collected for you is when you participate in developing a computer database. Even in these circumstances, the data may not come to you until much later, and by then it will begin to have characteristics of **secondary data.**

Under most circumstances data should be entered into your analysis data files (formats include Excel, SPSS, or the data files for some other software) in the form of a database. This principle is particularly important when there are many pieces of data or when the data are subject to change. Databases have these characteristics:

- Columns have unique column labels at the top

- Columns are adjacent

- Rows are adjacent

- There is a column that contains a unique identifier for each row; usually this is the first column

- Missing data are represented by leaving cells empty

- No formulas are entered into data cells; in some circumstances a column is a transformation of one or more other columns, in which case the entire column contains the effect of the same formula

- Different sets of data are entered in different databases; in the modern spreadsheet, this can be done by using a different tabbed sheet for each set of data.

Here are some of the problems of databases that you will face and some solutions to the problems.

Indicators vs. Measures

One problem is that the data may measure something other than what you wanted to measure. Secondary data may not measure what you want to measure. Instead, you may need to use **indicators,** that is, indirect **measures** of what you want to measure. For example you may want to measure how warm the temperatures are in apartments that are in a certain apartment complex. However, all you may be able to measure is the BTU output of the heating unit. Because of many other factors, such as the insulating efficiency of the windows, the BTU output does not fully measure heat, but you can be relatively sure that as BTU output goes up, heat goes up. The BTU output is an indicator. An even weaker indicator, but still an indicator, is the fuel consumption of that same heating unit. In contrast, periodic readings from thermostats in the apartments are actual measures.

Often, when using secondary data, you must opt for indicators because no one has made a data source available with data covering what you want to measure. It is important that indicators be realistically associated with what they are expected to indicate. Association between indicator and actual measure may be in four forms:

- The indicator may be thought to be strongly linked to the cause of the variable you want to measure. For example, the BTU output measures a major component of the cause of apartment heat.

- The indicator might be thought to be caused by the variable of interest. For example, housing quality might be caused by income and, thus, might be an indicator of income.

- The indicator and the variable of interest might have a common cause. For example, height and weight, at least among younger individuals, share common growth causes. So height may be treated as an indicator of weight.

- The indicator and the variable of interest may simply be highly correlated. For example, locus of residence in the United States is often treated as an indicator of political affiliation. In this last case, both in the example and the practice, the indicator is highly risky. The practice is particularly risky as unexplained correlations can end abruptly without explanation.

EXERCISE 1.   The "Exercise 1" tab in the "Exercises Appendix B" file contains several variables from the 1990 census for the twenty largest cities in the

United States. One variable it does not contain is the proportion of the population that lives in apartments or other mass housing. Choose the variable among those available that is the best indicator, and rank these cities from highest (1) to lowest (20) proportion living in apartments based on this indicator.

Data Are Not Ready

Data that are not ready can take several forms. Data may be presented to you on paper, but you may need the data electronically in order to carry out analysis; data may come to you in a "flat" (text) file, PDF file, or in a file format that is unfamiliar; or you may have variable identifiers and characteristics that you must somehow associate with the data.

Data presented on paper are actually not a problem if they are on a few pages, but they are a problem if they are on dozens or hundreds of pages. Flat files, PDF files, and other readable but unfamiliar file formats may be very similar to data on paper. The recent development of PDF has made very many more reports easily accessible but has in some ways reduced access to processable data.

Paper Files

When paper files are a few pages long, the easiest way to make them electronic is to manually enter them into the analysis entry software. After the number of pages has exceeded an entry tolerance level, which can only be determined by the analyst with whatever knowledge of resources he or she may have, the solution is to use a scanner and high-quality optical character recognition (OCR) software. Even high-quality OCR software will introduce errors. Consequently, the converted data must be examined for apparent errors. In addition, any striking, anomalous, or otherwise surprising findings should lead back to the data for verification.

Handwriting generally cannot be converted by OCR, so handwriting has to be entered.

EXERCISE 2. Enter the table below into an otherwise empty Excel spreadsheet. The totals should be computed, rather than entered. You will know that you have entered the correct data when totals match the totals in the table.

Flat Files and SAS, SPSS, and Similar Programs

It has long been the practice with SAS, SPSS, and possibly other sophisticated data analysis programs to supply data sets in flat files with files that contain processable records separate from those that contain data definitions and characteristics. Sometimes the analyst must take numerous steps to merge the data set with the data definitions. Sometimes the analyst does not have

Quarterly Sales Tax Historical Data

San Antonio	Year	Quarter	Gross sales	Amount subject to state tax	Outlets
	2003	1	11,311,608,818	3,087,049,921	23,579
	2003	2	12,409,623,017	3,314,867,517	23,738
	2003	3	12,561,038,538	3,232,526,033	23,664
	2003	4	16,694,692,407	3,553,285,739	38,767
Total			52,976,962,780	13,187,729,210	
	2004	1	13,027,280,715	3,258,989,861	23,815
	2004	2	14,179,391,209	3,494,192,071	24,203
	2004	3	15,085,013,472	3,485,982,264	24,839
	2004	4	19,297,704,842	3,791,342,974	40,756
Total			61,589,390,238	14,030,507,170	
	2005	1	16,973,715,119	3,499,319,801	25,129
	2005	2	17,261,486,059	3,724,910,861	25,255
	2005	3	18,806,638,266	3,795,075,602	25,502
	2005	4	24,335,891,266	4,230,613,112	42,007
Total			77,377,730,710	15,249,919,376	
	2006	1	18,723,209,205	3,982,621,381	25,542
	2006	2	22,298,125,390	4,194,297,940	26,156
	2006	3	22,373,348,938	4,203,954,940	26,298
	2006	4	23,043,345,590	4,576,142,657	40,095
Total			86,438,029,123	16,957,016,918	

access to any of the particular programming options that allow merging and must, consequently, work straight from the flat file and the data definitions.

Instructions in use of simple SAS or SPSS executable syntax files can be found on their respective Web sites (www.sas.com and www.spss.com). It is not the purpose to repeat those instructions here, particularly as this problem is gradually fading away.

Examples of a flat file are shown in Exhibit 1 for this appendix and a syntax file is shown in Exhibit 2. These have been downloaded from Interuniversity Consortium for Political and Social Research (ICPSR, www.icpsr.umich.edu). Only a few lines of the flat file are shown. The syntax file must be opened through the SPSS open syntax menu and requires editing before it can be used. Editing usually means that the path of the file that contains the data and the desired final filename must be added. In the example file there is a bolded statement that says:

DATA LIST FILE="physical-filename" /

The portion in quotes is the portion that needs to be edited by specifying where you have put the file on your computer. The following instructions

APPENDIX B, EXHIBIT 1
Example of Five Records from a Flat File from ICPSR Data

1975 1JAN 19752043152081719617 40012898106844049221454945297713684 85312 9456 8101
7810 9499 50344288528221211443361955442035280104 67857 5663 5999
92468213234912122159549811742572911833 11023588 55382 5701 5016 4666 6412
33434509054028869282695 840771263310630 880 917218675 67 29186123 6220286382051641002
6122 408 494 566 646 40041719113493254785026597395233312223465617 2

1975 2FEB 19752043152081593587 3683274190738524190054604267712000 80579 8555 7809
7366 9066 476982467011875443870416731389693 70671 59463 5034 5437
832031130046019371472441111935410113710483435 53182 5213 4865 4553 6082
3234247292375996354242 2 8267912080 9926 929 998210123 52 30187125 591834569185111 958
6160 315 475 553 702 411315399120542296704274813710303823839254853

1975 3MAR 19752043152081669654 39952956100336514170464482277611983 92386 9382 8896
849310274 55201254984191401415881791442907075930 63490 5340 6296
89520212614992206167849511314540811810573518 60590 5715 5649 5486 6865
367284854737744696226271 941971272510448 973 997231339 80 35182123 511923547217160 982
6751 348 565 685 695 44391584812182251576332387399233542273556119 8

1975 4APR 19752043152081573662 42723182105133774153184295243611529 94217 9207 8732
900910401 566642432421815274144716577447437 75142 61746 5285 7397
900319130353923101745549109354928123 29733706 61682 5767 5633 5637 6997
374534680736406703224 52 910201251210233 8371198227108 82 34235149 8319114881971711044
7398 372 588 766 803 486415722119762736707308223952318021549760156

1975 5MAY 19752043152081570736 49293694120334473143744237289212788107447
9914100261059012171 6457624501818172944021172444871 21 77680 63434 5479 8244
958974121854524001833542 983241781060 9423496 68739 6054 6202 6186 7680
4245244873352436598250 9 913361232710008 9391208231270 67 31238149 871735491171131 937
8027 344 587 865 827 53891489311420260072430062369128862595155874 4

APPENDIX B, EXHIBIT 2
An Executable Syntax File

```
*----------------------------------------------------------------------------------------*

            SPSS DATA DEFINITION STATEMENTS FOR ICPSR 6792
    UNIFORM CRIME REPORTS: MONTHLY WEAPON-SPECIFIC CRIME AND ARREST
        TIME SERIES, 1975–1993 [NATIONAL, STATE, AND 12-CITY DATA]
                    (PART 1: NATIONAL DATA)
                      FIRST ICPSR VERSION
                        OCTOBER 1998
```

SPSS setup sections are provided for the LRECL version of this data collection. These sections are listed below:

DATA LIST assigns the name, type, and decimal specification (if any), and specifies the beginning and ending column location for each variable. Users must replace the "physical-filename" in the DATA LIST statement with an appropriate filename for their system.

Continues

APPENDIX B, EXHIBIT 2   *(continued)*
An Executable Syntax File

VARIABLE LABELS assigns descriptive labels to all variables. Variable labels and variable names may be identical for some data files.

VALUE LABELS assigns descriptive labels to codes found in the data file. Not all codes necessarily have assigned value labels.

These data definition statements were tested using SPSS version 5.0 for UNIX.

--

* SPSS DATA LIST FOR 6792,
* UNIFORM CRIME REPORTS: MONTHLY WEAPON-SPECIFIC CRIME AND ARREST
* TIME SERIES, 1975–1993 [NATIONAL, STATE, AND 12-CITY DATA]
* (PART 1: NATIONAL DATA) .

DATA LIST FILE="physical-filename"

YEAR_	1–8	MONTH_	9–10	DATE_	11–18 (A)
VAR001	19–27	VAR002	28–31	VAR003	32–34
VAR004	35–39	VAR005	40–43	VAR006	44–47
VAR007	48–52	VAR008	53–57	VAR009	58–61
VAR010	62–65	VAR011	66–70	VAR012	71–76
VAR013	77–81	VAR014	82–86	VAR015	87–91
VAR016	92–96	VAR017	97–102	VAR018	103–108
VAR019	109–114	VAR020	115–119	VAR021	120–124
VAR022	125–130	VAR023	131–136	VAR024	137–142
VAR025	143–147	VAR026	148–152	VAR027	153–159
VAR028	160–163	VAR029	164–166	VAR030	167–170
VAR031	171–174	VAR032	175–177	VAR033	178–182
VAR034	183–186	VAR035	187–190	VAR036	191–200
VAR037	201–204	VAR038	205–210	VAR039	211–215
VAR040	216–220	VAR041	221–225	VAR042	226–230
VAR043	231–236	VAR044	237–241	VAR045	242–246
VAR046	247–250	VAR047	251–254	VAR048	255–260
VAR049	261–265	VAR050	266–270	VAR051	271–274
VAR052	275–278	VAR053	279–284	VAR054	285–287
VAR055	288–290	VAR056	291–293	VAR057	294–296
VAR058	297–299	VAR059	300–303	VAR060	304–306
VAR061	307–309	VAR062	310–312	VAR063	313–316
VAR064	317–321	VAR065	322–325	VAR066	326–329
VAR067	330–333	VAR068	334–337	VAR069	338–342
VAR070	343–347	VAR071	348–352	VAR072	353–356
VAR073	357–359	VAR074	360–364	VAR075	365–368
VAR076	369–372	VAR077	373–375	VAR078	376–378
VAR079	379–383				

APPENDIX B, EXHIBIT 2   *(continued)*

* SPSS VARIABLE LABELS FOR 6792,
* UNIFORM CRIME REPORTS: MONTHLY WEAPON–SPECIFIC CRIME AND ARREST
* TIME SERIES, 1975–1993 [NATIONAL, STATE, AND 12–CITY DATA]
* (PART 1: NATIONAL DATA) .

VARIABLE LABELS
YEAR_   "YEAR, NOT PERIODIC"
MONTH_   "MONTH, PERIOD 12"
DATE   "DATE. FORMAT: MMM YYYY"
VAR001   "TOTAL POPULATION"
VAR002   "TOTAL HOMICIDE"
VAR003   "TOTAL NEGLIGENT MANSLAUGHTER"
VAR004   "TOTAL RAPE"
VAR005   "TOTAL FORCIBLE RAPE"
VAR006   "TOTAL ATTEMPTED FORCIBLE RAPE"
VAR007   "TOTAL ROBBERIES"
VAR008   "TOTAL FIREARM ROBBERY"
VAR009   "TOTAL KNIFE/CUTTING INSTRUMENT ROBBERY"
VAR010   "TOTAL OTHER DANGEROUS WEAPON ROBBERY"
VAR011   "TOTAL STRONG–ARM ROBBERY"
VAR012   "TOTAL ASSAULTS"
VAR013   "TOTAL FIREARM ASSAULT"
VAR014   "TOTAL KNIFE/CUTTING INSTRUMENT ASSAULT"
VAR015   "TOTAL OTHER DANGEROUS WEAPON ASSAULT"
VAR016   "TOTAL HANDS, FISTS, FEET, ETC.– ASSAULT"
VAR017   "TOTAL OTHER ASSLTS—SIMPLE, NOT AGGRVTD"
VAR018   "TOTAL BURGLARIES"
VAR019   "TOTAL FORCIBLE ENTRY"
VAR020   "TOTAL UNLAWFUL ENTRY–NO FORCE"
VAR021   "TOTAL ATTEMPTED FORCIBLE ENTRY"
VAR022   "TOTAL LARCENY–THEFT"
VAR023   "TOTAL MOTOR VEHICLE THEFTS"
VAR024   "TOTAL AUTO THEFT"
VAR025   "TOTAL TRUCKS AND BUSES THEFT"
VAR026   "TOTAL OTHER VEHICLE THEFT"
VAR027   "GRAND TOTAL OF ALL ACTUAL OFFENSES"
VAR028   "TOTAL HOMICIDE CLEARED"
VAR029   "TOTAL NEGLIGENT MANSLAUGHTER CLEARED"
VAR030   "TOTAL RAPE CLEARED"
VAR031   "TOTAL FORCIBLE RAPE CLEARED"
VAR032   "TOTAL ATTEMPTED FORCIBLE RAPE CLEARED"

Continues

An Executable Syntax File

VAR033	"TOTAL ROBBERIES CLEARED"
VAR034	"TOTAL FIREARM ROBBERY CLEARED"
VAR035	"TOTAL KNIFE/CUT INSTRUMENT ROB CLEARED"
VAR036	"TOTAL OTHER DANGEROUS WEAPON ROB CLEARED"
VAR037	"TOTAL STRONG–ARM ROBBERY CLEARED"
VAR038	"TOTAL ASSAULTS CLEARED"
VAR039	"TOTAL FIREARM ASSAULT CLEARED"
VAR040	"TOTAL KNIFE/CUTTING INSTR ASSLT CLEARED"
VAR041	"TOTAL OTH DANGEROUS WEAPON ASSLT CLEARED"
VAR042	"TOTAL HANDS, FISTS, ETC.– ASSLT CLEARED"
VAR043	"TOTAL OTH ASSLTS—SIMPLE, NOT AGG CLEARD"
VAR044	"TOTAL BURGLARIES CLEARED"
VAR045	"TOTAL FORCIBLE ENTRY CLEARED"
VAR046	"TOTAL UNLAWFUL ENTRY–NO FORCE, CLEARED"
VAR047	"TOTAL ATTEMPTED FORCIBLE ENTRY, CLEARED"
VAR048	"TOTAL LARCENY–THEFT CLEARED"
VAR049	"TOTAL MOTOR VEHICLE THEFTS CLEARED"
VAR050	"TOTAL AUTO THEFT CLEARED"
VAR051	"TOTAL TRUCKS AND BUSES THEFT CLEARED"
VAR052	"TOTAL OTHER VEHICLE THEFT CLEARED"
VAR053	"GRAND TOTAL ALL ACTUAL OFFENSES CLEARED"
VAR054	"TOTAL HOMICIDE CLEARED UNDER 18 YR OLD"
VAR055	"TOTAL NEG MANSLAUGHTR CLEARD < 18 YR OLD"
VAR056	"TOTAL RAPE CLEARED UNDER 18 YR OLD"
VAR057	"TOTAL FORCIBLE RAPE CLEARED < 18 YR OLD"
VAR058	"TOTAL ATT FORC RAPE CLEARED < 18 YR OLD"
VAR059	"TOTAL ROBBERIES CLEARED UNDER 18 YR OLD"
VAR060	"TOTAL FIREARM ROB CLEARED < 18 YR OLD"
VAR061	"TOTAL KNIFE/CUT INSTR ROB CLEARD < 18 YR"
VAR062	"TOT OTH DANGEROUS WPN ROB CLEARD < 18 YR"
VAR063	"TOTAL STRONG–ARM ROB CLEARED < 18 YR OLD"
VAR064	"TOTAL ASSAULTS CLEARED UNDER 18 YR OLD"
VAR065	"TOTAL FIREARM ASSAULT CLEARED < 18 YR OL"
VAR066	"TOTAL KNIFE/CUT INSTR ASSLT, CLEARD < 18"
VAR067	"TOT OTH DANGEROUS WPN ASSLT CLEARED < 18"
VAR068	"TOTAL HANDS/FISTS–ASSLT CLEARED < 18 YR"
VAR069	"TOTAL OTH ASSLTS–SIMPLE CLEARED < 18 YR"
VAR070	"TOTAL BURGLARIES CLEARED UNDER 18 YR OLD"
VAR071	"TOTAL FORCIBLE ENTRY CLEARED < 18 YR OLD"
VAR072	"TOTAL UNLAWFUL ENTRY–NO FORC CLEARD < 18"
VAR073	"TOTAL ATT FORCIBLE ENTRY CLEARED < 18 YR"
VAR074	"TOTAL LARCENY–THEFT CLEARED < 18 YR OLD"

APPENDIX B, EXHIBIT 2   *(continued)*

VAR075	"TOTAL MV THEFTS CLEARED < 18 YR OLD"
VAR076	"TOTAL AUTO THEFT CLEARED UNDER 18 YR OLD"
VAR077	"TOTAL TRUCKS/BUSES THEFT CLEARED < 18 YR"
VAR078	"TOTAL OTH VEHICLE THEFT CLEARED < 18 YR"
VAR079	"GRAND TOT ALL ACTUAL OFFENS CLEARED < 18" .

* SPSS VALUE LABELS FOR 6792,

* UNIFORM CRIME REPORTS: MONTHLY WEAPON–SPECIFIC CRIME AND ARREST

* TIME SERIES, 1975–1993 [NATIONAL, STATE, AND 12–CITY DATA]

* (PART 1: NATIONAL DATA) .

VALUE LABELS

MONTH_	1	"January"
	2	"February"
	3	"March"
	4	"April"
	5	"May"
	6	"June"
	7	"July"
	8	"August"
	9	"September"
	10	"October"
	11	"November"
	12	"December".

---

apply to Microsoft operating systems. After you have edited "physical-file-name," it may look something like this:

DATA LIST FILE="C:\Documents and Settings**Your name**\My Document\
   SPSS**MyFile**.txt" /

The term "Your name" must be replaced with whatever identification you use with your computer. If you do not supply a user login and you are the sole user of the computer, the default is "admin" or "administrator."

The term "MyFile" should be replaced by the actual file name.

At the very end of the "syntax" you should add:

SAVE OUTFILE= "C:\Documents and Settings**Your name**\My Document\
   SPSS**MyFile**.sav" .
EXECUTE.

The bolded components should be edited. The second component requires the name you want to use.

If you want to use the data in an Excel spreadsheet, you should follow through with these lines. (You will see, below, that there are restrictions on what you can save from SPSS to Excel.)

```
SAVE TRANSLATE
OUTFILE='H C:\Documents and Settings\Your name\My Document\
    MyFile.xls'
/TYPE=XLS /VERSION=8 /MAP /REPLACE /FIELDNAMES
/CELLS=VALUES .
EXECUTE.
```

Again, the bolded components should be edited.

An example Excel file, using the data found in Exhibit 1 and the code in Exhibit 2 with the modifications discussed here, is shown on the accompanying CD in the file named FlattoExcel.xls.

These are instructions for SPSS. SAS is slightly different. For both of these programs, every single mark is relevant, and it is essential that the reader visit the SAS Web site.

Sometimes other editing is required. These skills usually can be acquired with just a few days of experience working with the software.

Sometimes flat files come with data labels on the first row and data in columns that are "beneath" the labels (on a wide enough sheet of paper). This may provide for simplified data importation. Or, if there are fewer than 256 variables (16,385 variables for Excel 2007), it may lead the analyst to import data through spreadsheet procedure.

This problem is gradually fading away as it is mostly associated with older data, collected when data storage was much more expensive than it is today. However, there remains a possibility that an analyst will have a data set that will be described by number of characters to a record and the number of characters, within a record, for each variable.

After the file is imported into SPSS, it can be exported to Excel format with certain restrictions. The most important of these are that Excel supports a maximum of 255 columns (variables) and a maximum of 65,536 rows (records) (Excel 2007 supports 16,384 columns and 1,048,576 rows); other further restrictions might include your computer's memory capacity.

EXERCISE 3. Using SPSS and using the files labeled Syntax.txt and Flat.txt on the CD, edit Syntax.txt as necessary and import Flat.txt into an SPSS (.sav) file, then into an Excel (.xls) file.

Flat Files and Microsoft Excel

Flat files can also be imported into spreadsheets with some restrictions:

■ There must be no more than 255 variables (16,384 for Excel 2007)

■ The flat file must have one continuous row of data for one record of data, and the row must break at the end of the record

■ It is highly desirable that the data be delimited

■ It is highly desirable that the first row of the data contain labels that are also delimited.

Delimited means there is a clear, unique, and not-otherwise-used mark at the end of each variable or variable label. A CSV file is a "comma separated values" file, which refers to a file in which data are delimited by commas. Other common delimiters are spaces and tabs. Any clearly identifiable delimiter will do, although CSV files enjoy especially easy treatment by Excel.

If the data are in a CSV file, Excel will automatically import the data into a spreadsheet, treating each comma as demarking a new cell.

It is relatively easy to make a CSV file. For example, take the data in the following brackets {3,5,7,8,9,2}. Open Notepad on your computer. Type the data, omitting the brackets but including the commas. Save the file, and at the end of the file name type ".csv" (omitting the quotation marks). Be sure you know where you saved the file.

Now open Excel and use the open file icon or use the file menu item to open a new file. Use the drop-down menu to select "all file types." Find the file and open it. Excel should automatically open it as an Excel spreadsheet. Now save the spreadsheet. Excel will provide a message asking you whether you want to save it as it is (not an Excel format). If you select no, it will proceed to menus that lead to converting the file to an Excel spreadsheet.

If, at the beginning, you save the file with an extension .txt instead of .csv—Notepad will default to .txt if you do not specify .csv—you can proceed through pretty much the same steps except that when you open the file Excel will do one of two things:

1. It will open in a menu that requires you to tell it which delimiter is used. The menu is intuitive; you should select comma.

2. It will import the whole string 3,5,7,8,9,2 as text.

If the second event happens, you can call up the menu that allows you to convert the string into cells of data. First highlight the cell or cells to be converted, next select "Data," then select "Text to Columns. . . ." The menu called up will permit you to tell Excel which delimiter separates the data. In Excel 2007, the "Text to Columns" icon is found on the "Data" ribbon.

The process just described also applies to other delimiters such as columns, spaces, or other characters.

The user will have difficulty importing text data into Excel if:

- The data do not have column labels; so after the data are imported, they still need to be identified.

- The importation disorganizes the labels with respect to the data in some way; this is a relatively high risk when text or html reports are posted on government Web sites. The user must go back to the visible report and validate that the labels are properly aligned with the data. Exhibit 3 demonstrates this difficulty. When the authors downloaded it from the Bureau of Labor Statistics and imported it into Excel, the default settings imported June, July, and August into a single column. The authors had to go back and reset the columns (the menus are relatively intuitive) to get the desired results. When the authors did this, the headings at the top of the table were broken into several pieces when some parts became uninterpretable. The result, with its broken heading rows, is shown on the accompanying CD in the file called "cpiai.xls." The user must be prepared to either edit such files or copy and paste the headers after importing the data rows.

- There are no reliable delimiters, or they change often throughout the source document. The user must make the text-to-columns conversion in tedious block-by-block steps.

- Delimiters are omitted when data are omitted. When the data set is relatively small, this means the data set must be carefully edited after conversion. When the data set is large or very large, it is worthless.

- The data are delimited by position only. This is the condition of some of the data demonstrated in Exhibit 1. That is, there are long strings of numbers where different numbers refer to different variables, and the only way to know which number refers to which variable is to know its position in the data set. The text-to-columns menu allows for separation of variables by position. It is important, in this case, to be very careful. In all likelihood, column labels will have to be added after importation. Also, this is a tedious process.

EXERCISE 4.   Download the most current file at the Bureau of Labor Statistics: ftp://ftp.bls.gov/pub/special.requests/cpi/cpiai.txt and import it to Excel. Make sure all columns of data are properly labeled with the correct column headings. (For those who do not have access to the Internet and who

APPENDIX B, EXHIBIT 3
File Lacking Organized Labels

U.S. Department Of Labor
Bureau of Labor Statistics
Washington, D.C. 20212
Consumer Price Index
All Urban Consumers — (CPI-U)
U.S. city average
All items
1982–84=100

														Percent change	
Year	Jan.	Feb.	Mar.	Apr.	May	June	July	Aug.	Sep.	Oct.	Nov.	Dec.	Annual Avg.	Dec–Dec.	Avg–Avg.
1913	9.8	9.8	9.8	9.8	9.7	9.8	9.9	9.9	10.0	10.0	10.1	10.0	9.9		
1914	10.0	9.9	9.9	9.8	9.9	9.9	10.0	10.2	10.2	10.1	10.2	10.1	10.0	1.0	1.0
1915	10.1	10.0	9.9	10.0	10.1	10.1	10.1	10.1	10.1	10.2	10.3	10.3	10.1	2.0	1.0
1916	10.4	10.4	10.5	10.6	10.7	10.8	10.8	10.9	11.1	11.3	11.5	11.6	10.9	12.6	7.9
1917	11.7	12.0	12.0	12.6	12.8	13.0	12.8	13.0	13.3	13.5	13.5	13.7	12.8	18.1	17.4
1918	14.0	14.1	14.0	14.2	14.5	14.7	15.1	15.4	15.7	16.0	16.3	16.5	15.1	20.4	18.0
1919	16.5	16.2	16.4	16.7	16.9	16.9	17.4	17.7	17.8	18.1	18.5	18.9	17.3	14.5	14.6
1920	19.3	19.5	19.7	20.3	20.6	20.9	20.8	20.3	20.0	19.9	19.8	19.4	20.0	2.6	15.6
1921	19.0	18.4	18.3	18.1	17.7	17.6	17.7	17.7	17.5	17.5	17.4	17.3	17.9	–10.8	–10.5
1922	16.9	16.9	16.7	16.7	16.7	16.7	16.8	16.6	16.6	16.7	16.8	16.9	16.8	–2.3	–6.1
1923	16.8	16.8	16.8	16.9	16.9	17.0	17.2	17.1	17.2	17.3	17.3	17.3	17.1	2.4	1.8
1924	17.3	17.2	17.1	17.0	17.0	17.0	17.1	17.0	17.1	17.2	17.2	17.3	17.1	0.0	0.0
1925	17.3	17.2	17.3	17.2	17.3	17.5	17.7	17.7	17.7	17.7	18.0	17.9	17.5	3.5	2.3
1926	17.9	17.9	17.8	17.9	17.8	17.7	17.5	17.4	17.5	17.6	17.7	17.7	17.7	–1.1	1.1
1927	17.5	17.4	17.3	17.3	17.4	17.6	17.3	17.2	17.3	17.4	17.3	17.3	17.4	–2.3	–1.7
1928	17.3	17.1	17.1	17.1	17.2	17.1	17.1	17.1	17.3	17.2	17.2	17.1	17.1	–1.2	–1.7
1929	17.1	17.1	17.0	16.9	17.0	17.1	17.3	17.3	17.3	17.3	17.3	17.2	17.1	0.6	0.0
1930	17.1	17.0	16.9	17.0	16.9	16.8	16.6	16.5	16.6	16.5	16.4	16.1	16.7	–6.4	–2.3
1931	15.9	15.7	15.6	15.5	15.3	15.1	15.1	15.1	15.0	14.9	14.7	14.6	15.2	–9.3	–9.0
1932	14.3	14.1	14.0	13.9	13.7	13.6	13.6	13.5	13.4	13.3	13.2	13.1	13.7	–10.3	–9.9
1933	12.9	12.7	12.6	12.6	12.6	12.7	13.1	13.2	13.2	13.2	13.2	13.2	13.0	0.8	–5.1
1934	13.2	13.3	13.3	13.3	13.3	13.4	13.4	13.4	13.6	13.5	13.5	13.4	13.4	1.5	3.1
1935	13.6	13.7	13.7	13.8	13.8	13.7	13.7	13.7	13.7	13.7	13.8	13.8	13.7	3.0	2.2
1936	13.8	13.8	13.7	13.7	13.7	13.8	13.9	14.0	14.0	14.0	14.0	14.0	13.9	1.4	1.5
1937	14.1	14.1	14.2	14.3	14.4	14.4	14.5	14.5	14.6	14.6	14.5	14.4	14.4	2.9	3.6
1938	14.2	14.1	14.1	14.2	14.1	14.1	14.1	14.1	14.1	14.0	14.0	14.0	14.1	–2.8	–2.1
1939	14.0	13.9	13.9	13.8	13.8	13.8	13.8	13.8	14.1	14.0	14.0	14.0	13.9	0.0	–1.4
1940	13.9	14.0	14.0	14.0	14.0	14.1	14.0	14.0	14.0	14.0	14.0	14.1	14.0	0.7	0.7

Continues

APPENDIX B, EXHIBIT 3   *(continued)*
File Lacking Organized Labels

Year	Jan.	Feb.	Mar.	Apr.	May	June	July	Aug.	Sep.	Oct.	Nov.	Dec.	Annual Avg.	Percent change Dec.–Dec.	Percent change Avg.–Avg.
1941	14.1	14.1	14.2	14.3	14.4	14.7	14.7	14.9	15.1	15.3	15.4	15.5	14.7	9.9	5.0
1942	15.7	15.8	16.0	16.1	16.3	16.3	16.4	16.5	16.5	16.7	16.8	16.9	16.3	9.0	10.9
1943	16.9	16.9	17.2	17.4	17.5	17.5	17.4	17.3	17.4	17.4	17.4	17.4	17.3	3.0	6.1
1944	17.4	17.4	17.4	17.5	17.5	17.6	17.7	17.7	17.7	17.7	17.7	17.8	17.6	2.3	1.7
1945	17.8	17.8	17.8	17.8	17.9	18.1	18.1	18.1	18.1	18.1	18.1	18.2	18.0	2.2	2.3
1946	18.2	18.1	18.3	18.4	18.5	18.7	19.8	20.2	20.4	20.8	21.3	21.5	19.5	18.1	8.3
1947	21.5	21.5	21.9	21.9	21.9	22.0	22.2	22.5	23.0	23.0	23.1	23.4	22.3	8.8	14.4
1948	23.7	23.5	23.4	23.8	23.9	24.1	24.4	24.5	24.5	24.4	24.2	24.1	24.1	3.0	8.1
1949	24.0	23.8	23.8	23.9	23.8	23.9	23.7	23.8	23.9	23.7	23.8	23.6	23.8	−2.1	−1.2
1950	23.5	23.5	23.6	23.6	23.7	23.8	24.1	24.3	24.4	24.6	24.7	25.0	24.1	5.9	1.3
1951	25.4	25.7	25.8	25.8	25.9	25.9	25.9	25.9	26.1	26.2	26.4	26.5	26.0	6.0	7.9
1952	26.5	26.3	26.3	26.4	26.4	26.5	26.7	26.7	26.7	26.7	26.7	26.7	26.5	0.8	1.9
1953	26.6	26.5	26.6	26.6	26.7	26.8	26.8	26.9	26.9	27.0	26.9	26.9	26.7	0.7	0.8
1954	26.9	26.9	26.9	26.8	26.9	26.9	26.9	26.9	26.8	26.8	26.8	26.7	26.9	−0.7	0.7
1955	26.7	26.7	26.7	26.7	26.7	26.7	26.8	26.8	26.9	26.9	26.9	26.8	26.8	0.4	−0.4
1956	26.8	26.8	26.8	26.9	27.0	27.2	27.4	27.3	27.4	27.5	27.5	27.6	27.2	3.0	1.5
1957	27.6	27.7	27.8	27.9	28.0	28.1	28.3	28.3	28.3	28.3	28.4	28.4	28.1	2.9	3.3
1958	28.6	28.6	28.8	28.9	28.9	28.9	29.0	28.9	28.9	28.9	29.0	28.9	28.9	1.8	2.8
1959	29.0	28.9	28.9	29.0	29.0	29.1	29.2	29.2	29.3	29.4	29.4	29.4	29.1	1.7	0.7
1960	29.3	29.4	29.4	29.5	29.5	29.6	29.6	29.6	29.6	29.8	29.8	29.8	29.6	1.4	1.7
1961	29.8	29.8	29.8	29.8	29.8	29.8	30.0	29.9	30.0	30.0	30.0	30.0	29.9	0.7	1.0
1962	30.0	30.1	30.1	30.2	30.2	30.2	30.3	30.3	30.4	30.4	30.4	30.4	30.2	1.3	1.0
1963	30.4	30.4	30.5	30.5	30.5	30.6	30.7	30.7	30.7	30.8	30.8	30.9	30.6	1.6	1.3
1964	30.9	30.9	30.9	30.9	30.9	31.0	31.1	31.0	31.1	31.1	31.2	31.2	31.0	1.0	1.3
1965	31.2	31.2	31.3	31.4	31.4	31.6	31.6	31.6	31.6	31.7	31.7	31.8	31.5	1.9	1.6
1966	31.8	32.0	32.1	32.3	32.3	32.4	32.5	32.7	32.7	32.9	32.9	32.9	32.4	3.5	2.9
1967	32.9	32.9	33.0	33.1	33.2	33.3	33.4	33.5	33.6	33.7	33.8	33.9	33.4	3.0	3.1
1968	34.1	34.2	34.3	34.4	34.5	34.7	34.9	35.0	35.1	35.3	35.4	35.5	34.8	4.7	4.2
1969	35.6	35.8	36.1	36.3	36.4	36.6	36.8	37.0	37.1	37.3	37.5	37.7	36.7	6.2	5.5
1970	37.8	38.0	38.2	38.5	38.6	38.8	39.0	39.0	39.2	39.4	39.6	39.8	38.8	5.6	5.7
1971	39.8	39.9	40.0	40.1	40.3	40.6	40.7	40.8	40.8	40.9	40.9	41.1	40.5	3.3	4.4
1972	41.1	41.3	41.4	41.5	41.6	41.7	41.9	42.0	42.1	42.3	42.4	42.5	41.8	3.4	3.2
1973	42.6	42.9	43.3	43.6	43.9	44.2	44.3	45.1	45.2	45.6	45.9	46.2	44.4	8.7	6.2

APPENDIX B, EXHIBIT 3   *(ontinued)*

Year	Jan.	Feb.	Mar.	Apr.	May	June	July	Aug.	Sep.	Oct.	Nov.	Dec.	Annual Avg.	Percent change Dec.–Dec.	Percent change Avg.–Avg.
1974	46.6	47.2	47.8	48.0	48.6	49.0	49.4	50.0	50.6	51.1	51.5	51.9	49.3	12.3	11.0
1975	52.1	52.5	52.7	52.9	53.2	53.6	54.2	54.3	54.6	54.9	55.3	55.5	53.8	6.9	9.1
1976	55.6	55.8	55.9	56.1	56.5	56.8	57.1	57.4	57.6	57.9	58.0	58.2	56.9	4.9	5.8
1977	58.5	59.1	59.5	60.0	60.3	60.7	61.0	61.2	61.4	61.6	61.9	62.1	60.6	6.7	6.5
1978	62.5	62.9	63.4	63.9	64.5	65.2	65.7	66.0	66.5	67.1	67.4	67.7	65.2	9.0	7.6
1979	68.3	69.1	69.8	70.6	71.5	72.3	73.1	73.8	74.6	75.2	75.9	76.7	72.6	13.3	11.3
1980	77.8	78.9	80.1	81.0	81.8	82.7	82.7	83.3	84.0	84.8	85.5	86.3	82.4	12.5	13.5
1981	87.0	87.9	88.5	89.1	89.8	90.6	91.6	92.3	93.2	93.4	93.7	94.0	90.9	8.9	10.3
1982	94.3	94.6	94.5	94.9	95.8	97.0	97.5	97.7	97.9	98.2	98.0	97.6	96.5	3.8	6.2
1983	97.8	97.9	97.9	98.6	99.2	99.5	99.9	100.2	100.7	101.0	101.2	101.3	99.6	3.8	3.2
1984	101.9	102.4	102.6	103.1	103.4	103.7	104.1	104.5	105.0	105.3	105.3	105.3	103.9	3.9	4.3
1985	105.5	106.0	106.4	106.9	107.3	107.6	107.8	108.0	108.3	108.7	109.0	109.3	107.6	3.8	3.6
1986	109.6	109.3	108.8	108.6	108.9	109.5	109.5	109.7	110.2	110.3	110.4	110.5	109.6	1.1	1.9
1987	111.2	111.6	112.1	112.7	113.1	113.5	113.8	114.4	115.0	115.3	115.4	115.4	113.6	4.4	3.6
1988	115.7	116.0	116.5	117.1	117.5	118.0	118.5	119.0	119.8	120.2	120.3	120.5	118.3	4.4	4.1
1989	121.1	121.6	122.3	123.1	123.8	124.1	124.4	124.6	125.0	125.6	125.9	126.1	124.0	4.6	4.8
1990	127.4	128.0	128.7	128.9	129.2	129.9	130.4	131.6	132.7	133.5	133.8	133.8	130.7	6.1	5.4
1991	134.6	134.8	135.0	135.2	135.6	136.0	136.2	136.6	137.2	137.4	137.8	137.9	136.2	3.1	4.2
1992	138.1	138.6	139.3	139.5	139.7	140.2	140.5	140.9	141.3	141.8	142.0	141.9	140.3	2.9	3.0
1993	142.6	143.1	143.6	144.0	144.2	144.4	144.4	144.8	145.1	145.7	145.8	145.8	144.5	2.7	3.0
1994	146.2	146.7	147.2	147.4	147.5	148.0	148.4	149.0	149.4	149.5	149.7	149.7	148.2	2.7	2.6
1995	150.3	150.9	151.4	151.9	152.2	152.5	152.5	152.9	153.2	153.7	153.6	153.5	152.4	2.5	2.8
1996	154.4	154.9	155.7	156.3	156.6	156.7	157.0	157.3	157.8	158.3	158.6	158.6	156.9	3.3	3.0
1997	159.1	159.6	160.0	160.2	160.1	160.3	160.5	160.8	161.2	161.6	161.5	161.3	160.5	1.7	2.3
1998	161.6	161.9	162.2	162.5	162.8	163.0	163.2	163.4	163.6	164.0	164.0	163.9	163.0	1.6	1.6
1999	164.3	164.5	165.0	166.2	166.2	166.2	166.7	167.1	167.9	168.2	168.3	168.3	166.6	2.7	2.2
2000	168.8	169.8	171.2	171.3	171.5	172.4	172.8	172.8	173.7	174.0	174.1	174.0	172.2	3.4	3.4
2001	175.1	175.8	176.2	176.9	177.7	178.0	177.5	177.5	178.3	177.7	177.4	176.7	177.1	1.6	2.8
2002	177.1	177.8	178.8	179.8	179.8	179.9	180.1	180.7	181.0	181.3	181.3	180.9	179.9	2.4	1.6
2003	181.7	183.1	184.2	183.8	183.5	183.7	183.9	184.6	185.2	185.0	184.5	184.3	184.0	1.9	2.3
2004	185.2	186.2	187.4	188.0	189.1	189.7	189.4	189.5	189.9	190.9	191.0	190.3	188.9	3.3	2.7
2005	190.7	191.8	193.3	194.6	194.4	194.5	195.4	196.4	198.8	199.2	197.6	196.8	195.3	3.4	3.4
2006	198.3	198.7	199.8	201.5	202.5	202.9	203.5	203.9	202.9	201.8	201.5	201.8	201.6	2.5	3.2

Source: Consumer Price Index, U.S. Department of Labor, Bureau of Labor Statistics, June 14, 2007, ftp://ftp.bls.gov/pub/special.requests/cpi/cpiai.txt.

want to perform this exercise, there is a February 20, 2008, version of this file, called cpiai.txt, on the disk.)

PDF Data

There are two kinds of PDF data. There are PDF graphics-only data and PDFs with underlying text data. Some PDF files are locked so that access to the underlying text data is inaccessible to the end user, although some off-brand PDF programs may ignore the locking mechanism. Whenever possible, the PDF program should be used to export the PDF text data to any permissible text format, where it can then be imported into Excel, if necessary. Under almost all circumstances, however, ABBYY PDF Transformer (a commercial product[1]) will extract the text data and a relatively high quality OCR of the graphics data and can save it as an Excel spreadsheet. It can also transform graphics-only text, which PDF programs may not be able to extract. If the files are huge, the conversion should be broken into parts.

Acrobat, beginning with version 4, offers "Column Select" and "Table Select" tools that make copying data simpler when there is underlying text. The availability of this option depends specifically on the precise nature of the Acrobat or Acrobat Reader software you may have. When you have the column select, and especially the table select option, it may be possible to copy an entire column or table to a spreadsheet without going through intermediate steps.

Exercise 5.   This exercise requires Adobe Acrobat Standard or Adobe Acrobat Professional. The precise process depends on the precise version you have (version 5 or higher, Standard or Professional). It will not work with PDF Reader, but it might work with alternative brands or PDF extractor programs.

There is a file provided labeled "censr-16-page-4.pdf." This is an extract from a report found at the U.S. Census Bureau site about the 2000 Census, Population and Housing, at www.census.gov/prod/cen2000/index.html. It is specifically a Census Special Report on "Areas With Concentrated Poverty." The download file URL is www.census.gov/prod/2005pubs/censr-16.pdf. Open the page 4 extract with Adobe Acrobat Standard or Professional. Using the Menus, save the file as text file, .txt. If given a choice, select Plain Text. From Excel, import the file using the procedure previously used for .csv and .txt files. You will find it necessary to delete the text-only material and to perform considerable reorganization. After some editing, most likely considerably less effort than keying the whole table from paper, you will have the table in the same organization within a spreadsheet.

If your software supports "Table Select," you can substantially reduce the effort using the "Table Select" feature. The image at the top of the next page shows the "Table Select" menu. First highlight the entire table and nothing else. Second, right click to call up the table select menu. Then click on "Copy

Poverty Thresholds (Annual Dollar Amounts) by Size of Family and Number of Related Children Under 18 Years Old: 1999

Size of family unit	Related children under 18 years								
	None	One	Two	Three	Four	Five	Six	Seven	Eight or more
One person (unrelated individual)									
Under 65 years	8,667								
65 years and over	7,								
Two people									
Householder under 65 years ..	11,								
Householder 65 years and over	10,								
Three people	13,								
Four people	17,			3,954					
Five people	20,			9,882	19,578				
Six people	23,			4,964	22,261	21,845			
Seven people	27,			6,595	25,828	24,934	23,953		
Eight people	30,			9,899	29,206	28,327	27,412	27,180	
Nine people or more	36,			6,169	35,489	34,554	33,708	33,499	32,208

Context menu (overlay):

Copy To Clipboard	Ctrl+C
Copy With Formatting	
Copy As Table	
Save As Table...	
Open Table in Spreadsheet	
Select All	Ctrl+A
Deselect All	Shift+Ctrl+A
Replace Text (Comment)	
Highlight Text (Comment)	
Add Note to Text (Comment)	
Underline Text (Comment)	
Cross Out Text (Comment)	
Add Bookmark	Ctrl+B
Create Link	

Source: U.S. Census Bureau, <www.ce...resh99.html>.

As Table" (to paste in a spreadsheet) or, for later versions such as this one, click on "Open Table in Spreadsheet."

If you have access to ABBYY PDF Transformer, you can directly import this table into an Excel spreadsheet. Results may still require some editing because, although PDF Transformer reads graphics and performs OCR transformation, it does not use any underlying text information. With this particular file, the authors found approximately equal amounts (but different kinds) of editing for the file with the two alternate text-oriented processes, but it was considerably less effort using the "copy as a table" process.

File Conversion

Briefly, SPSS, SAS, and many other programs are able to export files to either Excel format or to CSV format. Excel is able to import data from most databases (Access, Dbase, and others). For more sophisticated analysis, SPSS, SAS, and other powerful programs are able to import appropriately formatted data from Excel.[2]

Appropriate formatting strictly follows a proper database design, which is to make one record (row) for each observation unit and one variable (column) for each characteristic, while labeling each row with a variable name. It has been the authors' experience that SPSS does not respond well when the first data row (the first row following the labels) has any empty cell reflecting a missing value.

As with SPSS and SAS, these instructions assume that you will have other resources for developing skills for those purposes. These are instructions for getting data from those files into Excel for the kind of analysis typically performed in budgeting.

EXERCISE 6. There is a supplied file, Earmark.mdb (an Access Database file). It is paired with another file, Earmark.dbf (a Dbase file, that is used, in this case, by Access). This exercise requires first opening Earmark.mdb with Microsoft Access and using the tables feature, updating the location of Earmark.dbf to the location on your computer. Using Excel, use the open menus to open files of ALL TYPES. Find the file "Earmark.mdb" or "Earmark" with an Access database icon. Open it. A menu item will ask you whether you want to open the query to external data. Click "Yes." The result should be two columns. The first column is a list of entities who were reported as receiving earmarks in the database as downloaded from an Office of Management and Budget site, http://earmarks.omb.gov/download.html, on June 14, 2007. (This database was actually in a more user-friendly format and was converted to first a Dbase database and then an Access Query to create this exercise.) The second column is the reported total amount of earmarks that the recipient received.

Note that Excel can import entire Dbase or Access tables or it can import query results. Queries are used to summarize one or several columns keyed to some other column or columns. Where the Dbase or Access tables are small, it may be more effective to import the entire table. Where they are large, it is more likely that a query should be used as the first step to reduce the size of the file to be imported into Excel. If Access query functions are inadequate, another approach is to import the database into more powerful analysis software such as SPSS, SAS, or STATA and perform analysis there.

Data Require Collecting or Editing

The next set of data problems that can arise is not about access to the data, but they are problems with the data themselves:

- You might collect the data in pieces and have to build records.
- You might have multiple sources of data that are similar but with significant differences without a clear indication of which is more reliable.
- The data records may be missing data or may have uninterpretable values.
- The data records may have values that are extraordinary and improbable, but not subject to validation.

Data from Multiple Sources

A typical problem for practitioners is that before you can analyze your records you must construct your records. This does not mean that you must make observations and collect primary data. Instead, the observation units may be the frequent subject of reports, but the reports may be spread around to different locations.

For example, if you are interested in the population of your jurisdiction and other jurisdictions in your state, you will find data on the Web site of the U.S. Census Bureau. You may be interested in the local Consumer Price Index (CPI), which you will find on the Web site of the Bureau of Labor Statistics. You might be interested in median home values, which is information you can find from your own real estate appraisal office and, for other jurisdictions, possibly from a statewide report. We can go on adding variables of interest, but the point is that the data are not especially difficult to obtain, but they may not exist in a pre-existing data set.

There can, however, be difficulties with such data, and these difficulties may be subtle. One of the difficulties has to do with careful attention to observation units. The observation unit may vary from data source to data source, or even from variable to variable with the same data source.

For example, for the population, the Census Bureau can give you the actual population for the most recent census year, an estimate for the prior year, and a forecast for the current and future years. The population can be for the jurisdiction or for a smaller area known as a census block. The CPI, on the other hand, is available at the state level and for metropolitan statistical areas, which are usually multijurisdictional. A careful review of CPI material also reveals the frequent use of the word "urban." Non-urban jurisdictions are not represented in the data.

Thus, one way that observation units can vary is that the locale itself can vary from one data source to another. In some instances there may be at least a small leap of faith in believing that the data represent the locale at all. The user must be thoughtful in determining how this variation in observation unit impacts any analysis that may be conducted.

The second substantial source of variation is time. For example, a jurisdiction may have a July through June fiscal year and report all of its data consistent with this time period. If that jurisdiction is in Texas, the state fiscal year is September through August; or if it is in New York, the state fiscal year is April through March. State data will be reported consistent with that time period. The federal government and some other states have an October through September fiscal year and usually report data consistent with that time period. Some data are reported according to the calendar year. Thus, when data are reported as 2010 data, one must ask: Which 2010? Is it 2010 ending in April, June, August, September, December, or some other date? Treating data ending in periods far enough apart as parallel can confound some sorts of analyses. It may be necessary to make an adjustment. For example, if state data end in June and federal data end in September, it may be necessary to adjust the federal data by moving a quarter of each year's data forward to the next year.

The third substantial source of variation is the variation among the sources themselves. This problem is a bit tricky. The difficulty is that different information sources might be of different reliabilities and, thus, not agree with each other. Estimates of the number of homeless in U.S. cities differ by a factor of 100 among different sources. Typically, but not always, any official government statistic or estimate is likely to be less biased than estimates provided by advocacy or taxpayer groups.

Here are a few guidelines that are somewhat helpful:

- When possible, examine methodology descriptions to know exactly what published data are supposed to communicate.

- Prefer data supplied with supporting methodology descriptions to data supplied without.

- Prefer official government data unless you have specific reasons to be suspicious.

- When you have several competing sources of data and no clear reason to prefer one to another, average them. There is considerable evidence that averages of certain kinds of forecasts are less inaccurate (in the aggregate) than any specific forecast regardless of reason.

EXERCISE 7.   This exercise requires visiting several Web sites, so it is a bit complicated. The first site is the U.S. Census Bureau at www.census.gov/ Press-Release/www/2002/demoprofiles.html. The Census Bureau has been known to reorganize its Web site, so an example data set (for the state of Virginia) has been downloaded to the supporting disk; details are at the end of the exercise.

- At the Census Bureau Web site, click on the link for All Files beside the heading FTP Download (the direct URL to this location is www2.census. gov/census_2000/datasets/100_and_sample_profile/). Click on a selected state. This might be your state of origin in the United States, or, if you are not in the United States, a point of entry that you might use, or a state designated by your instructor.

1. Download two files.
   - The first file is labeled "2kh[##].pdf," where [##] stands for two digits. In the case of Virginia, it is 2kh51.pdf (on your disk); for New York, it is 2kh36.pdf.
   - The second file is labeled "ProfileData[ST].ZIP," where [ST] is replaced by a state abbreviation, such as OH for Ohio or VA for Virginia (on your disk it is ProfileDataVA.ZIP). You need the PDF file to inter-

pret the .csv files found inside the .zip file. Microsoft XP or higher should open the .zip file without a supplemental program. Inside the .zip file, there are four .csv files.

2. Import into Excel the one labeled "2kh[##].csv" (without a supplemental numeral at the end of the file name). Depending on your computer conditions, you may first have to extract the .zip file into a non-zip directory.

3. With the PDF file as a guide, locate the column that contains the community identifiers (names of jurisdictions) and the overall population of those jurisdictions in the 2000 census.

4. Save the file as a .xls; then (a) delete all other columns, (b) insert a row at the top of the file to column headings for the two columns that remain, and (c) provide brief headings for these two columns. Suggested headings are "Locality" and "Population." Finally, save the file again. The purpose of the first save, with the alternate file name, was to avoid damaging the original file if you needed to go back and use it again.

The second Web site to visit provides a list of metropolitan and micropolitan statistical areas (MSAs): www.census.gov/population/www/estimates/metrodef.html. The Census Bureau has a .txt version of this file at www.census.gov/population/estimates/metro-city/99mfips.txt (this version is also included on the CD and is labeled "99mfips.txt"), and a variety of Excel, PDF, and CSV files containing MSA information can be found at www.census.gov/population/www/cen2000/phc-t29.html. In addition, many other reliable Internet sites list MSAs. The current Census Bureau list at time of publication is on the disk as cbsa-01-fmt.csv and as CBSA03_MSA99.xls. For your chosen state, identify every locality that is in an MSA.

The third Web site is the Census Bureau's statistical abstract on consumer prices at www.census.gov/compendia/statab/2006/prices/consumer_price_indexes_cost_of_living_index/. The table listed as "Table 709. Cost of Living Index—Selected Metropolitan Areas" shows the relative cost of living of different communities. (This is a list of selected communities. A commercial product that is more complete is sold by the Council for Community and Economic Research, www.c2er.org/.) For the identified MSAs in your selected state, key the index number by all the localities within the MSA. For all other communities, average the value 100 and the value of the nearest MSA to produce an estimate. If no locality in your state is as high as 100, then for other localities average the two nearest MSAs.

For the sake of simplicity, this assignment stops here. The objective is to experience the search, download, and organize activities of collecting data from relatively friendly secondary data sources. Actual use of secondary data may be easier or considerably more difficult.

Data Require Editing or Imputation

When observation values are missing, uninterpretable, or improbable, the data may require editing or imputation.

If the values are missing or uninterpretable and there are numerous observations, then the substantial risk that one experiences is that the missing values may incidentally lead to a bias in any subsequent analysis. How does a bias arise?

First, the missing values themselves may be relatively inconsequential. However, during analysis with software such as SPSS the variable may seem somewhat interesting. The reason the value is missing for some observations may result from a biasing characteristic of the data. For example, people with other specific characteristics may decline to respond to ethnicity queries, thus leading to a missing or missing equivalent value in an ethnicity variable, and the ethnicity variable may be thought to be interesting to the analysis. If this variable is introduced into the analysis, it would have the effect of biasing the analysis. The reason will be that almost all software solves the missing-data problem by excluding records that have missing values.

Thus, one must be very sensitive to the effect of including variables with missing values on statistics of interest in other variables in the analysis. The first step is to watch the impact on the number of observations. If, with the introduction of a new variable, the number of observations that are included changes, the variable has missing values in records that did not have missing values prior to the introduction of the variable. Consequently, the analyst should determine the conditional mean and standard deviation of all the other variables, considering only those records that are included in the analysis with whole records after the introduction of the new variable, and compare them with the same two statistics before all whole records before the introduction of the new variable.

If there are any substantial changes in values, these changes, not the increased analytic effect of the additional variable, likely explain any changes in the analysis. In this case, remedial action must be taken. Remedial action may be to exclude the variable that introduces the bias. There are additional remedies as well:

- The best thing to do for missing values is to find the actual value and replace the missing value. In most cases, however, this is not possible.

- When data occur in a time series, the missing value can be interpolated through one of these processes:

  - If the data are not seasonal, the several observations before and after can be averaged, with the result substituted for the missing value. If the data show little randomness (move around very little), it is probably enough to average one observation each before and after. If there is a lot of randomness, it is probably best to include two or three observations from each period, before and after.

- If the data are seasonal (move in an obvious annual pattern), the same averaging approach can be used, but the observations should be taken from the year before and the year after.

EXERCISE 8. In the "Exercises Appendix B" spreadsheet, look at the tab labeled "Time Series." Interpolate the missing observation using the recommended method.

With **cross-sectional data,** the missing value can be interpolated through one of three approaches. The most reliable way is to find other variables in the data set that correlate with the variable that has missing values and build a regression or other correlation-based model to predict the value for those records where the value is missing. Substitute the model prediction for the missing values.

The next best method is to choose, based on at least quasi-expert opinion, five to ten other key variables in the data set, then match the observation with other observations using the missing value with these other variables. Using the matched records, do one of the following:

- Calculate the mean of the variable with the missing value and use it as a substitute,

- Use some other value such as the mode or median (particularly relevant for categorical or ordinal data), or

- Randomly choose a value (using random numbers, not haphazard methods) from among actual values observed.

If, for whatever reason, these methods are not available or fail (for example, no correlates and no matches), use one of the following:

- The mean of the variable,

- Some other value such as the mode or median, or

- A randomly chosen value from among values actually observed.

EXERCISE 9. There is a tab in the "Exercises Appendix B" spreadsheet labeled "Federal Data." Find at least two ways to interpolate the data.

Values Are Improbable

Sometimes the problem is not that the data are missing or uninterpretable, but the value itself causes concern. In this case, you might suspect that the value is an **outlier,** that it is an extreme value with respect to the other values.

One should keep in mind that, by definition, three standard deviations around the mean contain 99 percent of a data set, so with 100 observations, one should be outside three standard deviations. With a small data set, having a value outside three standard deviations from the mean is evidence on the face of it that it is an outlier. With a larger data set, the value should be substantially outside three standard deviations from the mean to be an outlier.

The correction for an outlier is to move it to three standard deviations from the mean on the same side of the mean as it already is. For time series, it should be moved to three standard deviations from a relatively short, for example, twelve or twenty-four period, moving average.

EXERCISE 10.   On the tab labeled "Federal Data" in the "Exercises Appendix B" file, the District of Columbia observations appear unusual. Determine whether each is an outlier. If so, determine the appropriate replacement value.

Sensitivity Analysis

When your data set has interpolated values (or any random values are used) and there several ways to interpolate the data, largely with cross-sectional data, it is likely worthwhile to make several alternative interpolated data sets and to conduct the same analysis with each set to determine the effect of the interpolation. When an outlier has been corrected, an alternative scenario can be tested without the outlier correction.

The use of multiple options or scenarios is called a **sensitivity analysis.** The purpose is to determine how much the final result you have is dependent on the specific choices you made during the process of analysis.

EXERCISE 11.   In the "Exercises Appendix B" file, for each of the four variables in the tab labeled "Federal Data," determine the average value for each alternative value used (missing value not changed, each interpolated value, both with and without any substitutions for outliers).

Data Definitions Change

You may know, or suspect, that the definitions of the variables have changed at specific points in time, or gradually over time, or at some time in the past although you are not sure when.

One of the more difficult problems with data is that the meaning associated with the data elements (variables) can change over time. For example, a jurisdiction may consolidate or lose territory as other jurisdictions are formed. Carelessness may incorrectly lead to the impression that associated characteristics—for example, area or taxable real property—do not substantially change when in fact they do.

There are many ways this problem may occur, and for long running data series it may be more common than the alternative, that there is no change in data definitions. It may take subtle attention to your data series to discover such changes. Following are some examples that may contribute to changing data definitions.

A series may be an aggregate of many smaller series. Over time, the smaller series may have additions and removals, thereby changing the definition of the data. For example, public employees operating ambulance and ambulance-like services may be moved from the public safety category to the public health category of a budget report. Consequently, the growth in public safety will be understated and the growth in public health will be overstated. The corrective action is to identify the employees and associated expenditures for the periods prior to the shift and adjust the amounts back to the beginning of the data series, thereby correcting the basis of the reporting.

An actual similar case the authors experienced involved Medicaid payments to physicians. During the early 1990s the federally based coding system for physician services was substantially changed. Consequently, physicians were forced to choose new codes for services they had long performed. These new codes led to "up coding," where physicians chose the higher paid of two codes in many instances where there was a choice. Consequently, following the change in the coding system, Medicaid expenditures were substantially higher than before the change. The underlying dynamic was a redefinition of the services that led to changing expenditures.

Another way a definition can change results is from deliberate change of the whole series definition at a point in time. The telltale sign of this sort of change is an abrupt change in the quantities associated with the series. Public policy changes sometimes have the effect of such abrupt changes by adding new people to service groups or adding new services for people in service groups. Well-documented time series may record these punctuated shifts.

A third way that a definition can change over time is from gradual definition shift. This sort of change may be the most difficult to discover. Gradual shift may result, for example, when data definitions are poorly documented at the beginning of data entry and updated with practice itself or as staff or management changes. Gradual shifts may be very difficult to discover.

EXERCISE 12. In the "Exercises Appendix B" file, on the tabbed sheet labeled "Terrorist," identify the year or years when the data may have experienced definition changes.

Analyzed Data Are the Only Data Available

You may receive previously analyzed data when you would prefer to have the records that were used to produce those analyses.

Perhaps the most frustrating data problem is to find the information you want, but not quite. You may be looking for information on people of a certain demographic, perhaps by gender, age, or economic strata. But what you find is a report that has more general information on a larger population. It includes the data you want, but also other people as well. The same result can arise with undesired service units, undesired service locations, or any other excess individual observation units.

What you, as the analyst, would like is the data set upon which the report you have found is based, along with an assurance that there is a variable that records the distinguishing characteristic you are interested in. Your first option might be to go to the source of the report and ask for just that. Often, however, pursuit of that option will be unsuccessful. What else can you do?

Rather than less analysis, what the report now needs is more analysis. Typically, what this additional analysis involves is **ratios** (also called proportions or percentages). It is likely that the ratio or ratios will come from other sources than the report you already have in hand. Using the ratios, you break down the information in the report to find the part you are interested in.

The ratio-breakdown method may be inexact and lead to substantial errors. Thus, it may be useful to also apply a sensitivity analysis. Alternative scenarios can be made by shifting ratios a tenth of their own size.

EXERCISE 13. In the "Exercises Appendix B" file, using only the information on the tab labeled "Federal Debt," find the gross domestic product for all years listed. Is a sensitivity analysis needed? Why or why not?

Sometimes pre-analyzed data are perfectly acceptable except for one difficulty. For whatever reason, the organization of the information as presented in the original report obscures the information you are looking for. Following is a very simple example: You may have a report that has two simple tables. The first table shows the number of children (under age nineteen) who are receiving a service and the percentage who are female. The second table shows the number of adults receiving a service and the percentage who are male. See the following example tables:

Children under the Age of Nineteen Who Are Receiving a Service	
Hypothetical Service: Children	
Children	250
Female (%)	46

Adults Who Are Receiving a Service	
Hypothetical Service: Adults	
Adult	400
Male (%)	35

You may be tasked to determine, among males, what proportion are children. These two tables contain the information, but you must analyze the data to find it.

First, you take the table about children and multiply 250 * 0.46, then subtract the result from 250. The result is

$$250 - (250 * 0.46) = 250 - 115 = 135 \qquad [1]$$

This is the number of male children served. Next, you multiply 400 * 0.35 to get

$$400 * 0.35 = 140 \qquad [2]$$

This is the number of adults served. Then you add the two results to get 275, which is the number of males served. Dividing 135 by 275 results in

$$135 / 275 = 0.490909 \approx 49.1 \text{ percent} \qquad [3]$$

So, the information was there, it simply had to be teased out.

EXERCISE 14.

1. For the hypothetical information given in Exercise 13, find the proportion of female children to all females.

2. For the hypothetical information given in Exercise 13, find the proportion of males for both children and adults together.

Where Can You Find Data?

You might be confident that there are relevant secondary data, but you do not know where to look for the data. There is no comprehensive solution to the problem of not knowing where to look for data. Following are some Web sites and strategies.

Federal Government Data

The most comprehensive source of federal government data is www.fedstats.gov. This site is intended to be a reference site for other federal government data sites. It is, however, aimed at the popular consumer. So, if you know what you are looking for, it is easier to go to the source site more directly.

Federal data related to budgeting may be found at www.census.gov (census data), www.bls.gov (consumer and producer price indexes), www.bea.gov (various economic data), and www.whitehouse.gov/omb (particularly official **discount rates** for present value calculations, but also other miscellaneous OMB publications and information). Other federal government sources are too numerous to list, but one that may not be apparent is the Central Intelligence Agency's *World Factbook* at https://www.cia.gov/library/publications/the-world-factbook/index.html.

State and Local Data

States generally post great quantities of data at their Web sites, which are generally found by www.[ST].gov, or www.state.[ST].us. For example, www.NY.gov gets the New York state Web site, while www.state.VA.us gets the Virginia Web site. State Web sites are too diverse to document here. The best approach is to begin at the top level Web site and use the menus to explore for the data you are looking for.

The official Web site format for local governments follows one of these formats www.ci.[CITY].[ST].us, or www.co.[COUNTY].[ST].us, or www.town.[TOWN].[ST].us. Some school systems use www.[CITY/COUNTY].k12.[ST].us. However, this practice is not universal, and there is much duplication in school district names, so the user will have to discover the particular practice within a particular state. Often local jurisdictions will register other domain names that end in .org or .gov.

Data access and availability are highly variable at the local government level. When looking for local government data, however, one should not omit looking at state or even federal sources. A good state source is the particular local government commission. A good federal source is the Census Bureau. Almost all federal agencies collect and widely publish data, so for particular kinds of questions, one should examine the Web sites of the relevant agencies. Often federal agencies publish contact information for requests for more extensive data.

Quasi-Private Sources of Data

Some of the more important sources of data on state government include:

National Governors Association, www.NGA.org

National Conference of State Legislatures, www.NCSL.org

National Association of State Budget Officers, www.NASBO.org

Some of the more important sources of data on local government include:

Government Finance Officers Association, www.GFOA.org

International City/County Management Association, www.ICMA.org

National Association of Counties, www.NACO.org

National Association of County Collectors, Treasurers, and Finance Officers, http://nacctfo.org/

Other Sources of Data

Governmental Accounting Standards Board, www.GASB.org. This site contains little data, but it is worthwhile to know about. It contains a subordinate page, www.seagov.org/index.shtml, which lists numerous performance measurement links. Some of these may contain data.

These are, of necessity, only partial listings with emphasis on sources that may have financial information. The ICMA and the GASB listings are of special interest as they may contain particular comparative information for performance measurement data or other useful material on performance budgeting implementation.

Notes

1. The authors are aware of no other similar product, although such products may exist.
2. Stat/Transfer can make conversions across many statistical, spreadsheet, and database platforms almost instantly. For more information, please see www.stattransfer.com/.

Appendix C

Spreadsheeting Basics

The objective of this appendix is to prepare students to use spreadsheets in budgeting. It is divided into two parts. The first part is for those people who have never used a spreadsheet or who have little understanding of what a spreadsheet is or does. The second part reviews some principles for using spreadsheets that maximize the usefulness of spreadsheets.

APPENDIX C, TABLE 1
Appearance of Excel in Office 2000, 2003, or XP

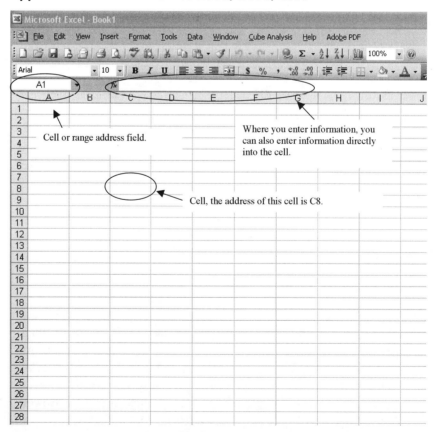

APPENDIX C, TABLE 2
Appearance of Excel in 2007

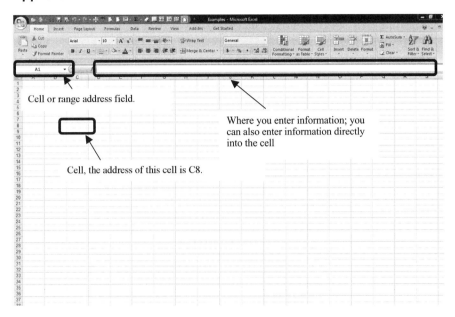

Cell or range address field.

Where you enter information; you can also enter information directly into the cell

Cell, the address of this cell is C8.

Principles for Use of Spreadsheets

A spreadsheet is a matrix or grid of mathematical cells. Each cell can contain a number or a formula (expression).

Cells

The basic unit of a spreadsheet is a cell. A spreadsheet is a matrix of cells that are in columns and rows. Each cell can:

- Contain information that is either text or numbers,

- Contain a reference to another cell or cells, and

- Contain a formula that may contain a reference to other cells.

WHERE THE ACTION IS. When you open your new empty Excel spreadsheet, you will see near the top of the spreadsheet screen a row that contains a white area with "A1" followed by, in most cases, a blue area ending in fx. After this is an empty white area that extends to the right end of the spreadsheet. Whatever is entered into a spreadsheet cell will appear in this area. By placing the cursor in this area, you can begin entering data in the cell. However, you can also enter your data and formulas directly into cells.

A cell may be "selected" by placing your pointer over it and clicking.

Excel has a default setting such that when you press enter, cell selection moves to the cell beneath the cell previously selected.

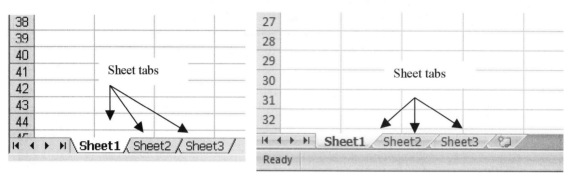

Earlier versions on left, Excel 2007 on right.

CELL ADDRESSES—ABSOLUTE AND RELATIVE. A formula refers to other cells by an "address," which is a label that is unique for a combination of column and row. In more complex spreadsheet "workbooks," the labeling can refer to tabbed-sheet, column, and row. In Excel, the column is specified by a letter from A to Z, then AA to AZ, and so forth until, IA to IV. This allows a total of 256 columns. Rows are specified by numbers from 1 to 65536. For Excel 2007 the highest column label is XFD (16,384 columns) and the highest row number is 1,048,576. A typical address would be "A1" (do not include the quote marks). By default, tabbed sheets are labeled Sheet1, Sheet2, and so forth. A typical address including the sheet label would be "Sheet1!A1."

Sheets can be renamed by right clicking on the sheet name and following the menu or by double clicking on the sheet name. Columns and rows cannot be renamed (very advanced users may find other ways of referring to them). When a sheet name has an empty space within it such as "Sheet One" it must be contained in SINGLE quotes when used, such as 'Sheet One'!A1.

While referring to a cell on the same sheet, you can omit the sheet label; however, it must be included when referring to a cell from another sheet.

Because one of the more flexible characteristics of spreadsheets is the copying of formulas, there is a feature that allows a distinction between an absolute cell address and a relative cell address. This distinction involves what happens when you copy a formula in a cell. When a cell address is absolute, the copied formula will contain the same cell address when it is later pasted in another cell. When it contains a relative cell address, it will refer to a cell in the same relative position when it is later pasted in another cell.

An address of the form A1 is a relative address. It is converted to an absolute address by placing a "$" symbol, sometimes called an anchor, in front of both the column and row addresses to become $A$1. There are also two intermediate or partial absolute cell addresses $A1 and A$1. These refer, respectively, to an absolute column location but a relative row location; and an absolute row but a relative column location.

All tabbed sheet addresses are absolute addresses.

C1			▼		fx	=A1

	A	B	C	D	
1	1		1		
2			1		
3			1		
4			1		
5					

This is a relative address. If you copy the entry in C1 to D1 or to C5, the result will be zero (0) because there is nothing in cell B1 or A5.

C2			▼		fx	=$A$1

	A	B	C	D	
1	1		1		
2			1		
3			1		
4			1		

This is an absolute address. You can copy it anywhere and it will still return the value in A1.

C3			▼		fx	=$A1

	A	B	C	D	
1	1		1		
2			1		
3			1		
4			1		
5					

This address is absolute with respect to column but not row. You can copy it to D1 and still receive the results from A1; however, if you copy it to C5, it will return zero (0).

189

C4	▼	f_x	=A$1

	A	B	C	D
1	1		1	
2			1	
3			1	
4			1	

This address is absolute with respect to row, but not column. You can copy it to C5 or any other row in column C and it will return the value from A1, but if you copy it to column D it will return zero (0).

C1	▼	f_x	=Sheet1!A1

	A	B	C	D	E
1			1		
2					
3					

This is a sheet label in an address. By including the sheet label, you can carry information from one sheet to another. The sheet label is always "absolute," although the rest of the address still follows the same rules as with the above for cases.

F1	▼	f_x	='Sheet One'!A1

	D	E	F	G	H
1			1		
2					
3					

This is a sheet label with a space in the middle of the label. Because of the space in the label, the label name is contained in single quote marks in the address.

USE OF THE EQUAL SIGN.   The equal sign, "=," is used in a spreadsheet for two purposes.

The most common use in Excel (and other products) is to distinguish a cell that refers to another cell or contains a formula from a cell that contains information. The equal sign means the cell refers to another cell or contains a formula.

When the first entry in the cell is an equal mark, the spreadsheet will interpret the cell contents as a formula.

If the formula is simply a cell address, the spreadsheet will return the content of the cell at the address in the cell containing the cell address.

If the formula is valid in the language of the spreadsheet, the spreadsheet will return the results of the formula.

The benefit of a spreadsheet is that the formula can combine mathematical operations with cell addresses, allowing operations to be broken down into tables that are easy to follow or update.

If the equal sign in a formula is found somewhere besides the beginning, it is a "logical operator," which is a term used in advanced spreadsheeting. If you are new to spreadsheeting, this is not the time to begin using this function.

The equal sign can be used along with sheet and cell address in combination to carry information from one tabbed page of a spreadsheet to another. Remember, if the formula is simply a cell address (or long address, including sheet) the returned information is the content of the cell address. Information produced on separate pages can be collected together with a simple equal-sign formula.

Mathematics in Spreadsheets

SYMBOLS.   Excel and most other spreadsheets recognize typical math symbols. These include the "+," "–," and "/" for add, subtract, and divide. Multiplication is symbolized with "*" to avoid confusion with the text "x."

C1			f_x	=A1+B1
	A	B	C	D	E
1	4	5	9		
2					

C5			f_x	=C3-C4
	A	B	C	D	
1					
2					
3			9		
4			7		
5			2		

FORMULAS.   A basic formula will be thus:

=A1+B1 or =C3–C4

Formulas can mix numbers and cell addresses, but we strongly advise against this practice.

Formulas can extend beyond one function and two cell addresses. If you are familiar with algebra, you will know that there are rules for how multiple actions will occur in a chain of mathematical processes, such as an addition followed by a subtraction, or two subtractions in a row. However, if you do not know or prefer a different order, you can take control through the use of parentheses. Parentheses must be used in pairs. The math rule for parentheses is simple: anything inside a pair of parentheses *must* be processed before anything outside the parentheses is processed. You do not have to worry about doing this. The spreadsheet will do it. What you need to do is used the parentheses to tell the spreadsheet to do it.

In spreadsheets, negative numbers entered in formulas should be entered inside parentheses.

B11	▼		*fx*	=SUM(B5:B10)
A	B	C	D	E
1				
2				
3				
4	15			
5	78			
6	23			
7	60			
8	42			
9	12			
10	31			
11	246			
12				

SUMMATION.   Almost all spreadsheet users use some functions. Here we learn a very basic one. It is called summation, or sum for short.

The formula for sum looks like this:

$$=SUM(B5:B10)$$

It can also look like this:

$$=SUM(Sheet1:B5:B10)$$

Any part of any cell address can have an absolute symbol. $B$5:$B$10, or $B5:B$10, or anything else. There are many options, and more turn out to be useful than the new user might think.

The formula has the same effect as

$$=B5+B6+B7+B8+B9+B10$$

It is more useful for several reasons, not all of which are discussed here. The most obvious one is that it takes less effort to write, especially as the number of cells gets larger.

B22			f_x	=SUM(B4:B10,B15:B20)	
A	B	C	D	E	F
1					
2					
3					
4	15				
5	78				
6	23				
7	60				
8	42				
9	12				
10	31				
11					
12					
13					
14					
15	45				
16	60				
17	97				
18	15				
19	38				
20	15				
21					
22	531				
23					

For your later use, we are going to learn that the part inside the parentheses is called an argument. Summation has a minimum of one argument, which, for summation, is a range such as B5:B10. The range of cells can be broken by a comma, such as (B5:B10,B15:B20), in which case there is more than one argument.

Point and Click

Spreadsheet development can be made much easier through use of point-and-click technology and the use of automated icons on the spreadsheet toolbar.

Point and click generally refers to using the mouse, roller ball, or other pointing device to identify some part of spreadsheet during development.

Two point-and-click features help ease spreadsheet development.

POINTING TO CELLS. Often when writing a formula, the cell of interest is off the screen or the cell address is long and cumbersome. With spreadsheets, the solution to this problem is to enter the mathematical operator of interest; then, using the pointer, locate the cell of interest and press the "Enter" key or the next formula operator. The spreadsheet will "capture" the cell address of the pointer and enter it into the formula for the user.

When you have completed the formula, you can edit the formula to add absolute cell address symbols as you might need. Edit the formula by selecting the cell and placing your cursor at the desired location in the formula area at the top of the screen.

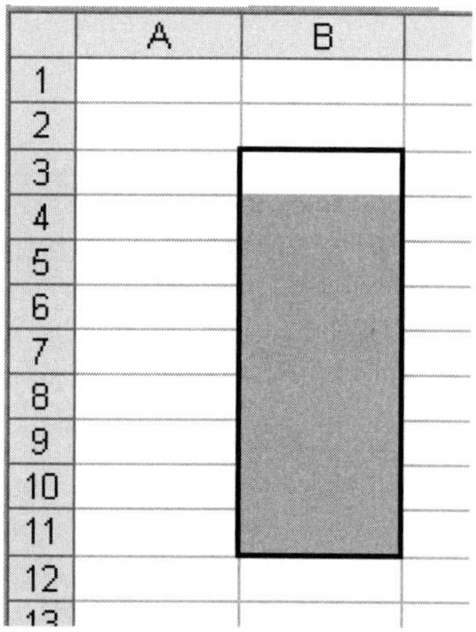

	A	B	
1			
2			
3			
4			
5			
6			
7			
8			
9			
10			
11			
12			
13			

HIGHLIGHTING CELLS. Functions and some other features often use a group of adjacent cells. Adjacent cells can be selected in a group by highlighting them. In the graphic, cells B3 through B11 are highlighted. Begin your function by typing the part of the formula from the equal sign to the open parenthesis. The only function we know at the moment is sum, so type

=SUM(

After typing this, use the pointer to find the first cell in the group to be summed. Click on it, and hold the pointer button down while scrolling to the last cell in the group. At this point release the button and type the closing parenthesis or just press enter.

Toolbars

For Users of Office 2000, Office 2003, and Office XP.

The toolbar is a row of icons (graphic symbols) usually located near the top of the spreadsheet. These icons are shortcuts for many features. Although you will need to learn these features as you progress, we will learn one now, together.

This icon is the capital Greek letter sigma that looks like this "Σ". This icon is a shortcut for the summation function. If you select the cell at the bottom of a column of adjacent numbers that are to be summed, then press the icon, you will find that the spreadsheet automatically enters a summation formula stretching to the top of the adjacent cells in the column. If you have effectively organized your data, all you have to do is press enter.

The function will also work for a row of adjacent cells. When there is a conflict (both row and column) the spreadsheet will select the column.

As you learn other spreadsheet functions, you can explore toolbar icons that might accelerate your development.

Quick Access Bar and Ribbon for Users of Excel 2007

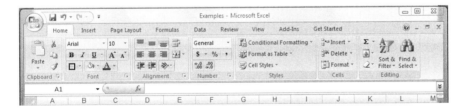

What was found on the toolbar in earlier versions of Excel is likely found on the "ribbon" in Excel 2007. The "ribbon" is an extensive menu of actions that can be carried out with the use of a mixture of icons and other graphic interface devices.

Different subsets of functions are found with the tabs at the top.

A vestigial toolbar, , is provided at the very top and is relabeled the "quick access bar." You can add icon shortcuts to the quick access bar as with older versions of Excel; however, the user is limited to one quick access bar. The bar can be repositioned below the ribbon if the user so prefers.

The Microsoft Office symbol, 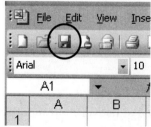, is a button that calls upon a drop-down menu to save or open files, see the most recently used files, print files, and take other common actions as shown in the next graphic.

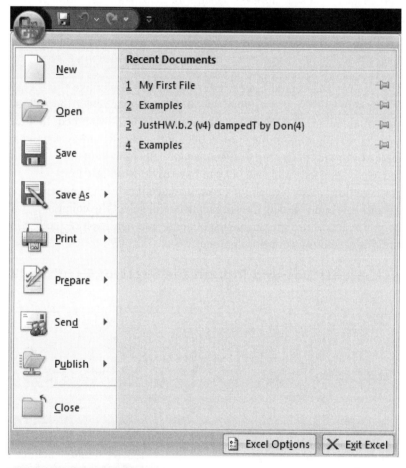

SAVING YOUR FILE. To save your file in Office 2000, Office 2003, and Office XP, begin by clicking on the disk icon at the top of your screen. For a previously unsaved file, the result should be the opening of a window that looks like the next graphic

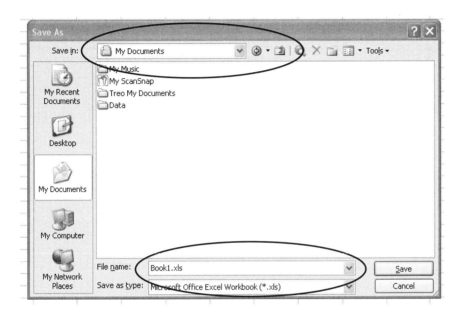

You can use the drop-down menu and icons at the top of the screen to change the location where the file will be saved. The default location is "My Documents," which is easy to access from your windows desktop.

You can use the box near the bottom of the screen to provide a name to your file. The default name is Book1.xls. Some settings on Windows may hide the .xls part.

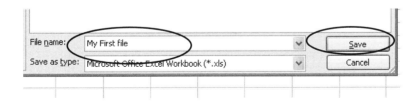

Supply a file name and click the "Save" button.

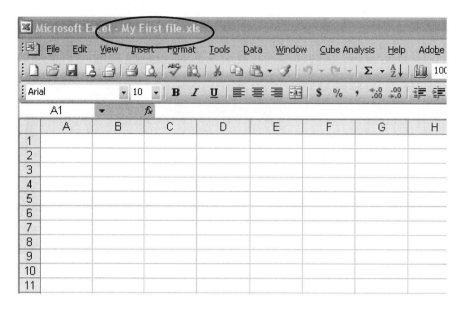

Your file name should now appear at the top of the screen.

You can now close your file by clicking on the "X" as shown in the graphic.

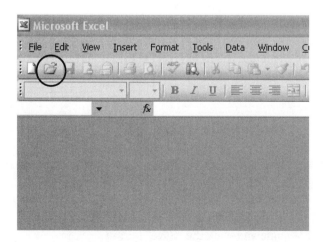

Next, click on the file-open icon.

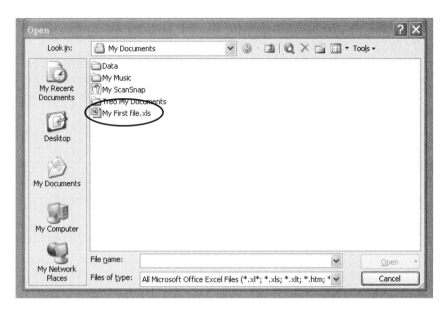

Your file is now in the list. Double click on it, and it opens.

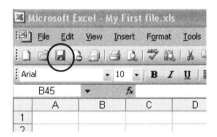

As you make updates to the file, it is a good idea to periodically click on the file-save button to make sure your saved file is consistent with the file as you have modified it. Although Excel saves a backup copy on a periodic schedule, your best protection against error is a current copy you have saved yourself.

To save your file in Excel 2007, click the icon in the quick access bar.

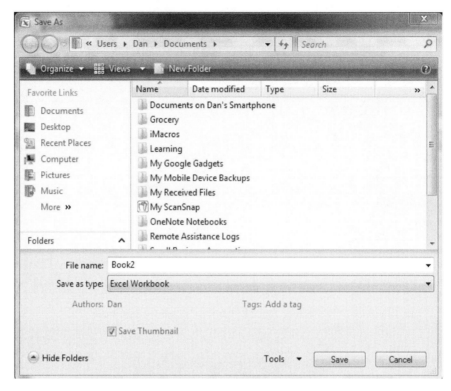

As a result you should receive a screen that looks somewhat like this. (Actual entries depend on your Windows operating system and your actual directory entries. This window reflects Windows Vista.)

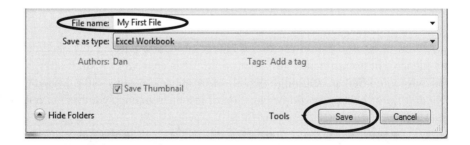

Supply a file name and click save.

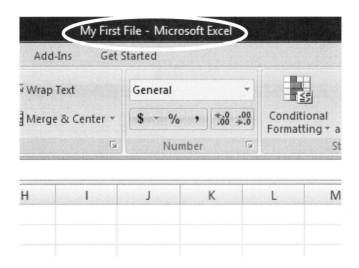

The file is now named and saved.

You can now close your file by clicking on the "X" as shown in the graphic.

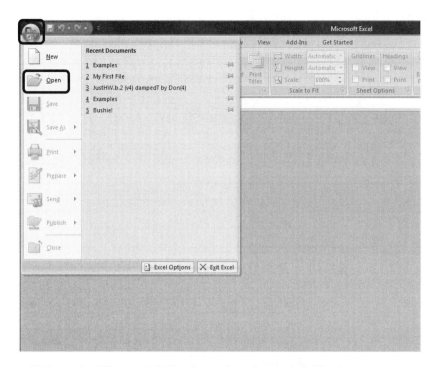

Click on the Microsoft Office icon, then the open-folder icon.

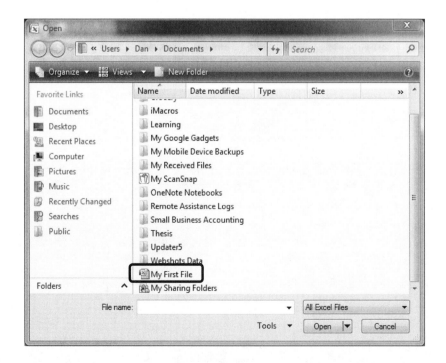

Your file is now in the list. Double click on it, and it opens. Note that if your operating system is Windows 2000 or Windows XP, some parts of the open dialog may look like the open dialog in earlier versions of Microsoft Office.

Although Excel auto-saves files every ten minutes, it may be a good idea to click on the ⬛ icon after making any important file change.

Printing your file. Excel defaults to printing all areas that are in use or have been used at some time by the user. It also prints in a generally unformatted, unfriendly manner. To change this default, the user must actively set print areas and organize print layout.

	A	B	C
1			
2			
3			
4		15	
5		78	
6		23	
7		60	
8		42	
9		12	
10		31	
11		246	
12			
13			
14			
15		45	
16		60	
17		97	
18		15	
19		38	
20		15	
21		270	
22			
23		531	
24			

Returning to Sheet1, we first highlight the area we want to print. Then we click on File and follow the menu to Print Area and Set Print Area.

Excel 2003 or earlier

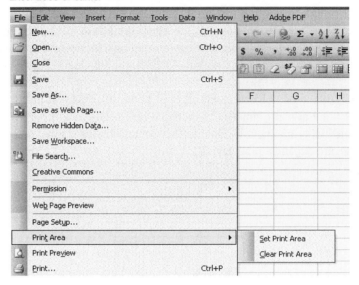

Excel 2007

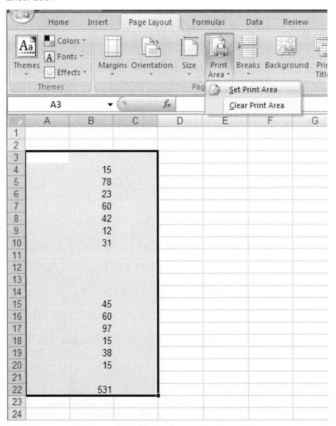

In Excel 2007, the procedure, after highlighting, is to select the "Page Layout" tab in the ribbon, and then select the print area graphic on the "Page Layout" tab. From there, select the option to set print area.

Excel now shows that we have successfully set the print area by showing Print_Area in the range name for the still-selected area and by outlining the print area with a dotted line.

Print_Area	▼	f_x	
	A	B	C
1			
2			
3			
4		15	
5		78	
6		23	
7		60	
8		42	
9		12	
10		31	
11		246	
12			
13			
14			
15		45	
16		60	
17		97	
18		15	
19		38	
20		15	
21		270	
22			
23		531	

For older versions of Office, if you do not want to adjust the print layout, you can then click ▱ to print the print area.

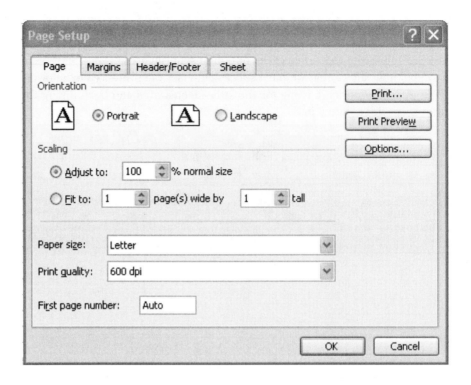

If you do want to adjust the layout, for example change the margins or change the layout from portrait (a vertical orientation, higher than it is wide) to landscape (a horizontal orientation, wider than it is high), you need to click on] File and find "Page Setup," which brings up the page setup menus. Various adjustments can be made, such as changing the font scale, forcing the entire output to be no more than one page wide or no more than one page tall (if both are selected, it means only one page), changing print quality, adjusting margins, adding headers and footers, and making other adjustments. When finished, the user can either click OK to save the settings or click Print to save the settings and send the output directly to the printer. Once returned to the main screen, the user can click ☒ to send the print area to the printer using the specified settings.

Generally, most settings will be saved for each tabbed page of the spreadsheet, so the user must click the correct tabbed page (the one you want to print) and gain focus on that page before clicking ☒ .

For Office 2007, we use the Microsoft Office button to call up this drop-down menu, then select print. If you want to continue without modifying options, select Quick Print. Otherwise select Print or Print Preview to select additional options. The page setup menu discussed previously can be accessed through the ribbon on the Print Preview screen.

The print button in the Print Preview screen will send the job to the printer. The job can also be sent to the printer from the OK button in the print menu, or from the Quick Print selection in the initial drop-down menu.

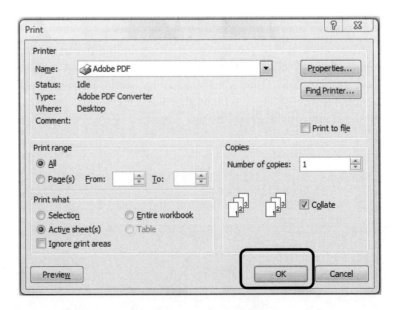

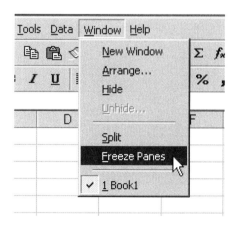

Reference Letter

Reference Number

Maximize the Usefulness of Your Spreadsheet

Add Columns or Rows

An entire column or an entire row can be added between two existing columns by highlighting the column to be moved to the right or the row to be moved down and then holding the "Control" key down and pressing the "+" key.

Highlight the entire column by clicking on the reference letter, or highlight the entire row by clicking on the reference number.

Delete Columns or Rows

An entire column or an entire row can be deleted by highlighting the column or row to be removed and then holding the "Control" key down and pressing the "–" key.

Freeze Panes

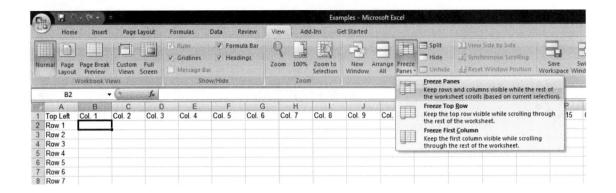

Freeze Panes is found on the Menu bar under "Windows" in older versions of Excel or on the "View" tab of the Excel 2007 ribbon.

Place your pointer at the location where you want your row headers and column headers to become permanently visible. In this example, cell B1 is selected. Row 1 and Column A will become permanently visible. Select Freeze Panes as in the previous graphic. In Excel 2007, you can select whether to freeze rows, or columns, or both. In earlier versions, both are selected by default unless you place your cursor in row 1 or column A.

	A	O	P	Q	R	S	T	U	V	W
1	Top Left	Col. 14	Col. 15	Col. 16	Col. 17	Col. 18	Col. 19	Col. 20	Col. 21	Col. 22
22	Row 21									
23	Row 22									
24	Row 23									
25	Row 24									
26	Row 25									
27	Row 26									
28	Row 27									
29	Row 28									
30	Row 29									
31	Row 30									
32	Row 31									
33	Row 32									
34	Row 33									
35	Row 34									
36	Row 35									
37	Row 36									
38	Row 37									
39	Row 38									
40	Row 39									

Afterward, you can scroll down or to the right, but row 1 and column A do not scroll off the screen. This feature is particularly helpful when working with large tables.

Wrap Text

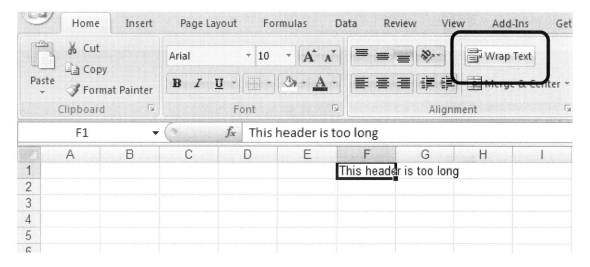

When your header is long, you can wrap the text onto several rows in the same cell. On the "Home" tab in the ribbon, select "Wrap Text."

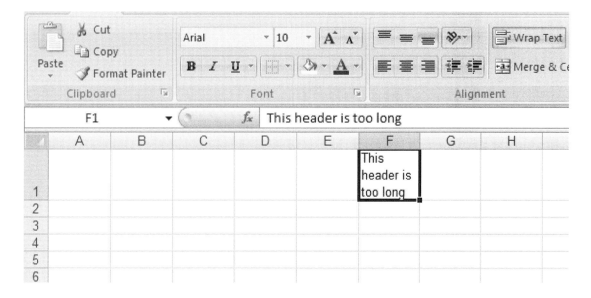

The result is demonstrated in this graphic.

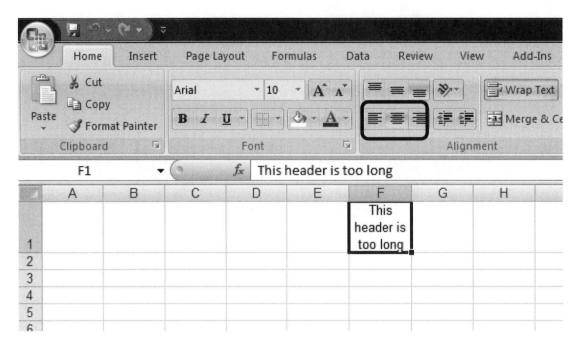

The text might look better if you center it by using the centering icon. The process in older versions of Excel is shown here:

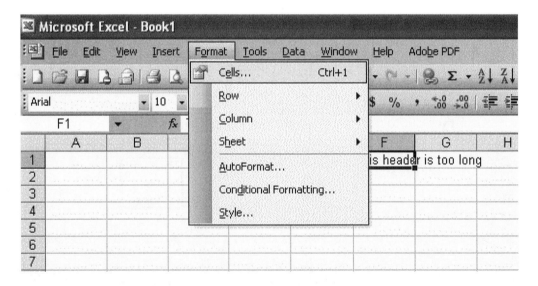

Select Format Cells from the Format menu

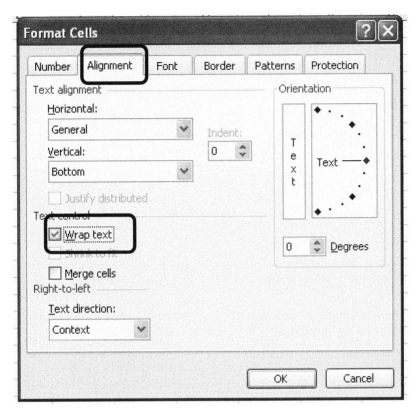

In the interactive menu, click on the "Alignment" tab and click on the Wrap text box to add a check.

Finish by clicking on the center text icon.

Error Messages

A1	▼	*fx*
	A	B
1		#REF!
2		
3		#DIV/0!
4		
5		#VALUE!
6		
7		#NAME?
8		
9		#NUM!
10		

#REF!. The message #REF! usually occurs while you are developing a spreadsheet; it occurs for one of two reasons. First the developer copies a formula with a relative address. When it is pasted, the relative location is outside the matrix of the spreadsheet. The correction for this is to rewrite the formula.

Second, the developer deletes a column or row in which there is a cell to which a formula refers. The correction for this, provided that the spreadsheet has not been saved, is to undo the delete using the undo icon ⟳ . If the spreadsheet has been saved, the correction is to rewrite the formula.

#DIV/0!. The message #DIV/0! arises when there is a division by zero. Division by zero is not valid. Occasionally this message arises with a more complex function such as AVERAGE, where there are no values entered into the column to be averaged. More commonly it arises because there is some division in a formula that is copied and pasted to many cells. Sometimes the divisor is zero, and the error message results. If, for report purposes, this message is undesired, see the solution explained with the IF function in Appendix E.

#VALUE!. The #VALUE! message arises because the formula refers to a cell that has an illegitimate value for the formula. Typically this mismatch is a text value where the formula calls for a number. The correction is to find the text and replace it with a legitimate value, or to rewrite the formula.

#NAME?. The #NAME? message arises when an invalid function or range name is entered. The correction is to edit the formula and replace the invalid name with a valid one.

#NUM!. The #NUM! message arises when a function or formula gives rise to a mathematically invalid result. For example, negative numbers have no square roots, so a function that asks for the square root of a negative number will receive this error message.

CIRCULAR ERROR MESSAGE. This message is shown by:

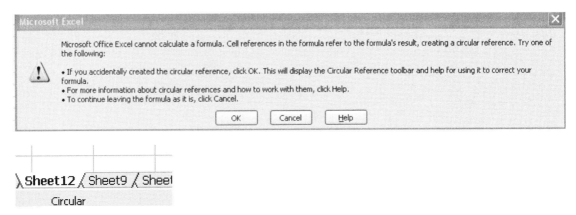

Circular

or

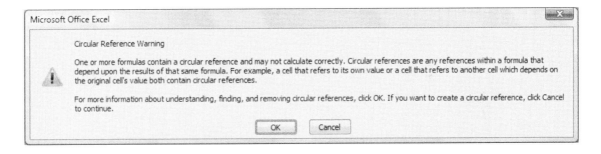

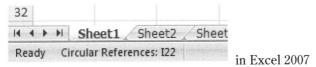

in Excel 2007

The circular error message arises when a formula refers to the cell that contains it. Excel cannot process such a formula. The formula must be rewritten.

How to Make an XY Plot in Excel 2003 or Earlier

These procedures are parallel to those in Chapter 4, which review how to make an XY plot using Excel 2007. These procedures create the same plot using Excel 2003 or earlier. Users of Excel 2007 are referred to Chapter 4.

Highlight the columns that contain the data. Columns can be found in the sheet labeled "Tbl 4.2" in "Budget Tools Chapter 4 (for student).xls."

		Period	X_t
5			
6		Period 0	
7		1980	2,210.0
8		1981	2,320.6
9		1982	2,488.3
10		1983	2,767.7
11		1984	3,082.9
12		1985	3,348.8
13		1986	3,430.8
14		1987	3,943.7
15		1988	3,656.3
16		1989	4,083.9
17		1990	4,021.0
18		1991	4,254.9
19		1992	4,772.5
20		1993	4,979.3
21		1994	4,968.9
22		1995	4,894.3
23		1996	5,173.8
24		1997	5,648.2
25		1998	6,547.3
26		1999	6,871.8
27		2000	6,749.2
28		2001	7,209.0
29		2002	5,762.6
30		2003	5,661.4
31		2004	6,653.4
32		2005	7,635.3
33		2006	8,245.0
34		2007	8,647.8

The column that will serve as the X-axis label must be the leftmost of the columns highlighted. Start at the labeled header row. You can skip a column or row by holding the "Control" key down and beginning the highlight again at the next column or row you want to include. If the labels are not immediately above the data, you can either enter labels manually or hold the "Control" key down and then highlight the row that contains the labels. Take note, the labels row must be in the same order as the data.

Next, select the chart wizard icon (see below) to start making the chart.

Third, on the first menu select XY (scatter); see image below.

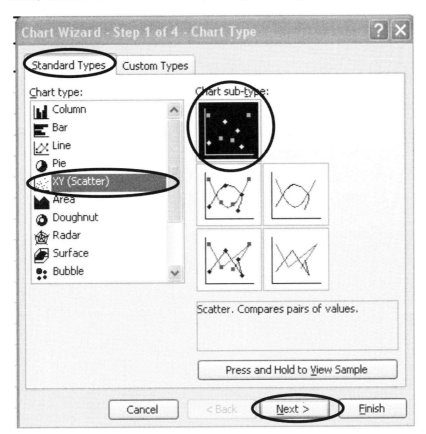

Later you may want to explore various subtypes, but for now, select the default subtype and select next.

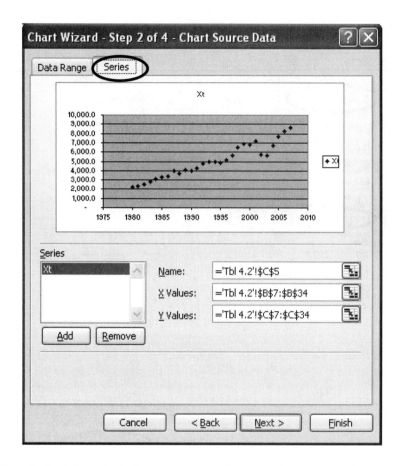

Fourth, the "Step 2" displays two tabs at the top and a small version of your plot in the main screen. You usually simply select next, to accept this screen. For now, first look at the tab labeled "Series" and make sure the labels are satisfactory. If not, click "Cancel" and start over. Be very careful about what you highlight. For your first try, it may be best to use only contiguous rows and columns. When you get to this step again, if the labels are not satisfactory, click on each series in the left-side box and type in the label you want in the "Name" box. Then click Next.

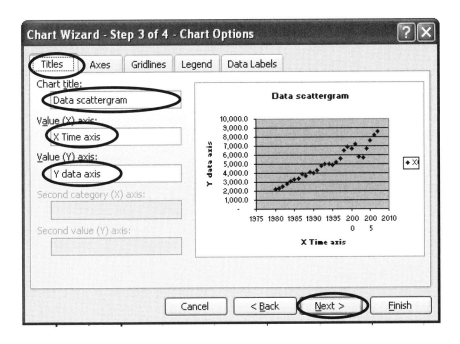

Fifth, in step three you enter a Chart title and labels for the X and Y axes. You can also select the other three tabs on this screen to improve the format of the chart. We recommend removing the distracting gridlines and moving the legend to the bottom as shown in the following four images.

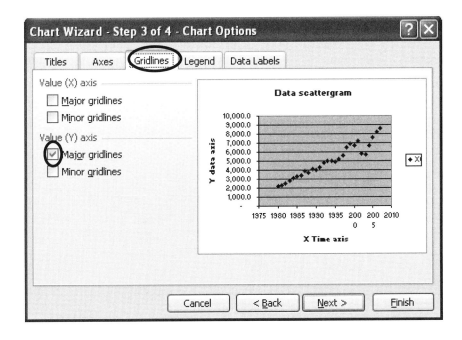

Change to:

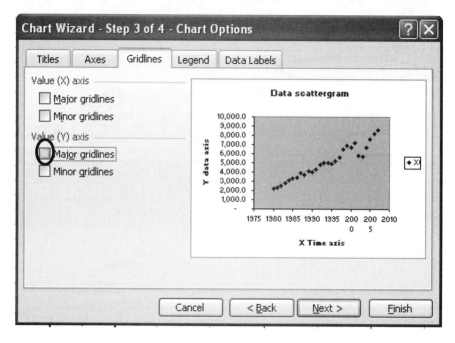

and

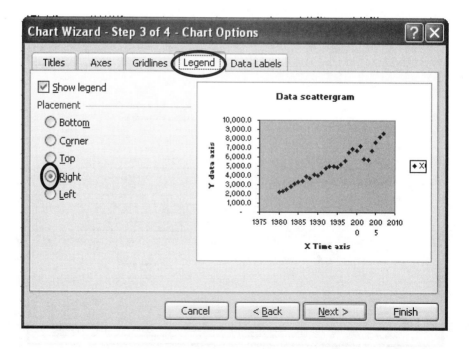

Change to:

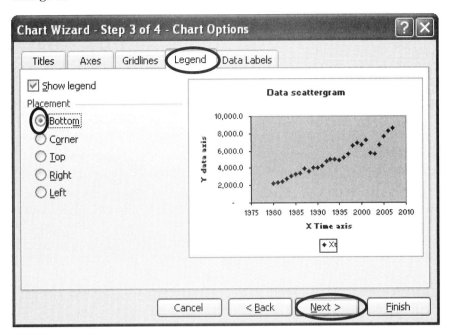

Select "Next" once more.

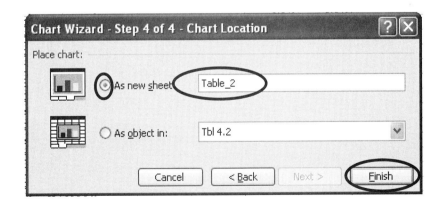

At Step 4, select a location for the chart. You will have more control if you select "As new sheet" and enter a name of your choosing in the box. Then select "Finish."

In this case the resulting chart looks like this:

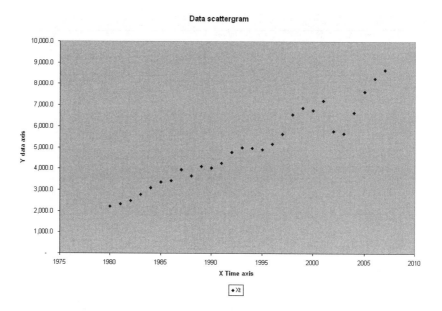

Double click on the Y (vertical) axis to bring up this menu (the menu may open in any of the tab pages listed at the top):

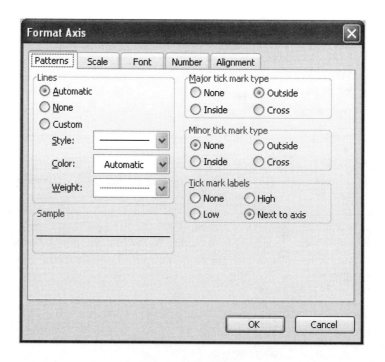

Select Scale and restrict the Minimum to 2000 and Maximum to 9000.

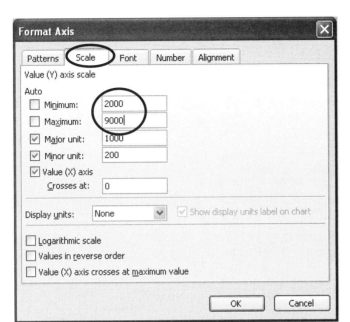

Select number and change the format to Currency with zero (0) decimal places and click OK.

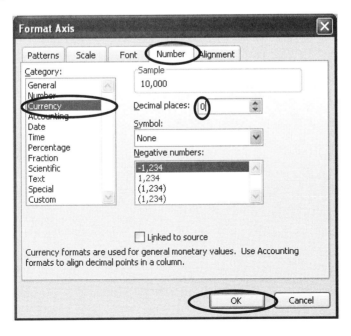

Select the x axis and adjust as shown.

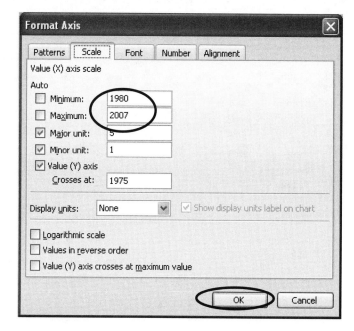

The gray background can be removed by clicking in the gray area and pressing the "Delete" key.

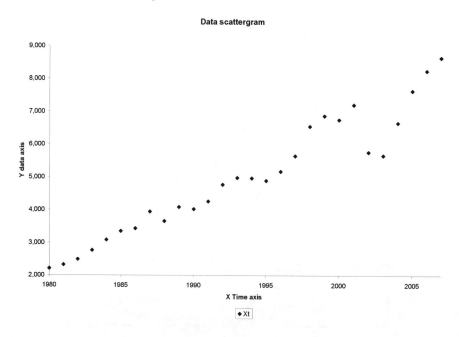

Your plot should now look like this. You can explore the menus and effects of double clicking to further format the plot.

Exercises

Note to students: Later exercises likely will call back to earlier exercises. You may want to copy the files you make to removable media that you can take with you.

Exercise 1.

This exercise provides practice in the principles of spreadsheets.

1. Open a blank spreadsheet.

2. Before making any entries, save the empty file using your last name and first initial as the file name. Particularly for students, it is helpful to use your name in file names you submit to other individuals; it is best to start that practice now.

3. Rename Sheet1 as "Practice."

4. On the renamed sheet, enter the following values: In Cell A1 enter 15, in Cell B1 enter 5.

5. In Cell C1, add cells A1 and B1.

6. In Cell C2, subtract B1 from A1.

7. In Cell C3, multiply A1 by B1.

8. In Cell C4, divide A1 by B1.

9. Click on Sheet2 (for the instructions for the following problems) and enter the following numbers in cells B2 through B8 {15, 78, 23, 60, 42, 12, 31}.

10. Enter the following numbers in cells C2 through C8 {45, 60, 97, 15, 30, 38, 15}.

11. Place your pointer in cell B9 and use the [Σ] icon to total (sum) cells B2 through B8.

12. Keeping your pointer in cell B9, click the [icon] icon to copy your formula.

13. Place your pointer in cell C9 and click the [icon] icon to paste your formula.

14. Place your pointer in cell B12 and enter a function/formula that sums all the entries in cells B2 through B8 and all the entries in cells C2 through C8 using two (2) arguments.

15. Print out your work from "Practice" and "Sheet2."

Spreadsheet Principles

The purposes of these principles are to make your spreadsheets easily verifiable and to reduce risk associated with buried or inconsistent information. Another important consideration is to take maximum advantage of the power of spreadsheets.

DATA.   Under many circumstances data should be entered in the form of a database. This principle is particularly important when there is a lot of information or when the information is subject to change. Databases have these characteristics:

- Columns have unique column labels at the top.

- Columns are adjacent.

- Rows are adjacent.

- There is a column that contains a unique identifier for each row; usually this is the first column.

- Missing data are represented by leaving cells empty.

- No formulas are entered into data cells.

- In some circumstances a column is a transformation of one or more other columns, in which case the entire column contains the effect of the same formula.

- Different sets of data are entered in different databases. In the modern spreadsheet, this can be done by using a different tabbed sheet for each set of data.

FORMULAS.   Spreadsheet cells can contain data, and they can contain formulas. An error arises when they contain both. There can be several reasons for this error:

- The data part disappears.

- The highest functionality of the spreadsheet is to easily change data, which is not possible when the data are hidden inside formulas.

- Often in spreadsheet development, formulas are copied, in which case hidden "hard coded" data can lead to errors.

TABLES.   Tables are where most budget spreadsheeting occurs. Tables bear a lot of similarity to a database. The difference is that some columns or rows contain data and some are calculated. Other rules are largely the same.

- Tables should not involve gaps between columns to improve appearance, and gaps between rows should be minimized.

- Under most circumstances, one table should appear on one tabbed sheet.

- Columns and rows should be clearly labeled with unique labels.

- No cell should contain both a formula and data.

- Where data are carried from one tabbed page of the spreadsheet to another, it is best to reveal them, rather than bury them inside a formula.

- Tables may be used for presentation, so guidelines for formatting provided in Appendix D should be followed.

SIMPLIFICATION.   If you know two ways to accomplish something in a spreadsheet and one of them is simpler, use the simpler one unless you have a very good reason to use the other. For example, we know two ways to add all the cells from cell B5 to B10:

$$=SUM(B5:B10)$$

and

$$=B5+B6+B7+B8+B9+B10$$

The simplification principle says to use the first way. Advanced users sometimes have very good reasons not to use the simplification principle. Professors sometimes use more complicated methods so students will see what is going on. New users usually do not have a good reason to avoid the simplification principle.

ROUNDING VS. NOT ROUNDING.   Prior to the rise of computerized mathematics, analysts had to decide before calculating at what level of specificity to round. Even if one stops at some very insignificant decimal place, you are rounding somewhere. The typical practice is to round quickly, as the digits beyond the first few have little impact on the magnitude of the final number.

In the computerized environment, matters are different. It can be more work for both the analyst and the computer to round than to not round. There is rounding, of course, but the rounding occurs at some insignificant location eight to sixty-four decimal places or further after the zero.

Sometimes, analysts do not like to work with such specific numbers and tend to force rounding near zero or even before zero. This forced rounding is unnecessary.

The most effective approach is to calculate in all the glorious specificity, but represent the final numbers at a level of confidence that is reasonable for the data analyzed. Typically, for example, a budget in millions of dollars might be confident at the hundred thousand level. Digits below that may be misleadingly specific. When, later, techniques are provided for rounding, this rule should be considered.

As a general practice when calculations are performed before rounding, or whenever summations may appear awkward with rounding involved—as with percentages—the following disclaimer should appear: "Totals may not sum because of rounding."

POWER OF THE SPREADSHEET. The spreadsheet is not a word processor. Its function is to calculate, not merely to present. Wherever information flows from one location to another, the information should travel through formulas. No calculations should be conducted offline with the results entered into the spreadsheet. Nor should they be copied by retyping. Use the spreadsheet for its power, which is to take your newest bit of information and recalculate your results without intervening manual steps.

DOCUMENTING SPREADSHEETS.   Spreadsheets are useful only if they can be interpreted. When a creator first makes one, he or she knows what every cell represents. But soon this knowledge dissipates. Text entries should be included throughout the spreadsheet to explain what cells are doing, what the calculations are intended to accomplish, and where information in cells originated.

COPY AND PASTE TO WORD DOCUMENTS.   Results produced in spreadsheets are often used in reports. Appendix D provides tips on table formatting. However, one additional consideration is how to incorporate results directly into word processing files. More and more reports are communicated electronically.

Transmitting portions of reports in Excel files can be problematic for several reasons. First, it may require considerable effort to ensure that the recipient knows how to navigate the file in order to find the report. Second, formatting for the reader requires consideration of what the reader might do to print the file; a report that looks attractive on the screen might print poorly unless considerable additional work is done. Third, possession of the spreadsheet may tempt the report recipient to second-guess the analyst on analysis or assumptions.

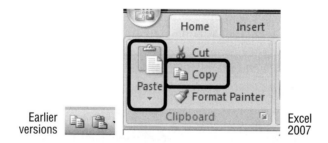

When transmitting the report electronically, it is best to copy specific tables into the appropriate sections of the word processing document. Using the universal copy-paste functions of Windows-based software may lead to additional formatting effort, but it will pay off in the end. The two icons in the graphic shown above and found on the tool bar will greatly speed your use of the copy (left) and paste (right) functions.

EXERCISE 2.

This exercise provides practice in using copy-and-paste techniques.

1. Copy your print areas from Exercise 1 in this appendix: copy them from Excel to Microsoft Word.

2. Save the results in a Word file. Print out the Word file. (Note, no guidance is provided in this text for Microsoft Word.)

Did you follow the file naming guidelines suggested in Part 1?

Here we look at formulas and functions that have special application in budgeting. This section does not explain the use of functions in budgeting; it provides practice in how to get the spreadsheet to do them.

B11	▾	f_x =SUBTOTAL(9,B5:B10)		
	A	B	C	D	E
4		15			
5		78			
6		23			
7		60			
8		42			
9		12			
10		31			
11		246			
12					

B21	▾	f_x =SUBTOTAL(9,B15:B20)		
	A	B	C	D	E
4		15			
5		78			
6		23			
7		60			
8		42			
9		12			
10		31			
11		246			
12					
13					
14					
15		45			
16		60			
17		97			
18		15			
19		38			
20		15			
21		270			
22					

SUBTOTAL.   Subtotal is a function that is similar to summation. It has a minimum of two arguments. The FIRST argument is a number from 1 to 11 that tells subtotal what specific function to perform. For budgeting we are interested in the number 9, which tells the spreadsheet to perform summation. The second and subsequent arguments are ranges of cells that contain the data to be summed.

So, the formula looks like this:

$$=SUBTOTAL(9,B5:B10)$$

The specific benefit of the subtotal function is that when two or more instances of subtotal are calculated and one includes the cell that contains the other, the included subtotal is not calculated in the containing subtotal. This is very useful when summing up a long column of numbers where there are intermittent subtotals within, which happens quite often within budgeting. So, if the first five entries are subtotaled, then the next seven, then the next twelve, etcetera, to the bottom of the spreadsheet, using the summation formula, the analyst must then hunt for the specific totals and add them up using: =B11+Bxx+Byy+ . . . .

	B23	▾	ƒx	=SUBTOTAL(9,B4:B21)	
	A	B	C	D	E
4		15			
5		78			
6		23			
7		60			
8		42			
9		12			
10		31			
11		246			
12					
13					
14					
15		45			
16		60			
17		97			
18		15			
19		38			
20		15			
21		270			
22					
23		531			

However, using the subtotal function, the analyst simply sums the whole column using the subtotal function rather than the summation function.

For this function to work, it must be used in both the internal subtotals and at the grand total. Also, the grand total must total all the values contributing to the internal subtotals.

PERCENTAGES. There is a general formula that is widely known to the effect that percentage is found by:

$$n/N * 100, \text{ where}$$

n is the number of observations or other value of a subgroup, and

N is the number of observations or other value of the whole group.

The "times 100" simply moves the decimal point two places to the right, thereby changing the representation of the number from a decimal to a percentage.

To CALCULATE with a percentage thus produced, the first step is to DIVIDE by 100.

Spreadsheets have rendered this approach obsolete. This obsolescence is because the visual presentation of a number can differ from the information contained in the cell. For example, the cell can contain the number 0.01, but it can visually present it to the screen and to the printer as 1%. The "%" icon on the toolbar will do this in one easy step.

This means that for the spreadsheet it is unnecessary to multiply or divide by 100 to achieve a visual presentation, which can, instead, be achieved through data formatting.

C5		f_x =ROUND(B5,-3)	
	A	B	C	D
4				
5		345,678	346,000	
6				

ROUNDING. Earlier we discussed rounding as compared with not rounding. The recommendation is to not round until calculations are completed. Rounding can be troublesome in some of the same ways that percentages are troublesome. Thus, rounding should be preformed only at the very end of a series of calculations.

The function for rounding is ROUND, and it has two arguments. The first argument gives the cell address for the number to be rounded. The second argument gives the decimal place for the rounded number. Positive numbers are spaces to the *right* of the decimal (smaller than one); negative numbers are spaces to the *left* of the decimal (larger than one).

An example might be

$$=\text{ROUND}(B5,-3)$$

The effect of this would be to round the number in B5 to thousands.

Suppose I have the number 345,678 in cell B5. If I use the function =ROUND(B5,–3), the spreadsheet will not only present, *but also calculate with* the information 346,000.

When producing a table that contains rounded information, it is best to round only the final product, the number that the table produces. At the end of the table, first show the exact number produced by the calculation then, on the next row, show the rounded number. Use the rounded number in related text.

If the table contains several rounded numbers that are summed, these considerations apply. First, all numbers should be rounded to the same decimal level. Second, the spreadsheet should contain a second shadow table that has the same calculations without rounding to determine the effect of rounding. Third, the reported table should contain the disclaimer, "Totals may not sum due to rounding." Fourth, under no circumstances should such a table be produced if multiplication or division, more complex math, or variances are in the analysis.

REBUILDING AN INTEREST RATE.   Interest rates can be represented two remarkably different ways. For example five percent can be represented by either 0.05 (5%) or it can be represented by 1.05 (105%). The first number represents the *change* from period one to period two achieved through interest rate growth. The second number represents the *whole number transformed into the next whole number.*

There are times, especially when multiplying, that it is necessary to calculate in the whole number rather than just the change value. The simple method of doing this is to enter the number 1 in one cell and the "interest rate" (the change part) in another cell. Then in a third cell add them together. Reference the third cell for subsequent calculations. This leaves the change part of the interest rate available for alternate scenario values.

Suppose we have 1 in cell A1, 0.05 in cell B1, and the formula =A1+B1 in cell C1. Subsequent calculations refer to cell $C$1 (using absolute cell addresses to avoid copy and paste errors, if necessary). Later we come to believe that the correct interest rate is 3%. We adjust cell B1 and all other relevant cells adjust automatically.

C1		▼	f_x	=B1+A1	
	A	B	C		
1	1	0.05	1.05		
2					

E1		▼	f_x	=$C$1^D1	
	A	B	C	D	E
1	1	0.05	1.05	5	1.276282
2					

THE EXPONENTIAL. The exponential is a special number in math that tells the computer (either human or electronic) how many times to multiply a number by itself. This information is particularly interesting when working with, for example, interest rates. If you want to know the effect of an interest rate five years in the future, the answer is to multiply the rate by itself five times. Assuming our interest rate is 1.05, as described in the last section, then this would be represented by 1.05^5 or $(1.05)^5$. Spreadsheets do not have an effective way to process a function merely by changing the font, so instead they use a symbol "^". Let us assume that we have the value 1.05 in cell C1 as described in the last section. In cell D1 we enter the number 5. In cell E1 we enter the formula

$$=C1\text{^}D1$$

The effect of this will be to tell the spreadsheet to return the value of:

$$1.05*1.05*1.05*1.05*1.05$$

If you multiply the result of that formula by some actual amount, it will tell you what the resulting amount should be after five years.

		f_x	=NPV(B1,G1:G10)		
B	C	D	E	F	G
0.05					45
					45
					45
					45
					45
					45
					45
					45
					45
					45
					$347.48

NET PRESENT VALUE.   The Net Present Value function is used to calculate the effect of an interest rate on flows of money. It may produce a shortcut to some of the calculations discussed above. The function has two arguments. The first one is an interest rate as expressed in cell B5 in the two previous sections, that is, the change amount, not the whole amount. The second one is the flow of money in equally spaced periods beginning with period ONE (1). A flow of money is a set of amounts such as the amount of income you receive at the end of each year. Take note, if there is an amount associated with period ZERO (before any interest accrues) it should not be included in the flow that is considered in the NPV formula.

Suppose you have a flow such as {45, 45, 45, 45, ... ,45} representing $45,000 a year in income beginning in year one, in cells G1 through G10. You have the interest rate of 0.05 in cell B1. In cell G12 you have the formula

$$=NPV(B1,G1:G10)$$

This formula returns the amount $347.48, which is the value in year zero of this flow of money. Note, this amount is less than the sum of this column. An explanation will occur in the Capital Budget section.

SORTING DATA.

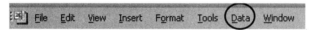

From the menu bar, select data and follow the menus to " Sort ..." *Do not select the from the task bar unless you are sure that you have a simple sort.* The menu bar option will take you to the next menu.

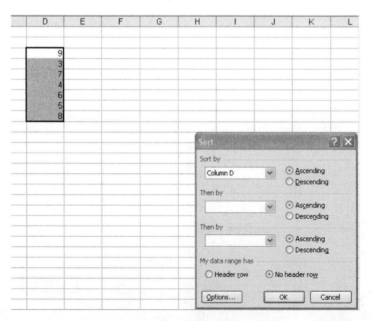

With the older Excel menu, you can select up to three key columns for the sort. For each column you can select "Ascending" (A to Z or 1 to 10) or "Descending" (the reverse). Generally the menu will default to the bullet "My data has" header row, particularly if there is text in the first row and numbers in the other rows. If the first row of data is among the data to be sorted, click instead on the "No header row" radio button. Generally you will not need to click on the options button unless your sort data contain dates, in which case you should follow the menus.

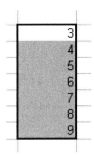

After you click OK, the data are sorted.
In Excel 2007 you find sort on the Data tab.

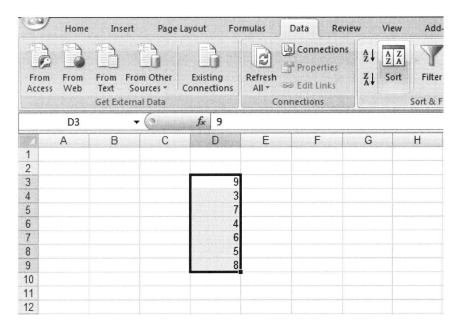

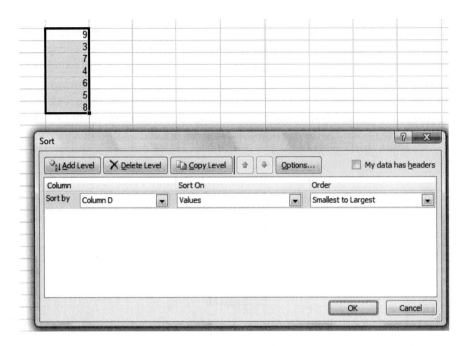

With Excel 2007 you can add multiple sort levels up to the number of columns you have using the Add Level button. Generally, you will have no reason to change the default Sort On "Values." The "Options" button allows you to select sort left to right rather than the default top to bottom. The "Order" drop-down menu allows smallest to largest, largest to smallest, or a custom list which may be used for certain calendar entries. Check the header box as appropriate.

NAMED RANGES. Spreadsheets use named ranges to reduce the difficulty of referring to a cell, group of cells, or table repeatedly. They are particularly useful when a table is produced for use elsewhere in the spreadsheet. The named range is used instead of a cell or range address. For example, if we have named the range G1 through G10 as RangeOne, we can use the following formula

$$=SUM(RangeOne)$$

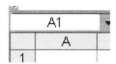

It will have the same effect as:

$$=SUM(G1:G10)$$

There are some rules:

Only contiguous areas can be named ranges.

Range names cannot contain empty spaces.

Range names cannot be equal to cell addresses (A1 through IV65536; see also larger addresses for Excel 2007).

Range names cannot be equal to function names.

There are a few other special words used by spreadsheets that should not be used as range names, but it is usually through misfortune or deliberate risk that gets you there.

To name a range:

Highlight the entire area that is to be named.

Above the top left cell of the visible spreadsheet there will be a white area that contains the cell address of the top left cell of the area you have just highlighted.

Place your pointer in that area and click.

Type the name you have selected for the range name and press enter.

The range name should now appear where the cell address previously was at the beginning of step 2.

Beside the area you have just typed in there is a small drop-down arrow, if you place your pointer on it and click, you should see a list with the range name you have just created.

Range named "Salaries"

	A	B	C	D
1				
2				
3				$ 45,000
4				
5				Clarke, Roland
6				
7	Name	Position	Emp. Anv.	Salary
8	Amos, Joe	Supervisor	June	$50,000
9	Barabas, Susan	Executive	March	$75,000
10	Clarke, Roland	Skilled	September	$45,000
11				

Formula bar: D3 =VLOOKUP(D5,Salaries,4)

VERTICAL LOOKUP.   Vertical lookup is a database function. It allows the user to use one bit of information to find another. Perhaps you know a person's name and have a sorted list of names and salaries. Vertical lookup allows you to use the name to find the income. This is a very useful function for skilled spreadsheet users. Vertical lookup has three arguments. The first one is the target information, such as the name of the employee. The second one is the range in which the database can be found—typically a named range. The third one is the number of columns, beginning with the first column as 1, from the key column (which must be the first column) to the column that contains the information. By definition a database should be wider than one column.

Suppose you have a salary database in a range named Salaries. In cell D5 you have the name of a person whose salary you want to use in a calculation (spelled exactly as in the database). In the database the first column is the name. In the second column is the job classification. In the third column is the salary information by year. In the fourth column is the salary information. For your purposes, it is the salary information that you want. There could be other information in other columns. In another cell you enter the formula using the function as follows:

=VLOOKUP(D5,Salaries,4)

This function will work properly only if the database is sorted by the names column in the database and only if the names are spelled the same in both locations.

f_x	=RANK(F1,F1:F10,1)	
E	F	G
	30	
	18	
	29	
	56	
4	43	
	90	
	12	
	56	
	45	
	31	

RANKING DATA. The Excel ranking function is not exactly equal to the statistical ranking function, but it is sufficient for ordinary communication. It has three arguments. The first argument is the cell address of the number you want ranked. The second argument is the range of cells that contain the other numbers to which this number is to be compared. The third argument is either 0 or 1. If it is 0, the smallest number will have the largest number rank, if it is 1, the smallest number will have the smallest number rank. So an example might be:

$$=RANK(F1,F1:F10,1)$$

Suppose {30;18;29;56;43;90;12;56;45;31} are in cells F1 through F10. The example formula returns the resulting rank of 4.

D5	▼	f_x	=AVERAGE(B5:B10)	
	A	B	C	D
1				
2				
3				
4				
5		43		46.16667
6		90		46.16667
7		12		
8		56		
9		45		
10		31		

AVERAGE.   To calculate a statistical mean, Excel uses a function labeled "Average." Assuming that you have some data in cells B5 to B10 for which you want an average, the formula looks like this:

$$=AVERAGE(B5:B10)$$

This will have the same effect as:

$$=SUM(B5:B10)/N \text{ [N is not a spreadsheet function!]}$$

where N is the count of the cells from B5 to B10 that contain an entry.

You can determine N with a function "Count," so you can also determine the average with:

$$=SUM(B5:B10)/COUNT(B5:B10)$$

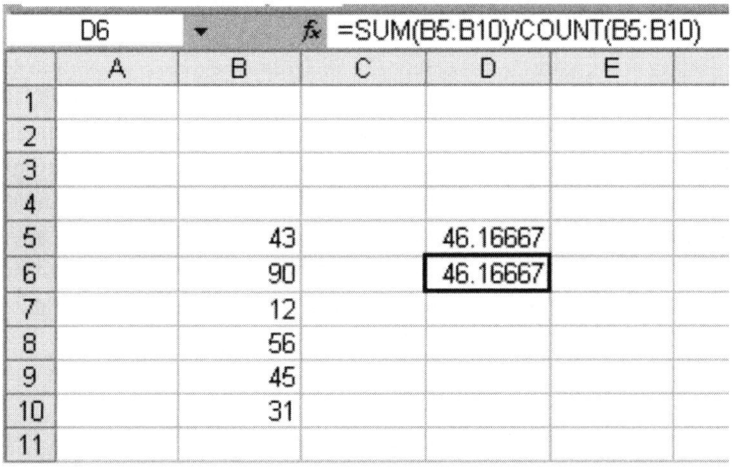

	D6	▼		*fx*	=SUM(B5:B10)/COUNT(B5:B10)	
	A	B	C	D	E	
1						
2						
3						
4						
5		43		46.16667		
6		90		46.16667		
7		12				
8		56				
9		45				
10		31				
11						

However, this violates the simplicity principle discussed in Section 2, so should not ordinarily be used. It is shown here to explain what the Average function does.

If you want an average of two non-contiguous ranges, you can include two arguments in your formula. Suppose you want the average of B5 through B10 and B12 through B17, but not B11. The formula would be:

$$=AVERAGE(B5:B10, B12:B17)$$

The effect is shown in the graphic.

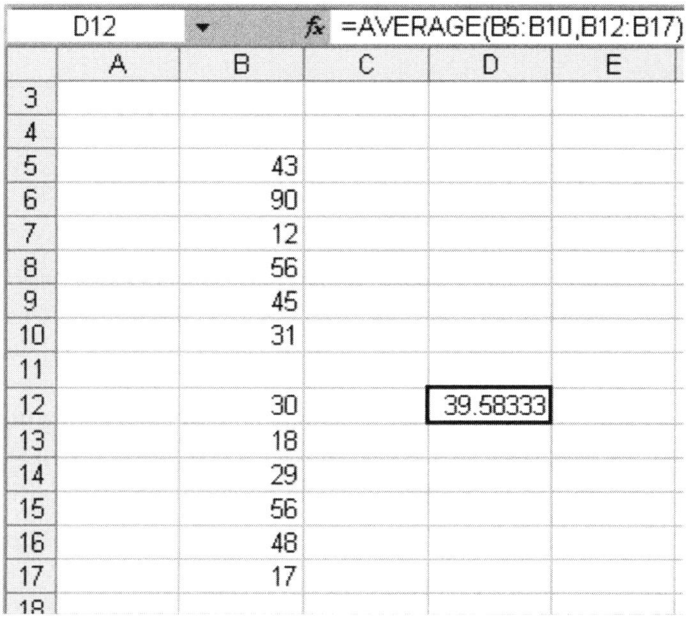

D12	▼		_fx_ =AVERAGE(B5:B10,B12:B17)	
	A	B	C	D	E
3					
4					
5		43			
6		90			
7		12			
8		56			
9		45			
10		31			
11					
12		30		39.58333	
13		18			
14		29			
15		56			
16		48			
17		17			
18					

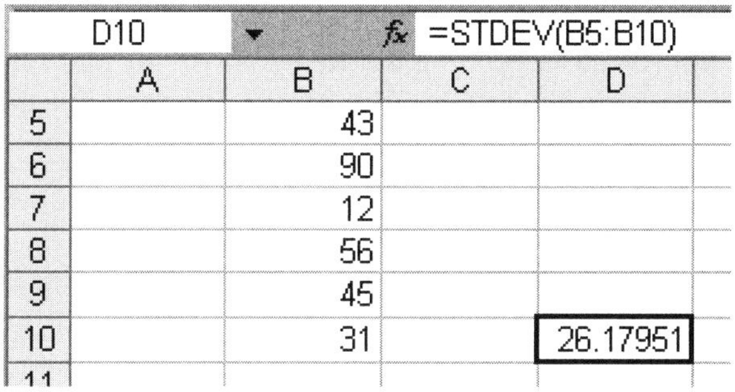

D10	▼		_fx_ =STDEV(B5:B10)	
	A	B	C	D
5		43		
6		90		
7		12		
8		56		
9		45		
10		31		26.17951
11				

STANDARD DEVIATION. Standard Deviation is a very common statistic. When used without any other reference it is the standard deviation of the mean (average). There are two different concepts known as the sample standard deviation and the population standard deviation. Under almost all circumstances where their values are sharply different the sample standard deviation is likely the right one to use. When in doubt, use sample standard deviation. Excel will produce either. Following is the function for sample standard deviation. Assuming that we have the same data we have just used to calculate the mean. We would also like to know the standard deviation. The function is:

=STDEV(B5:B10)

241

Any common statistics book will explain the math underlying this procedure.

DATES.

	A
1	7/25/07
2	7-25-07
3	25-Jul-07

Budget spreadsheets commonly contain date information. In the "bad old days" it was somewhat difficult to enter dates. Today, you can enter a date in standard American format, such as "7/05/07." The spreadsheet interprets any valid date in the two slash format as a date. You can also enter it as "7-25-07" or July 25, 2007. The graphic shows the effect of entering the date in these three formats, respectively. All three of these are valid dates in Excel.

EXERCISES. Use the spreadsheet called "Budget Tools Appendix C Exercises." The tabbed sheet is labeled "Part 3." The problems described here should be completed there with the data that can be found there.

EXERCISE 1.

In the yellow highlighted cells, compute the subtotals for the component tables, and in the green highlighted cell compute the total for the entire column.

EXERCISE 2.

Use the appropriate spreadsheet method to demonstrate the numbers as percentages.

In the yellow highlighted cell show the percentage for 45 / 50.

EXERCISE 3.

In the first column there are numbers to be rounded to the degree shown in the second column. Put the results in the yellow highlighted area in the third column.

EXERCISE 4.

1. In the highlighted cell, show the first year of interest on $250 at 5 percent.

2. In the highlighted cells show the cumulative value for each year from year 1 to year 10 on $500 compounded at 3 percent per year. What is the final total value of the deposit?

EXERCISE 5.

1. Sort the information in the table by name.

2. Name the table that contains the data, but not the headers, "Ages."

3. Use Vlookup to find Henderson's age.

4. Use Vlookup to find Wilson's gender.

EXERCISE 6.

1. Find the rank for all cells with the largest value having the rank of 1, place in the highlighted cells.

2. Find the average of the data; place in the highlighted cell.

3. Find the standard deviation of the data; place in the highlighted cell.

EXERCISE 7.

Enter today's date in the highlighted cell. Use a traditional numeric entry such as ##/##/## (for example, 07/27/07).

Enter today's date in the highlighted cell. Use a text form such as Month ##, 20## (for example, July 27, 2007).

Appendix D

How to Produce
Clear, Attractive Reports

After students learn how to use a spreadsheet, students should turn their attention to making that spreadsheet readable and attractive. Students will discover that, in the workplace, the readability and attractiveness of their work is as important as the work itself.

How to Use Labels

In a spreadsheet, labels are in the top row of the data and in the left column. The labels explain what is the row or column. It is extremely important that labels are chosen with care so that the reader immediately understands what is in that column. For example, "wmyrsed" is not very clear while "women mayors yrs. of ed." is quite clear, and the latter label can fit in the top two rows of a column. Your supervisor does not wish to spend time finding out what each label means. The label should be intuitive. This is not the case in SPSS, in which there is a limit of eight characters for labels. Spreadsheets have no limit to the number of characters in a label. We are limited only by our common sense.

How to Use Bold Text

Bold your labels in the top row and center the labels. Compare these two spreadsheets; Table 1 is unformatted; Table 2 has formatting for the column heads.

Already the spreadsheet on types of hospital payments looks far better because we bolded the labels of the columns. How much better does this chart look if you take the title out of the spreadsheet and place it above the table, in bold? See Table 3.

Now the spreadsheet really sings. It is simple, clear, and attractive to the reader. Another method to make your spreadsheet highly polished is to set off the header rows with rules. See the same spreadsheet with rules in the header rows (Table 4).

APPENDIX D, TABLE 1
Sample Table without Formatting

Types of Hospital Payment by Department (%)

	Medicaid	Medicare	No insurance	Private insurance
Cardiology				
Emergency				
Ophthalmology				
Pediatrics				
Podiatry				

APPENDIX D, TABLE 2
Sample Table with Formatting

Types of Hospital Payment by Department (%)

	Medicaid	**Medicare**	**No insurance**	**Private insurance**
Cardiology				
Emergency				
Ophthalmology				
Pediatrics				
Podiatry				

APPENDIX D, TABLE 3
Sample Table with Title in Prominent Position

Table 1: Types of Hospital Payment by Department (percent)

	Medicaid	**Medicare**	**No insurance**	**Private insurance**
Cardiology				
Emergency				
Ophthalmology				
Pediatrics				
Podiatry				

APPENDIX D, TABLE 4
Sample Table with Rule Outlining the Header Rows

Table 1: Types of Hospital Payment by Department (percent)

	Medicaid	**Medicare**	**No insurance**	**Private insurance**
Cardiology				
Emergency				
Ophthalmology				
Pediatrics				
Podiatry				

How to Use Indentations and Careful Categorization

Often a fiscal analyst is asked to create a budget with revenues, expenditures, and net. This can be done accurately yet be poorly formatted, or it can be accomplished with a great deal of finesse that requires little time, only sophistication.

Table 5 is readable, but because of the way it is formatted, it is not very informative.

Table 6 is far more readable and easy to understand, with lots of clear information.

What is so special about the second spreadsheet is the bolding of labels, the careful creation of subcategories that are helpful to the reader, and the indentation used for categories. All of these details make for a far more readable spreadsheet.

APPENDIX D, TABLE 5
Sample Table without Formatting and with Embedded Title

	Smithtown's Operating Budget
Revenues	
Property taxes	$20,000,000
Federal aid	1,500,000
State aid	8,600,000
Sales tax	3,000,000
User fees	750,000
Total revenues	$33,850,000
Expenditures	
Salaries	$21,000,000
Benefits	5,880,000
Supplies	2,000,000
Equipment	3,000,000
Travel	340,000
Other	1,500,000
Total expenditures	$33,720,000
Net	$130,000

APPENDIX D, TABLE 6
Sample Table with Formatting, Prominent Title, and Indents

Table 1: Smithtown's Operating Budget, FY 2007

	Budget
Revenues	
Property taxes	$20,000,000
Federal aid	1,500,000
State aid	8,600,000
Sales tax	3,000,000
User fees	750,000
Total revenues	$33,850,000
Expenditures	
Personnel services	
Salaries	$21,000,000
Benefits	5,880,000
Subtotal, personnel services	$26,880,000
Nonpersonnel services	
Supplies	$2,000,000
Equipment	3,000,000
Travel	340,000
Other	1,500,000
Subtotal, nonpersonnel services	$6,840,000
Total expenditures	$33,720,000
Net	$130,000

How to Use Rules

Rules delineating specific cells in spreadsheets can indicate that some columns belong together and others do not belong to them. In Table 7, program services are separated from support services, which has two categories, fund-raising and administration. Now the reader understands that support services comprises both fund-raising and administration.

How to Build Assumptions into a Spreadsheet

Creating proposed budgets can be complicated. It may remain complicated, but it is essential that the proposed budget be clearly laid out in a way that the reader understands the assumptions made in the creation of the proposed budget. In Table 8 the assumptions are situated in a format that can be used to create formulas and to be easily presented to the reader.

APPENDIX D, TABLE 7
Sample Table Showing Rules That Span More than One Column

Table 1: Martin Luther King Settlement House, Statement of Functional Expenses, FY 2007

Expenses	Program services	Support services		Total
		Fund-raising	Administration	
Salaries and benefits	$300,000	$40,000	$60,000	$400,000
Depreciation	10,000	0	0	10,000
Equipment	5,000	2,000	4,000	11,000
Office expenses	15,000	10,000	5,000	30,000
Professional fees	1,000	750	500	2,250
Rent	12,000	1,000	3,000	16,000
Travel	900	2,500	1,500	4,900
Total expenses	$343,900	$56,250	$74,000	$474,150

APPENDIX D, TABLE 8
Sample Table with Formatting and Assumptions Following the Table

Table 3: Proposed Budget for Fire Department, FY 2007

Positions	Salary FY 2006	Salary increases	Salary FY 2007	Health insurance	Pension	Social Security	Disability	Total benefits	Total salary	No.	Total budget
Chief	$70,000	—	$70,000	$8,400	$14,000	$4,200	$1,400	$28,000	$98,000	1.0	$98,000
Shift commander	50,000	$2,500	52,500	6,300	10,500	3,150	1,050	21,000	73,500	3.0	220,500
Firefighter 2	40,000	2,000	42,000	5,040	8,400	2,520	840	16,800	58,800	12.0	705,600
Firefighter 1	30,000	1,500	31,500	3,780	6,300	1,890	630	12,600	44,100	26.0	1,146,600
Clerical	20,000	1,000	21,000	2,520	4,200	1,260	420	8,400	29,400	1.5	44,100
Total proposed budget										43.5	$2,214,800

Assumptions:
1. 5 percent increase for all salaries except for the chief of firefighters.
2. 12 percent of each salary is for health insurance.
3. 20 percent of each salary is for pension.
4. 6 percent of each salary is for Social Security.
5. 2 percent of each salary is for disability.

Often budgets have assumptions built into them. For example, salaries may include 3 percent of the salary for health insurance and 20 percent of the salary for the pension fund, so that the true cost of a position is higher than just the salary. The true costs include the fringe benefits. In Table 8, there are several assumptions, which are listed in the assumptions following the spreadsheet.

APPENDIX D, TABLE 9
Sample Table with Formatting and Assumptions Embedded in the Table

Table 3: Proposed Budget for Fire Department, FY 2007

Positions	Salary FY 2006	Salary increases	Salary FY 2007	Health insurance	Pension	Social Security	Disability	Total benefits	Total salary	No.	Total budget
						Benefits					
Assumptions		5%		12%	20%	6%	2%				
Chief	$70,000	—	$70,000	$8,400	$14,000	$4,200	$1,400	$28,000	$98,000	1.0	$98,000
Shift commander	50,000	$2,500	52,500	6,300	10,500	3,150	1,050	21,000	73,500	3.0	220,500
Firefighter 2	40,000	2,000	42,000	5,040	8,400	2,520	840	16,800	58,800	12.0	705,600
Firefighter 1	30,000	1,500	31,500	3,780	6,300	1,890	630	12,600	44,100	26.0	1,146,600
Clerical	20,000	1,000	21,000	2,520	4,200	1,260	420	8,400	29,400	1.5	44,100
Total proposed budget										43.5	$2,214,800

In addition, the spreadsheet is designed in such a way that the readers understand how much each position costs before the total budget is calculated. This is very useful for any analysis that might be needed about the proposed budget.

Table 8 shows one way to present this information. However, a more useful way to organize the data is to place the assumptions in the spreadsheet (see Table 9). This has two advantages. The first is that the reader can easily see the effect of the assumptions, and the second is that the fiscal analyst can use the numbers to create formulas for the spreadsheet. As much as possible, assumptions should be clearly stated in the spreadsheet.

Exercise

Below are data that need to be placed in a spreadsheet. The challenge is to create a proposed budget for the public library of Smithtown. Here is all the information you need:

Proposed budget:

- 5 percent increase in salaries except for clerical staff, who get a 6.5 percent increase
- Assume fringe benefits are the same as in the Fire Department's proposed budget
- One chief librarian at a salary of $75,893
- Two librarian positions at Level II at a salary of $61,234 each
- Four librarian positions at Level I at a salary of $54,469 each

- One management information system position at a salary of $71,089
- Five clericals, three of whom are budgeted for half time at a full-time salary of $31,789, and the other two are full time.

Create the spreadsheet and answer the following questions:

1. What is the salary plus fringe benefits for one Level II librarian?
2. What is the total number of positions, not people?
3. How much is the library spending on health insurance for a Level I librarian in the proposed budget?
4. What is the total proposed budget for the library?

Appendix E

Advanced Spreadsheeting for Budgeting

These spreadsheet skills are for the user who has attained the skills in Appendix C. They are more advanced skills that are used for more complex spreadsheet purposes. All the skills demonstrated here are used in spreadsheets supporting this text.

Logic Functions

Logic functions are functions that test a cell for a truth condition and either return a truth value, or perform another operation depending on the truth value. The most common logic functions are "=," ">," and "<" (equal, greater than, and less than).

D1	▼	f_x =C1=E1
C	**D**	**E**
35	TRUE	35

D1	▼	f_x =C1=E1
C	**D**	**E**
35	FALSE	10

The simplest use of a logic function is to test a cell for its truth value. Suppose you have the value 35 in cell C1 and a value in Cell E1. In Cell D1 you enter the formula =C1=E1. This is equivalent to the question: Is the value in E1 equal to the value in C1? In the first graphic, the result is "TRUE." In the second graphic, it is "FALSE."

Sometimes values past the decimal are hidden on purpose, or there is a long column of numbers to be checked, so simply returning the value true or false is all that the user needs.

	D1	▼		f_x =(C1=E1)*1	
	C	D	E	F	
1	35	0	10		

However, other times, the user wants to condition some calculation on the truth value. There are two ways to condition calculations on the results of this logical test. The first (less complex, but involving more skill) rests on the partial equivalence of "TRUE" with "1" and "FALSE" with "0." Thus, the formula =(C1=E1)*1 will equal 1 if C1 is equal to E1 and will equal 0 otherwise. Use of this binary value can frequently be used to produce conditional formulas because the formula takes a value when multiplied by 1 but fails to take a value when multiplied by zero.

	F1	▼		f_x =IF(C1=E1,C1,0)	
	C	D	E	F	G
1	35		10	0	
2					

The other, somewhat more elegant, but also more complex, method of conditional formulas uses the IF formulation, which has three arguments.

$$=IF(C1=E1,C1,0)$$

The first argument is the logic query, the second argument is the formula to use in the case that the logic query returns a value of true, and the third argument is the formula to use in the case that the logic query returns a value of false. The given example has the same effect as the formula given in the previous graphic.

	F1	▼		f_x =IF(C1=E1,C1+E1,C1-E1)	
	C	D	E	F	G
1	35		10	25	
2					

However, with the IF formulation, the conditional formulas can be entered directly into the second and third arguments.

$$=IF(C1=E1,C1+E1,C1-E1)$$

251

In the example in this graphic, if the conditional returns "true" C1 and E1 are added, if it returns "false," as it does, E1 is subtracted from C1.

The IF function can be used to prevent #DIV/0! errors as shown in this graphic.

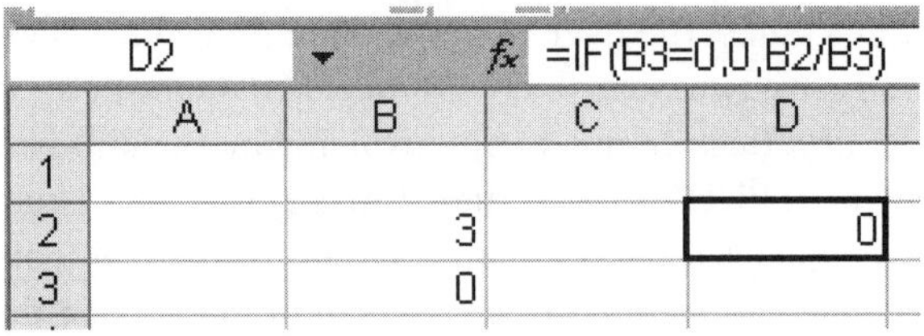

D2			f_x =IF(B3=0,0,B2/B3)	
	A	B	C	D
1				
2		3		0
3		0		

AND Function and OR Function

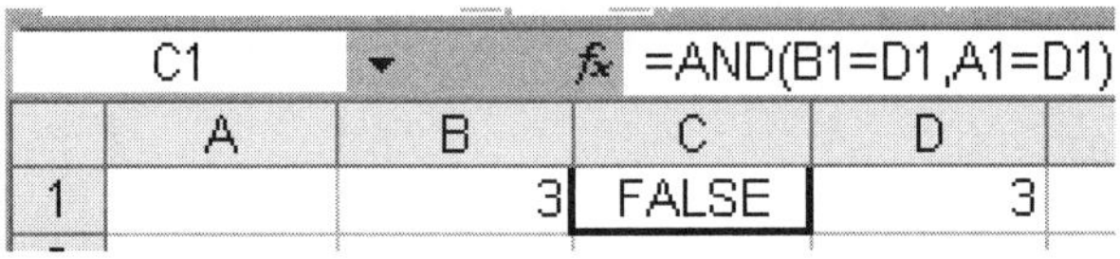

C1			f_x =AND(B1=D1,A1=D1)	
	A	B	C	D
1		3	FALSE	3

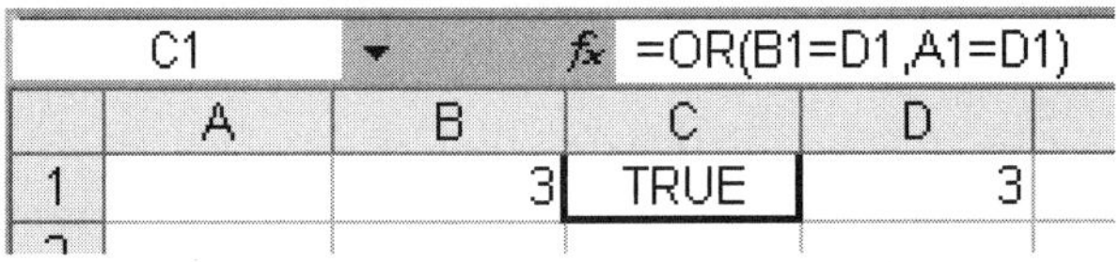

C1			f_x =OR(B1=D1,A1=D1)	
	A	B	C	D
1		3	TRUE	3

The "AND" and the "OR" functions concatenate multiple logic statements. The AND function will return "FALSE" unless all of the individual statements are true. The OR statement will return "TRUE" if at least one of the individual statements is true. In the graphic,

=AND(B1=D1,A1=D1)

returns "FALSE" while

=OR(B1=D1,A1=D1)

returns "TRUE."

In both cases cell A1 is empty and not equal to D1, while B1 and C1 both contain the value 3.

C3		▼	*fx* =IF(AND(B1=D1,A1=D1),B1+D1,B1*D1)			
	A	B	C	D	E	F
1		3	FALSE	3		
2						
3			9			

C3		▼	*fx* =IF(OR(B1=D1,A1=D1),B1+D1,B1*D1)			
	A	B	C	D	E	F
1		3	TRUE	3		
2						
3			6			

The AND and OR statements can be embedded in the IF statement to produce more advanced conditional statements. Here, when true, B1 is added to D1; when false, B1 is multipled by D1.

$$=IF(AND(B1=D1,A1=D1),B1+D1,B1*D1)$$

returns 9, which is 3*3, while

$$=IF(OR(B1=D1,A1=D1),B1+D1,B1*D1)$$

returns 6, which is 3+3.

CELL Function

C2		▼	*fx* =CELL("address",$E$2)		
	A	B	C	D	E
1					
2			$E$2		

The CELL function looks up characteristics of the designated spreadsheet cell. In the example formula, it looks up the cell address. This function has two arguments. The first is the characteristic desired (for other possible characteristics, refer to the Excel help screen). The second is the desired cell. Regardless of whether the address in the formula is relative or absolute, the returned address will be displayed as absolute.

$$=CELL("address",$E$2)$$

There are times when the spreadsheet developer wants to put a reference cell address in another cell. Because it is relatively easy to add or delete rows or columns, this fixed reference to a cell address can be unreliable. By using this function, the explicitly listed cell address will keep up with the actual cell address.

D2	▼		*fx* =INDIRECT(C2)		
	A	B	C	D	E
1					
2			$E$2	30	30
3					

The INDIRECT function treats the cell address in the referenced cell as if it were entered in the formula at the location of the indirect function. The function takes one argument, the cell that contains the indirect cell address.

Suppose you have a number in cell E2. For whatever reason, reasons usually involve spreadsheet complexities, you do not want to insert E2 in your formula. You enter E2 or =CELL("address",E2) in cell C2; in cell D2 you enter:

=INDIRECT(C2)

The indirect formula returns the same result as if you had entered =E2 in cell D2. Sometimes, this function can produce a relatively easy way to make a table referring to non-contiguous source data. There are also other uses of this function for more sophisticated spreadsheeting.

D2	▼		*fx* =ABS(C2)	
	A	B	C	D
1				
2			-3	3
3				

The ABS function takes one argument. It returns the absolute value of the number in the referenced cell. Suppose you have negative three in C2. In cell D2 you insert the function

=ABS(C2)

The result is the absolute value, which is positive three.

Maximum and Minimum

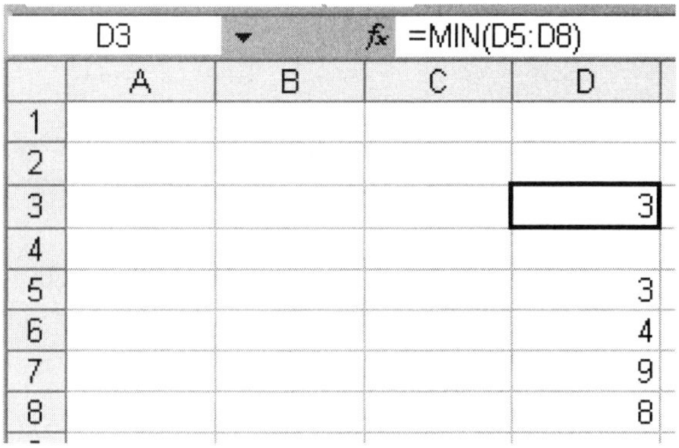

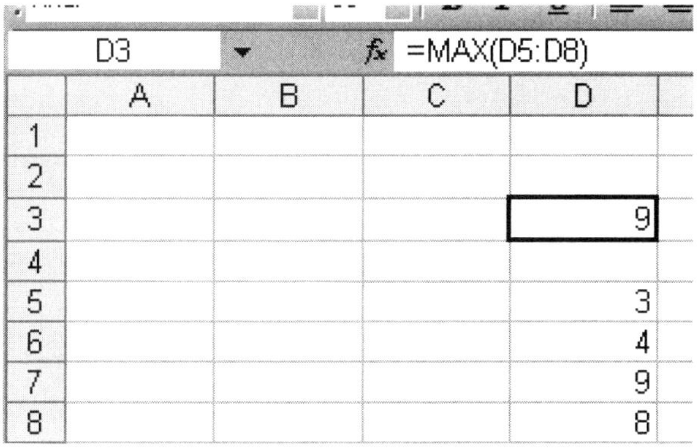

The MIN and MAX functions test a range of data to find the minimum or maximum values. In the graphic

$$=MIN(D5:D8)$$

returns 3, the lowest value, while

$$=MAX(D5:D8)$$

returns 9, the highest value.

Square Root

D2	▾	*fx*	=SQRT(C1)	
	A	B	C	D
1			81	
2				9

Square root is used in finding RMSE, which is explained in the glossary. It is also a common mathematical function that finds the number that, when multiplied by itself, results in the queried number. In the graphic,

=SQRT(C1)

returns 9, which is the number that, when multiplied by itself, results in 81 (the queried number).

Parsing Dates

D1	▾	*fx*	=DAY(A1)	
	A	B	C	D
1	7/25/2007			25
2				7
3	25-Jul-07			2007

D2	▾	*fx*	=MONTH(A1)	
	A	B	C	D
1	7/25/2007			25
2				7
3	25-Jul-07			2007

D3	▾	*fx*	=YEAR(A3)	
	A	B	C	D
1	7/25/2007			25
2				7
3	25-Jul-07			2007

Sometimes the user wants only a part of a date, the day, month, or year. Excel has functions that promptly find this information.

The function

$$=DAY(A1)$$

returns 25, the day of the month in the example. The function

$$=MONTH(A1)$$

returns 7, the month in the example. The function

$$=YEAR(A3)$$

returns 2007, the year in the example. The alternative format is shown to demonstrate that Excel is interpreting the underlying information, not the format.

Truncating Data

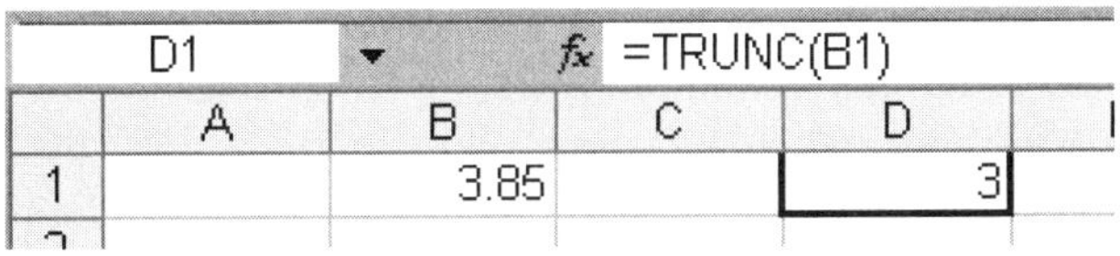

D1		f_x =TRUNC(B1)		
	A	B	C	D	I
1		3.85		3

On rare occasions it is appropriate to delete the portion of a number that follows a decimal rather than to round it. For example, one may have a contract where one pays only for full hours of service, so partial hours are not paid at all rather than paid at a scaled rate. After determining the precise number of hours, one may still need to determine the number of paid hours. WARNING: Deleting decimal values is not equivalent to rounding and should never be confused with rounding.

The function for deleting the portion after the decimal is TRUNC. In the graphic

$$=TRUNC(B1)$$

returns 3. If this number had been rounded, it would be 4.

Developing Excel Macros

Developing Excel macros should be attempted only by experienced Excel users. This guidance is for the user who already knows the basics of macros but may want to apply that knowledge to forecast fitting. To learn basic macro skills, the user should consult Microsoft or other instruction material. The guidance will be useful for the student who already knows how to call up the macro writing screens within Excel (Microsoft Visual Basic, within Excel).

Typically macro functionality requires development of both spreadsheet elements and macro elements. In the spreadsheet, "Budget Tools Appendix E macro.xls" (Office 2003 and earlier) or "Budget Tools Appendix E macro.xlsm" (Office 2007), there is only one tab, "Table 5 for Macro."[1] Macros make sense only in the context of extending some functionality. This spreadsheet extends the forecast functionality from Chapter 4. The rest of this section follows on from the material in Chapter 4. First, the spreadsheet itself must be further developed. The additional development is shown in columns N through R in rows 1 through 6, columns N through R in rows 7 through 149, and in cells F4 and G4. Also, the initialization formulas in F6 and G6 have been slightly modified for the special case where β is zero.

This is what the changes do: The changes in rows 7 through 149 in columns N and O provide an extended grid (pairs of values α and β) to search. Column P in the same rows is reserved for output (RMSE for each of 143 different pairs) from the macro. Columns Q and R in these rows and the formulas in cells P6, Q6, and R6 are used to identify the α and β values associated with the smallest RMSE generated by the 143 pairs.

The entries in cells N1 and O1 are used by the macro to sequentially search through all 143 pairs, they are copied by formula into F4 and G4. Cell P1 is copied by the macro sequentially into the column P7 through P149 as N1 and O1 update. This is the critical grid search. The entry in P1 is the RMSE value also found in cell H3. Cell N2 is the switch that is set to 1 or 0. Cell N2 is also the named range "Signal." When it is set to 1, the table reads the values in N1 and O1 into the cells F4 and G4 to generate the forecast; when it is set to 0 (after the optimal RMSE has been identified), it reads the values from N6 and O6 into the table to generate the forecast.

To use this table along with the original table to generate a grid search and optimal forecast, use the following macro, the execution of which is explained in Excel Help menus. (As stated at the beginning of this discussion, macros should be attempted only by experienced users.)

```
MACRO (note, this line is not part of the macro)
Sub FitMac()
Let Range("Signal") = 0
Sheets("Table 5 for Macro").Select
Range("p7:p149").ClearContents
Range("N1").Select
```

```
For a = 6 To 148
For b = 0 To 1
Let ActiveCell.Offset(0, b) = ActiveCell.Offset(a, b)
Let ActiveCell.Offset(a, 2) = ActiveCell.Offset(0, 2)
Next b
Next a
Let Range("Signal") = 1
End Sub
END OF MACRO (note, this line is not part of the macro)
```

This macro is included in the spreadsheet. As the first line of the macro says, the macro is labeled "FitMac." The experienced user will know how to invoke it, so standard invocation guidance is not provided; however, if the spreadsheet has macro permission, the user can invoke this macro with key combination control-p. The second line turns the switch (in the named range, "Signal") to zero. The effect of this is to tell the spreadsheet to look to N1 and O1 for α and β. The third and fifth lines locate the cursor at a definite location. The line between these empties out cells P7 through P149 of any prior content (this step is not strictly required, but it makes the effect of the macro more visible to the user). The next two lines begin an outer and an inner loop. The next line (the inner loop) copies α and β values from the column N7:O149 in pairs to N1 and O1. The next line (the outer loop) copies the resulting RMSE from P1 to P7:P149 beside the correct pair of α and β values. The next two lines close the inner and outer loops. The next line turns the switch to 1, which has the effect of using the best RMSE to select the associated α and β values using the logic-math formulas in columns Q and R. The last line ends the macro.

Exercises

Use the spreadsheet named "Budget Tools Appendix E Exercises" and the tabbed sheet "Part 5."

Exercise 1.

In the highlighted cell, test the two values above for equality.

Exercise 2.

In the highlighted cell, write a formula that divides cell A5 by cell A4 if they are not equal and multiplies them if they are equal.

Exercise 3.

1. If cell A5 is equal to cell A4 and if cell A5 is greater than cell A4, add them together, otherwise return the value zero.

2. If cell A5 is either greater than or less than cell A4, subtract cell A5 from cell A4, otherwise add them together.

Exercise 4.

In the highlighted cell, write a formula that finds the cell address for the value 25 in problem 1.

Exercise 5.

In the highlighted cell, write a formula that uses the highlighted cell in Exercise 4 to display the value of the referenced cell.

Exercise 6.

In the highlighted cells show the absolute value for each number in the column.

Exercise 7.

In the highlighted cells show the minimum and maximum values for the original and absolute value columns of problem 6.

Exercise 8.

1. Using the highlighted cells, find the square root for each of the associated values in the column.

2. What is the square root of –1? What is the meaning of this result?

Exercise 9.

Using the highlighted cells, extract the day, month, and year out of the given date.

Exercise 10.

For each of the numbers shown, first truncate each number in the labeled column, then round it to zero decimal places in the labeled column. Why are some cells in agreement and some not?

Note

1. Depending on the version of Office software, various steps must be taken to enable the use of macros. These steps may involve changing the Excel security level or simply clicking an "OK" button to allow use of a macro.

Glossary

Absolute percent error. Absolute value of the forecast value minus observed value all divided by observed value.

Activity measures. Measure of the activities of the organization; for example, the hours of work performed by employees of a certain class.

Actuals. Expenditures.

Allocative stage. Stage in the budget process when the budget is changed to reflect the legislative agreement.

Allotment. Specific amount of money that has been provided for a particular agency for a certain period of time.

Annual data. One observation that accounts for all the data for a whole year.

Annualization. Process by which a dollar amount, such as salaries, is spread out over the entire fiscal year rather than only a portion of the fiscal year. *— page 13*

Assets. Anything a person or company owns—such as money or property—that is of value.

Assumptions. Those factors or circumstances taken for granted as true without proof and that underline an argument or problem. *— page 14.*

Average costs. Total costs of a product or program; these total costs are divided by the total number of units involved.

Balance sheet. Statement of total assets and liabilities at one point in time for a governmental entity or corporation.

Base case. The most likely case upon which the cost-benefit analysis is initially conducted.

Benchmarks. Adoption of the achievement level of other similarly situated organizations.

Breakeven. Analysis required to determine the exact volume when the revenue equals the cost of the activities.

Budget implementation. Monies are spent according to the budget during a certain time; this usually refers to the fiscal year of the governmental agency or organization.

Calendarization. Process by which we break up expenses or revenues into monthly amounts; a cash flow spreadsheet laying out the fiscal year by the month is a calendarization of the revenues and expenditures.

Capital assets. Something that has a useful life or a defined period of time of more than one year and is usually obtained using borrowed dollars; most organizations set a minimum life expectancy and minimum value on an item before classifying a good or group of goods a capital good.

Capital budget. Document that indicates the proposed long-term investments in buildings and equipment.

Capital fund. Sum of money established to finance the acquisition of fixed assets, such as buildings or equipment.

Capital improvement plan (CIP). A planning document for a defined period of time that indicates the time, number, volume, and dollar amount of all acquisition and construction for an organization or government.

Capital spending. All charges used to support the capital budget, which supports construction and other expensive major long-term acquisitions.

Chart of accounts. Listing of categories of all transactions in a financial system with a numeric-alpha system to track the categories.

Classification and coding. Chart of account classifies every transaction into categories and codes these categories for easy reference.

Compounding. Process of earning interest on interest; compounding can be used to determine the future value of a current amount, in which the current interest is added to the principal in computing interest for the next period.

Consumer price index (CPI). Measure of the change in the prices of consumer goods and services over time.

Cost. Resources used to produce a good or service, often in monetary terms.

Cost-benefit analysis (CBA). Economic evaluation in which both the costs and the benefit are expressed in monetary units.

Cross-sectional data. Data that are a series of observations about a particular data set that varies according to a variable at the same point in time.

Debt service fund. Sum of money in which money is set aside to pay for a debt.

Discount rate. Interest rate used to calculate the present values of future amounts.

Discretion. Ability of the public employee to make substantial decisions about the activities of government to achieve the democratically defined outcomes.

Early stage outcome. Outcome that occurs during or soon after the organization has performed its service.

Efficiency measure. Ratio of the output to the input.

Equity. fairness, particularly with respect to the distribution of public services.

Expenditure codes. Five-digit codes that are arranged by functional unit and object of expenditure or expense.

Expense codes. See *expenditure codes*.

Exponential smoothing. Process for finding the local mean value of a time series based on a weighted average between the older part of the series and the most recent observation, where the weights are the opposite shares of one or more parameters; the mean found by this method is used as a forecast.

Fiduciary funds. Funds that track transactions in which government acts as a trustee, such as collecting and tracking workmen's compensation or Social Security payroll taxes and then depositing those funds with the state.

Financial efficiency. Efficiency that can be measured in monetary units.

Financial plan. Planning document that indicates how an organization is going to use its resources over a specific period of time; the plan includes projected budgets usually over a period of four or five years.

Financial statement. Report stating the financial condition of a government or corporation in separate statements.

Fixed cost. Cost that remains constant over a given period of time or a cer- — *page 13* tain volume of activity.

Forecast. Estimated value for a period, based on information from previous periods.

Fund accounting. System of accounting in which assets and liabilities are grouped according to the purpose and restriction for which they are to be used.

Fund source. Specific part of an appropriation account that has been set aside to fund a particular work to be performed.

General fund. In governmental accounting, a sum of money set aside for day-to-day expenses, and not for special purposes.

General ledger codes. Three-digit codes arranged in balance sheet order; assets, followed by liabilities and fund equity.

Governmental funds. Usually refers to any fund operated by any level of government; these funds use the modified accrual accounting method.

Income statement. Statement of all revenues and expenditures over a defined period of time.

Index. Numerical scale of change in a particular subject area; a common index is a stock index.

Indicator. Indirect measure of what is to be calculated.

Indicators. Indirect measures of what you want to measure.

Inflation. Increase in general prices over time that reduces consumer purchasing power.

Input. Amount used to invest in a given activity.

Interim outcome indicator. Indicator, sometimes called a proxy, that measures something instead of the desired outcome as a substitute until the outcome can be more directly observed.

Level. Frequency at which data are recorded: weekly, monthly, quarterly, annually, and so forth.

Liability. Anything that is owed to someone else; in government or nonprofit accounting, liability refers to all the debts that organization owes.

Life cycle costing (LCC). Analytical method used to determine the total cost of ownership, including acquisition, operation, maintenance, and disposal.

Line item. Itemized account or appropriation usually in a budget or appropriation bill.

Line item veto. The veto of one item from a list of items in an appropriation; some governors and mayors possess this power by law.

Loss function. Summary value that measures the effectiveness of the forecast.

Marginal cost. Cost incurred by government or nonprofit organizations that results from producing one more unit or from adding one more client to an existing program.

Mean error (ME). A bias measure, the sum of the errors divided by the count of the errors.

Mean square error (MSE). A statistic that quantifies the accuracy of a forecasting procedure; it begins with the forecast minus the observed value for each observation of a forecast, these values are squared, summed, and then the average is found; the resulting value is the mean square error of the forecast.

Measures. In budgeting, measures are variables that can be used in analysis.

Measures of process. Measures of way the organization uses inputs to achieve outputs and outcomes.

Measures of satisfaction. Measures of the response of a target audience to the activities, outputs, or outcomes of an organization; generally measured through surveys.

Midpoint forecast. Forecast of the middle of the range of likely values; actual value will involve some random variation (this part cannot be predicted).

Net assets. The total assets minus all the liabilities that an organization owes.

Net present value (NPV). Difference between the present values of the benefits and the present value of the costs often associated with a long-term project.

Nonpersonnel services (NPS). Budget items not included in personnel services; common categories of NPS are supplies, equipment, travel, construction, consultants.

Nonseasonal data. Data that do not exhibit a repeating pattern each year.

Object code. Classification to identify the type of purchase, or service, or any other charge received in a financial system.

Objects of expenditure. Expenditures can be classified by agreed upon codes in different types of categories, such as travel costs, contractual services, and so forth.

Operating expenditures (funds). All charges used to support day-to-day operations of an agency and that are expenditures other than capital expenditures.

Other than personnel services (OTPS). See *nonpersonnel services.*

Out year. The year beyond the current fiscal year. Often used in plural in a discussion of forecasting data several years into the future.

Outcome. Long-term achievement of what was originally established that the agency would achieve.

Outlier. Data that are extreme in respect to other values.

Output. Immediate short-term measure of an activity.

Pay as you go. Financing capital assets through fees, taxes, or other operating revenues (also known as pay go).

Percentage change. Units after a time period minus units before the time period divided by units before the time period (represented as times 100); definition should include the formula $(X_2 - X_1) / X_1 * 100$.

Percentage of total. Units (such as dollars) for a part (such as part of a budget) divided by units for the whole and represented as times 100; definition should include the formula $(X_i) / X * 100$.

Performance measurement. General term referring to various ways of observing the performance of an organization.

Permanently restricted funds. Funds that usually cannot be spent although the interest earned on the funds may be used.

Personnel services (PS). Those budget items relating to salaried employees, including salaries and fringe benefits.

Post hoc accountability. Reporting achievement to a policy-making body rather than following detailed procedures issued by that body.

Primary data. Data collected directly through an instrument or observation, typically for use in analysis by those who collect the data.

Process efficiency. Ratio output/input with respect to any process.

Process measures. See *measures of process.*

Program code. Number related to the accounting system that defines where the transactions concerning a particular program are categorized.

Proprietary funds. Funds in a governmental unit that are set up to account for activities that are similar to those in the private sector; proprietary funds are self-supporting in that the services are financed through user charges; proprietary funds use the economic resources measurement focus and the accrual basis of accounting.

Ratio analysis. Study, using ratios, of the financial condition of a government entity or nonprofit.

Ratios. Relative relationship that is calculated between two numbers.

Reference groups. Organizations, governments, or other entities that are similarly situated (compared with your organization) with respect to the information you are analyzing or communicating.

Revenue codes. Four-digit codes that are arranged by source.

Revenues. Broad general term referring to any money coming to a government or other entity for its own expenditures, in other words, all the money received by a governmental unit or nonprofit group; funds can come from many different places and be used for a variety of purposes.

Root mean square error. A loss function; the square root of the sum of the squared errors divided by the count of the squared errors.

Secondary data. Data collected by someone else, at an earlier time or under a different circumstance and made available through a data set or database.

Sensitivity analysis. Process of varying parameters in a given model to assess the level of change in its outcome.

Simulation. Method of forecasting in which the forecaster can forecast all the elements of an entire system.

Special revenue fund. Funds in governmental accounting set aside for specific purposes, unlike a general fund.

Standard. Setting targets based on guidelines established by authoritative bodies.

Step-fixed costs. Costs that remain constant within a given range of activities and length of time but that can change stepwise beyond these critical points.

Target. Proposed and budgeted level of performance.

Temporarily restricted funds. Funds that are restricted in use and cannot yet be spent.

Time series. Data that periodically gain a new observation from the same process.

Time value of money (TVM). Principle that money received in the present is worth more than the same amount received in the future; TVM is the basis for discounted cash-flow calculations.

Trend. Tendency for the series to increase or decrease from period to period.

Unrestricted funds. See *operating expenditures*.

Vacancy rate. Calculation of the percentage of positions that are vacant.

Variable costs. Costs that vary with volume.

Variance. Difference between what is budgeted and what is actually spent.

Variance analysis. Process of comparing a budget that has already been created with the actual expenditures.

About the Authors

Greg G. Chen is an associate professor at Baruch College, City University of New York; he has had broad working experience in China, Canada, and the United States. Professor Chen was the budget manager for the Ministry of Finance and the premier's office of British Columbia, Canada, and senior policy adviser and senior researcher in various government agencies and public authorities in British Columbia before taking his professorship in the United States. Professor Chen conducts research and publishes papers on the subjects of public and corporate finance, budgeting and cost-benefit analysis, traffic safety and injury prevention, school safety and student achievement, comparative health care systems, research methodology, and program evaluation.

Dall W. Forsythe, a professor of practice at the Wagner School at New York University, has extensive management experience in the government, private, and nonprofit sectors. In government, he served as budget director for the State of New York and for the New York City Board of Education. In the private sector, he worked as a managing director in the public finance department of Lehman Brothers. In the nonprofit sector, Forsythe served as chief administrative officer of the Episcopal Diocese of New York for four years. He is author of *Memos to the Governor: An Introduction to State Budgeting* (2004), and in 1998 he received the S. Kenneth Howard Award, a career achievement award from the Association for Budgeting and Financial Management.

Lynne A. Weikart is associate professor at Baruch College, City University of New York. Before her academic career, she held several high-level government positions, including budget director of the Division of Special Education in New York City's public schools and executive deputy commissioner of the New York State Division of Human Rights. For several years, she also served as the executive director of City Project, a progressive fiscal think tank that focused on reforming New York City's resource allocation patterns. Her current research focuses on resource allocation in urban areas as well as the budgeting process and gender issues, and she has published several articles about these subjects. Professor Weikart won the Luther Gulick Award for

Outstanding Academic, New York Metropolitan Chapter of the American Society for Public Administration, in 2001. Her book, *Follow the Money: Who Controls Urban Mayors? A Case Study of Decision Making during Fiscal Crises,* is in press.

Daniel W. Williams is associate professor at Baruch College, City University of New York. Before joining the faculty at Baruch, he held several high-level positions in government, including the budget directorship of the Virginia Department of Medical Assistance Services. His research focuses on the history of performance measurement. His articles have appeared in *Administrative Theory & Praxis, Public Administration Review,* and *Administration & Society.* He also conducts research into technical forecasting.

Index

Note: Tables and boxes are indicated by *t* and *b,* respectively.